THE HINGE

The Hinge

CIVIL SOCIETY,
GROUP CULTURES, AND
THE POWER OF LOCAL
COMMITMENTS

Gary Alan Fine

The University of Chicago Press   CHICAGO AND LONDON

The University of Chicago Press, Chicago 60637
The University of Chicago Press, Ltd., London
© 2021 by The University of Chicago
Published 2021

30 29 28 27 26 25 24 23 22 21   1 2 3 4 5

ISBN-13: 978-0-226-74552-7 (cloth)
ISBN-13: 978-0-226-74566-4 (paper)
ISBN-13: 978-0-226-74583-1 (e-book)
DOI: https://doi.org/10.7208/chicago/9780226745831.001.0001

Library of Congress Cataloging-in-Publication Data

Names: Fine, Gary Alan, author.
Title: The hinge : civil society, group cultures, and the power of local
commitments / Gary Alan Fine.
Description: Chicago : University of Chicago Press, 2021. | Includes
bibliographical references and index.
Identifiers: LCCN 2020026471 | ISBN 9780226745527 (cloth) |
ISBN 9780226745664 (paperback) | ISBN 9780226745831 (ebook)
Subjects: LCSH: Social interaction. | Intergroup relations. | Civil
society. | Community life.
Classification: LCC HM1111 .F55 2021 | DDC 302—dc23
LC record available at https://lccn.loc.gov/2020026471

To
My Sociological Mentors at the University
of Pennsylvania (1968–1972)

E. DIGBY BALTZELL

ERVING GOFFMAN

PHILIP RIEFF

CONTENTS

INTRODUCTION

A Mesoworld

*To love the little platoon we belong to in society is the first principle ...
of public affections. It is the first link in the series by which we proceed
towards a love to our country, and to mankind.*

EDMUND BURKE, *Reflections on the French Revolution*

Edmund Burke is right. The little platoon is the basis of political
commitment. When we watch or participate in an organized demonstration, we are a platoon. When our family celebrates Thanksgiving
together, carving a turkey around the dining room table, we are a platoon. When we gather to clean a local park or river, we are a platoon.
These may not be military engagements, but it is engagement none-
theless. Bands of brothers are not only found on killing fields but can
be squads of siblings in hospitals or sisters in street carnivals. Group
performance is evident in accounts of the debates over America's
founding, the challenges of dealing with Cold War Cuba, organizing
for Civil Rights activism, and the people's revolution in Cairo's Tahrir
Square in the Arab Spring. An array of careful accounts of local spaces
emphasizes that society depends on group action. These are little platoons, to which we are firmly attached.

Social fields—constellations of linked actors with shared concerns—
are organized through group commitment. Burke's platoons help explain a violent revolution, a democratic transition, a conspiracy by
shadowy elites, a totalitarian regime, or a cultural renaissance. We
find this in the genesis of the First World War, the French Revolution,
the Civil Rights movement, the stable governance of a midwestern
farming town, or the performance of an activist theater troupe. Both
ethnographic and historical accounts reveal this process. Small communities, working together and, on occasion, enmeshed in conflict,
create the conditions for political action. Both dramatic changes and
long-term continuities happen because groups commit to political
projects and then coordinate with others. In their performances, they

can change the debate by revealing that individual trauma is not personal distress but societal dysfunction (Alexander 2017).

According to management theorist Mary Parker Follett (1918: 3), the group organization of society constitutes the essence of democracy and the soul of popular government. Citizens develop a civic imagination through which they address issues, but they rarely do this alone. Those who share a social field think together, but this thinking becomes powerful when acting in concert. Thinking is social: minds work in concert (Zerubavel 1997). When we look at ethnographic sites—mushroom hunters, political volunteers, art collectors, chess competitors, or senior citizen progressive activists—we find that gatherings provide the basis by which individual perspectives meld into a shared worldview. Collective activities bolster commitments, both locally and when facing a wider community.

We often believe that we belong within a like-minded community. We share an identity and a fate. With this commitment, we speak of groups as acting, even while recognizing that this involves individuals engaging in a joint performance. The recognition of a "we" overrides a platoon of "I"s. We live in a world of first-person plurals.

Despite ideological imaginaries of individualism, there are no self-made men and women. As First Lady Hillary Clinton wrote, it takes a village to produce a child—and a citizen.[1] Strong neighborhoods provide a safe and watched environment for children. At least certain 'hoods in close-knit urban areas, leafy suburban sites, and small towns afford these benefits. What is crucial is that residents know and care about each other. In Durkheim's (1964 [1893]) terms, articulated in *The Division of Labor in Society*, this constitutes "precontractual solidarity." Although rational contractualism plays a role, group-based identity constitutes the core of sociality. We are activists, players, or naturalists, but typically in the context of a group, that through its culture creates a self.

We imagine communities to which we aspire, which we value, and to which we are devoted. Focusing on the local, on the civic, and on the institutional, we act in ways that reveal familiar and patterned linkages between the personal and the structural. This intersection constitutes the platform on which the linkage of micro and macro depends. *The Hinge*, my metaphorical title, asserts that the two realms—personal and institutional—are never fully autonomous. Microlocal action and extralocal structures fit together with each operating in light of the other's constraints.

Sociologists often begin with Thomas Hobbes who, it is said, provided the discipline's core challenge: How is social order possible? Hobbes proposed that without limits on rival personal interests, the security necessary for routine tasks would be absent. Although in *Leviathan* Hobbes does not refer to "social order," his problem is ours. Hobbes (1651) writes,

> Whatsoever therefore is consequent to a time of Warre, where every man is Enemy to every man ... wherein men live without other security, than what their own strength, and their own invention shall furnish them withal. In such condition, there is ... no Society; and which is worst of all, continuall feare, and danger of violent death; And the life of man, solitary, poore, nasty, brutish, and short.

In such dire circumstances, how can orchards be fruitful, libraries filled, villages peaceable, and people die in their beds? Hobbes's solution to a world of uncoordinated interests is a realm of control. Authority is assigned to the Leviathan, an "artificial" or corporate person. Society is organized either from above or from within. Hobbes dismisses the latter, posing a world of solitary self-interest against a world of central power and surveillance. He poses a stark choice lacking a middle: both individuals and institutions lack self-governing social stability. However, democracy exists and self-determination is possible because there *is* a middle: a teeming world of tiny publics that acts and responds.

This mesoworld, this middle, is the Hinge, the linkage of external structures and personal interest. Order operates horizontally, not only vertically. Even vertical control depends on the existence of groups at each level of authority. Oppression relies on interactional routines as does democracy. In contrast to Hobbesian red-in-tooth-and-claw individualism, localism and social relations create security and routine. The place to search for a haven from epistemic turmoil is in tight communities and meaningful connections. Society requires a mesh of groups, a world of crosscutting dialogues (Cohen and Arato 1992: 252; Back and Polisar 1983; Sennett 2012).

Circuits of action—as I will term behavioral routines that provide consistent expectations for participants—while occurring in local spaces, can potentially diffuse as individuals participate in numerous such scenes: family, church, neighborhood, club, team, school, and workplace. Devout hermits are scarce, and so are quasi-loners, belonging to only a single group. Because organizations are isomorphic, having similar structures (DiMaggio and Powell 1983), the routines in one locale are often duplicated in others. For instance, expectations of what constitutes legitimate cross-gender contact (hugging, erotic compliments, unwanted touching), learned in one context, may be displayed elsewhere. At least they are until participants reject them through disapproval or sanctions, challenged, for example, as feminist movements (#MeToo) demand new rules. Unfamiliar routines are awkward until they become taken for granted. These diverse and widespread expectations are a way in which social change, readily achieved in one group, becomes challenging as proponents strive to institutionalize them in many groups. As local cultures respond to institutional enforcement and the existence of counternorms through media reports, groups may change in similar directions, but the process is rarely immediate. Further, when local traditions are defined as distinct and desirable, differentiation, rather than alliance and conformity, is common. Those domains that still embrace Mad Men culture are slow to realize that Time's Up.

~

Relationships among groups constitute the foundation of civil society. It is in our sociality—our lives that depend on others—in which we find the coordination, friendships, and conflicts that make for the fabric of society. Large ideas—power, structure, nation, or humanity—do not exist as they are imagined—that is, society is not created by them, only described by them. Instead, as Howard Becker (1986) argues, society from top to bottom is created by people *doing things together*.

Ideas of community and sociability cover much ground. Georg Simmel (1971: 24) writes, "Sociation ranges all the way from the momentary getting together for a walk to the founding of a family, from relations maintained 'until further notice' to membership in a state, from the temporary aggregation of hotel guests to the intimate bond of a medieval guild." Echoing Simmel, Danny Kaplan (2018) provocatively and persuasively argues that the nation develops from a sense of "social club sociability."

This does not mean that everyone can join that club. Further, not all within a political entity will know each other, and some may embrace a national identity without participating in a recognized group. Even if, as Benedict Anderson (1991) famously suggested, nations are imagined communities, this does not suggest that the imagining inevitably shapes patriotic behavior. Still, Kaplan's metaphor of the nation as a social club suggests that something akin to George Herbert Mead's (1934) concept of the "generalized other" defines our shared belonging.

That friendship and group participation transform populations of strangers into comrades encourages a recognition of civic belonging. How strangers become friends is central to the establishment of collaborative citizenship. Institutions permit relations that create narratives of national pride.

Despite the role of group sociability as the basis of civic engagement, many analyses of the structure of political engagement take one of two forms: either they examine how institutional structures set conditions for politics, erasing the agency of the individual, or they examine how individual attitudes and backgrounds are the basis for political decisions. While sociologists have long contributed to the mesolevel analysis of civic culture, these other approaches— the macro and the micro—have dominated. In both, ongoing relations are dismissed and links among local communities downplayed. But the problem goes deeper than this marginalization of the group. Many who examine the mesolevel treat it as an end in itself, disregarding that groups have relations with other groups and to the institutions of which they form a part. This limits our understanding of how local communities fit into larger worlds. By focusing on a single case, we ignore that each group culture is shaped through a web of myriad groups.

A foundation of shared politics is based on the reality that sociable groups depend on prepolitical behavior (Feigenbaum 1959). Interpersonal trust generates collective engagement. Productive civic action consists of people working together to improve their common lot (Giddens 1984). This model echoes the American Political Science Association's "Civic Education Project for the Next Century" that focused on "the civic work of ordinary people who, located in diverse, plural communities, work on behalf of their communities and seek eagerly for common goods, both heroic and mundane" (Ehrenberg 1999: x). An embrace of group culture depends on ongoing obligations that, when recognized, encourage the performance of shared identity (Lichterman and Eliasoph 2014: 815).[2]

The awareness of group influence in public life, while often eclipsed by a focus on the individual, the institution, the society, or the global, has been growing in contemporary social science. There is increased attention to neighborhood effects (Sampson 2012; Vargas 2016), community organizations (Eliasoph 2012), and sites of affiliation (Goldfarb 2006). As a result, mesolevel scholars draw on several extensive bodies of research to address how civil society, political process, and community organization are locally produced. The goal is not to ask whether a mesolevel approach does or should exist but to specify how best to think about groups in civic culture, both through their internal characteristics and their public ones.

Examining mesolevel traditions has a long lineage, evident in accounts of participatory democracy, township governance, and political friendships. The value of friendship in the construction of the state dates to Aristotle in his *Politics* and to the nineteenth-century sociologist Ferdinand Tönnies (2001: 43), who in *Community and Society* describes the clan as the "the family before the family and … village before the village." Of course, many political systems are larger than families and villages, making full participation impossible, but even in representative systems (as well as in dictatorships) interacting partners shape decision-making. As political scientist Jane Mansbridge (1980: 34) points out, every parliamentary system depends on face-to-face meetings of the elected representatives. These gatherings may be of those jointly tasked with solving a problem or those who are developing partisan strategies to achieve conflictual goals. But governmentality always involves the working out of commitments.

Consistent with both Alexis de Tocqueville (1966 [1835]) and Richard Sennett (1977: 31), thriving societies depend on a web of social relations. In this way, I emphasize the image beloved of sociologists: "where the action is" (Goffman 1967). Interpreting *collective* and *coordinated* action is essential for any model of social organization and, ultimately, for civil society.

The Civic Hinge

I present a set of analytic tools to provide strategies for a locally based appreciation of civic life. Politics, as defined broadly, involves the distribution of resources, power, and status, and this covers but also extends beyond voting, protesting, and legislating. It includes civil order, civic action, communal identity, and governmental responses. With such a broad view of politics, how does local culture shape affiliation and participation? As James Jasper (2010) points out, we must bracket "big structures" to discover the centrality of interaction. Polities, communities, and institutions depend on interpersonal coordination. People see the world in similar ways as their close associates, whether or not they intend a common future. Even ostensibly apolitical groups, such as leisure clubs—like mushroom-hunting societies that engage in naturework and worry about the environment (Fine 1998)—potentially link their commitments into political culture, no matter if the commitments remain unrecognized (Kjølsrød 2013: 1207). Based on their perspectives and interests, many groups develop what sociologists Robert Merton and Elinor Barber (2004) refer to as "sociocognitive microenvironments." We do not live with millions, but with a few, and these few shape our worldview.

Throughout this book, I treat politics and civil society broadly, preferring expansive definitions to narrow ones. A constrained idea of politics, focusing on state legitimacy, its monopoly on violence, and governmental surveillance is too limited for understanding the sociality that stands behind resource distribution and informal power arrangements. These additional forms of interpersonal politics have great weight in shaping lives. To this end, I examine group influence as evident in government decision-making, in demonstrations, in town meetings, in coffee-shop discussions, and in terrorist cells.

While few scholars deny the salience of the group in creating social order, and while influential studies have contributed to that level of analysis, often an emphasis on structures or on the rational considerations of individuals ignores collective action and sociability. We lose if we enshrine a microeconomic model of behavioral choice or if we erase interaction by stressing larger institutional, state-based, or global entities. Both approaches have merit, but they ignore the places and relations that motivate action. For a social system to thrive, groups must create systems of recognized meaning and establish rules of order or of dispute.

My goal is not simply to assert that we need additional studies of the social basis of civic action—a point none would deny—but to provide tools and concepts for research. Each of the seven substantive chapters presents a mesolevel "building block" of civil society: coordination, relations, associations, place, conflict, control, and extensions.

While these map civic society, by themselves they are merely topics. To give them power, more is needed: a set of analytic strategies. Treating civic order as a site of local action builds on four themes about which I have previously written. I use interaction order, group culture, circuits of action, and tiny publics as analytic strategies, revealing how this semiautonomous mesolevel analysis serves as the *hinge* through which micro- and macrolevels are linked. These themes represent my attempt to integrate performance, experience, routine, and engagement in a mesolevel analysis of communal politics. It is to these themes to which I turn.

A Mesolevel Agenda

Although *culture, interaction*, and *structure* are central to any model that attempts to link levels of analysis, these concepts in themselves are too broad to be useful for theorizing. Almost anything can be treated as culture, interaction, or structure. While the intersection of these concepts forms the basis of a mesolevel sociology, integrating action and order, more specific themes permit us to see how civic order results from communal practices. I draw on four conceptual themes, which, while they overlap, address different aspects of the linkage of micro and macro through a mesolevel analysis. Together they operate as the conceptual basis of the Hinge of my title: the interaction order, group culture, circuits of action, and tiny publics.

INTERACTION ORDER

Consider first the *interaction order*, a concept outlined by Erving Goffman in 1983 to explain how social structures develop from interaction. Goffman long emphasized the importance of performance in the creation of social order, and the dramaturgical metaphor has been central to both symbolic interaction (Brissett and Edgley 2005) and the strong program of cultural analysis, pioneered by Jeffrey Alexander (2017) and his students (Reed 2006). Today we recognize that people do not merely think and act; they perform for others, collectively presenting meaning.

In emphasizing the interaction order, Goffman argued that, through its performance, interaction could be orderly and routine, even allowing for the preferences of participants. Goffman composed his American Sociological Association presidential address while terminally ill, so this text leaves analytic gaps and is largely devoid of those rich empirical examples for which his early writings are so beloved. Still, the idea of the interaction order asserts that even with a recognition of the importance of agentic action, people accept the reality of structures and widely held understandings. This relies on the claim that shared practices arise from the structure of interaction itself. Such a framework incorporates both action and meaning into an orderly and recognizable world that is essential for behavioral predictability and ontological security. The interaction order establishes an integrative sociology that treats civic action as a domain of well-recognized actions, even if, on occasion and with costs, these actions may be challenged.

To make his point, Goffman (1983: 4) argues that "at the very center of interaction life is the cognitive relation we have with those present before us, without which relationship our activity, behavioral and verbal, could not be meaningfully organized." By participating in an interaction order, group members recognize their associations and their practices as stable and consequential. This solidity does not depend on the immediate encounter but results from routines tied to ongoing social relations. Extending Goffman's insight, Anne Rawls (1987: 136) addresses the "interaction order sui generis," suggesting that "imperatives that are not structurally defined" are organizing principles that build local commitments. The commitments derive from responses to expectations and then lead to a solidification of those expectations. In this way, culture is both cause and effect of interaction and affiliation.

Goffman's interaction order provides a basis for examining social systems comparatively and historically. A spontaneous performance does not, in itself, generate a communal relation, but, rather, the relation depends on a shared experience.[3] In contrast to the view that interaction is continually renewed in each meeting, an interaction order asserts that present choices are built on past routines. The building of local worlds means that imagined communities are everywhere, not only at the level of the state and nation. Civil society is not merely an appendage of the state or nation but is built in localities. We imagine ourselves tethered to some worlds that are large and others that are small—those that are more or less powerful. These connections can be cognitive (through cultural logics), emotional (through cohesive affect), or behavioral (through common experiences), but together they produce action routines.

Because we imagine past interaction as a template for the present, Goffman (1983) argued that we build society through tacit agreement to transform behavior into orderliness. As a result, comforting routines generate trust (Misztal 2001). Interaction orders explain social systems from the dyad to the globe and from the bedroom to the state, a point consistent with Collins's (1981) account of how microstructures develop macrostructural understandings.

GROUP CULTURE

While the interaction order emphasizes the structuring of interaction as a set of ongoing practices, the role of local culture is only implicit. However, we must bring in cultures to provide interaction with a solidifying content that grows from the internal dynamics of the group. I have argued that group cultures—what I have termed "idiocultures" (Fine 1979)—reveal that culture is more than an amorphous mist (Ghaziani 2012). In contrast, it is a concrete set of beliefs and practices held by people with ongoing relations. While some cultural traditions are widely known and utilized, they are known and utilized within group contexts. Other cultural traditions are particular to small communities. But whatever their spread, culture provides the basis for action: tools within a tool kit (Swidler 1986). As a framework, I argue that idioculture

consists of a system of knowledge, beliefs, behaviors, and customs shared by members of an interacting group to which members can refer and that serve as the basis of further interaction. Members recognize that they share experiences, and these experiences can be referred to with the expectation that they will be understood by other members, thus being used to construct a social reality for the participants. (Fine 1987: 125)

Knowing that others share one's experience can be empowering in creating civic commitment. When many groups in similar circumstances have parallel experiences, this can provoke a wider civic allegiance or promote a common desire for change. We see this in the discussions of sexual harassment and assault in the #MeToo movement in which group discussions (once labeled "consciousness raising") reveal the frequency of what seemed to be hidden and idiosyncratic personal experience. These gatherings provide the basis for communication within networks or through media extensions, establishing new and powerful grievance frames.

I combine Goffman's recognition of how interaction creates an orderly social process with the recognition, often absent in microanalytic studies of interpersonal relations, that meanings are frequently situated within (relatively) stable group cultures. As numerous ethnographies demonstrate, families, clubs, teams, and cliques exemplify local cultures that shape interaction orders. Experiences and collective memories are essential if individuals are to believe that they are part of a public with common interests or linked fates (Dawson 1995; Olick and Robbins 1998). As Eviatar Zerubavel (1997) emphasizes, thinking is neither individual nor universal, neither psychic nor physiological. It is communal. The future as a space for interaction is built on a knowable past.

Drawing on the approach of Ann Swidler (1986), I believe that culture can be considered a tool kit. However, tools are not generic but used in local ways (Fine and Harrington 2004). Participants must learn how they have been used (the collective past) and imagine the ways that they might be used (the prospective future). Group cultures gain power because of this temporality, linking past, present, and future. By working together, solving problems and recognizing that some disagreements are intractable, organizational arrangements are solidified. This perspective demands an approach that anchors action in culture, emphasizing the centrality of performance, transactions, and coordination in producing a behavioral narrative (Jasper 2010).

A mesolevel analysis recognizes that idiocultures serve as a bulwark of civil society, providing the content—the "stuff"—of the interaction order. Norms of conduct, rituals, routines, idioms, and practices are the basis of propriety. The shared actions and discourses of groups establish a civic imagination, shaped by social location, personal and political experience, and tradition (Baiocchi et al. 2014: 69).

The group culture approach is evident in Muzafer Sherif's Robbers' Cave experiment, a study of the development and then mitigation of group conflict through the evolving traditions of two cabins of preadolescent boys. The summer camp setting permitted the boys to create nicknames, songs, and rituals that reflected group needs and moral accountings. Sherif and his colleagues saw these local cultures as establishing rivalry through battles over resources and contrasting identities. Later the cultural norms shifted and hostility was overcome through the recognition of superordinate goals that required all campers to work together to achieve the interests of both groups. Each cabin came to recognize that it needed the other to benefit (Sherif et al. 1961). Ultimately, any theory of the local must address how the specific forms of culture connect interaction orders to ongoing commitments both within and between groups. However much we emphasize interaction and structure, moments of togetherness must be filled with recognizable substance: they are about *something*.

CIRCUITS OF ACTION

The theory of the Hinge draws an analytic link between individual actors and larger social structures. Social systems are held together through shared culture and through a commitment to well-established interaction practices. From this perspective, actors who recognize the likely responses of others stand at the heart of sociology. They do not engage in action in isolation but in context.

I postulate the value of "circuits of action" in which actors respond to constraints. I define a circuit of action as a system of civic participation in which interactional choices are filtered through an actor's awareness of what the group with which they identify and in which they participate considers culturally appropriate. Circuits of action mirror the rules of the interaction order and the content of group cultures in light of the necessity for predictable action. Personal desires, group pressures, and institutional control channel the options from which circuits of action are established. This approach emphasizes the negotiations and adjustments on which civic action depends while accepting established practices. Anselm Strauss (1978) and David

Maines (1977) have been central thinkers in pointing to negotiation as a tool for building flexible but durable relations, not starting afresh each time but in light of an understood context. Politics is performed in the immediate presence of others[4] but with the awareness of a meaningful, referential past.

To understand circuits of action, I emphasize that face-to-face interaction requires a twined phenomenology of self and other. For phenomenologist of the social Alfred Schutz (1967), face-to-face interaction originates with an "Other orientation" (163) or "Thou-orientation" (173). This orientation creates the possibility of what Schutz refers to as "we-relationships," which he claimed are at the heart of sociality (Tuomela 2005). However, addressing the mesolevel construction of civil society, Schutz goes deeper. He quotes Max Weber's *Economy and Society* to argue that when we consider collective entities, we imagine actions that occur through face-to-face interaction. Weber (1978: 14) writes in *Economy and Society*,

> For sociological purposes ... there is no such thing as a collective personality which "acts." When reference is made in a sociological context to a "state," a "nation," a "corporation," a "family" or an "army corps," or to similar collectivities, what is meant is, on the contrary, only a certain kind of development of actual or possible social actions of the individual persons.

People act with regard to each other. Schutz (1967: 199), in turn, extends Weber,

> Every "action" of the state can be reduced to the actions of its functionaries, whom we can apprehend by means of personal ideal types and toward whom we can assume a They-orientation.... From the sociological point of view, therefore, the term "state" is merely an abbreviation for a highly complex network of interdependent personal ideal types. When we speak of any collectivity as "acting," we take this complex structural arrangement for granted.... We forget that, whereas the conscious experiences of typical individuals are quite conceivable, the conscious experiences of a collective are not.

While Schutz insists on a sociology of minds together, he downplays the phenomenology—and the organization—of joint action as part of an ongoing circuit of adjustment to established pasts and imagined futures. This negotiation is crucial. When parties are copresent (as in families or on teams), what generates collective action depends on communal understandings. More than separate minds, groups rely on routine lines of action, recursive and negotiated, created through shared expectations and common anticipations.

TINY PUBLICS

In joining the micro and the macro, I adopt the model of *sociological miniaturism*, the approach that John Stolte, Karen Cook, and I postulated (Stolte, Fine, and Cook 2001). This perspective asserts that microsociological concepts are an interpretive framework through which a grounded, action-oriented structural analysis is possible. A mesolevel analysis of civic action depends on groups being constituted as "publics." In other words, many groups have an implicit politics and communal face. A *tiny public* is a group with a recognizable interaction order and culture that strives to play a role within a civic structure, democratic or authoritarian. This concept leverages the interaction order and group culture to support the civic realm of the Hinge. Such communities may be small, but they contribute to a broader politics, embracing values on which shared commitment depends. The diversity of tiny publics and their widespread placement allows for a mesoanalysis of both the street corner and global financial markets.

In considering tiny publics, I stress their role in civil society, in the public sphere, and in governance. These domains overlap, although they are not identical: the first emphasizes the organization of extended communal systems, the second refers to forms of action and discourse as engaged citizens, and the third addresses groups within institutions of the state. The civil society and the public sphere often are linked to democratic political systems, although small groups are also found in authoritarian systems, sometimes in opposition to those totalizing systems but not invariably so (Riley 2010). We must avoid the naive error of assuming that groups are necessarily committed to freedom or equality, or that they will inevitably resist larger, more powerful systems. Perhaps tiny publics are virtuous spaces in that all members can participate (Putnam 2000; Alexander 2006), but we should be cautious of assigning virtue to publics simply based on their modest size (Kaplan 2018: 53). Little platoons do not necessarily fight for justice, however that slippery concept is defined.

If the image of tiny publics is useful, it should explain how groups are a lens to understand political involvement and governmental control. These publics are "society itself." As John Dewey (1954: 42) understood in *The Public and Its Problems*, "The intimate and familiar propinquity group is not a social unity within an inclusive whole. It is, for almost all purposes, society itself." In Dewey's civic pragmatism, the "propinquity group" [the tiny public] constitutes society with knowledge interpreted socially, justifying Dewey's canny metaphor that in democracy the ear is more powerful than the eye: personal communication trumps what an individual can perceive: "Vision is a spectator; hearing is a participator" (Dewey 1954: 218–19). The presence of those who provide an earful promotes complying with moral demands, not just relying on an internal compass.

While I emphasize consensus and concord in civil society, publics—tiny and large—need to cope with external threats as well as with internal divisions. Tiny publics divide and sometimes battle. Civic vice occurs just as does civic virtue. Contentious disputes also reflect a hinge between micro and macro. As I describe in chapter 5, a mesolevel analysis demands addressing the presence—and sometimes the merits—of conflict and disruption without presuming accord. The challenge, as Muzafer Sherif realized, is to create conditions that permit group cultures to respond productively to their shared context (Sherif et al. 1961).

Tiny publics are far from perfect, often because smooth interaction becomes such a compelling ideal that groups that are conflict-averse, as many are, may avoid controversies that should be addressed or may bow to the wishes of the most influential. Jane Mansbridge (1980: 34), accounting for "adversary democracy," points to the challenge of consensus,

> When citizens have a common interest, face-to-face contact—which allows debate, empathy, listening, learning, changing opinions, and a burst of solidarity when a decision is reached—can bring real joy. But in the face of conflict, emotions turn sour.... Fear of conflict leads those with influence in a meeting to suppress important issues rather than letting them surface and cause disruption. It leads them also to avoid the appearance of conflict by pressing for unanimity.

Groups are powerful when they, as in the archetypal Quaker meeting, constitute themselves as systems of consensus, papering over disagreements. However, enshrining a one-voice model can silence a valuable diversity of opinions.

The existence of an array of tiny publics suggests that affiliation need not end at the boundary of interaction but extends to imagined connections with other groups felt to have similar character. We often consider ourselves members of a set of groups, creating, in effect, a vast public from a set of tiny publics. Microcultures balloon into subcultures. Once this broader civic affiliation is recognized, actions (voting, contributing, or demonstrating) generate a more consequential set of commitments and identities. Such connections are part of a search for a "good society," a domain of mutual respect and moral virtue (Bellah et al. 1991). Good societies depend on good publics. This imaginary develops from a belief that the strong ties of family, friendship, and neighborhood can be extended through caring communities: villages in the interaction order. This is true even if the community is internally split or has disputed boundaries—a culture of complaint (Weeks 2004)—as long as participants feel that they have resources or norms that are worth disputing.

As political theorist Michael Walzer (1992: 107) recognizes,

> Civil society itself is sustained by groups much smaller than the *demos* or the working class or the mass of consumers or the nation. All these are necessarily pluralized as they are incorporated. They become part of the fabric of family, friends, comrades and colleagues, where people are connected to one another and made responsible for one another.

Walzer asserts that civil society connects to what amounts to a network of tiny publics, proclaiming that the good life is possible only in a civil society that depends on sociable members, freely associating and communicating. This is what tiny publics can achieve.

By examining group action in the form of tiny publics, I extend a political sociology that recognizes that a range of publics—elites, conformers, the marginal, and the resistant—all depend on the meanings, the social relations, and the structural possibilities provided by local communities.

Elaborating the Hinge

In building a theory of the Hinge, I organize my text by using seven building-block concepts that, taken together, provide for a mesolevel analysis of civic action: coordination, relations, association, place, conflict, control, and extensions. After surveying previous research and extending it in light of my theoretical approach, I present three empirical cases that exemplify how these concepts have been used in distinct ways. Several of these twenty-one cases build on multiple studies. Each provides an entry to how groups order civil society in interaction, not only people in mind and institutions in structure. Through the diversity of cases, I provide a wide lens: some are closely tied to sites of power and others are more distant. Hinges take various forms, differently situated institutionally with varying amounts of structural leverage and cultural capital.

Chapter 1, "Coordination," asks how people do things together. Coordination is essential for civic engagement, the commitment to an interaction order, and the production of a group culture. It is not that coordination inevitably depends on full consensus but rather that individuals fit lines of action together. The negotiated order is part of politics from the ground up. Participants recognize that they share communal spaces and collaborate for mutual ends. This recognition— and the problems that ensue—is expressed in the problem (sometimes labeled the "tragedy") of the commons. How can citizens with private interests that might overload the carrying capacity of a system moderate their desires, satisficing but not maximizing individual outcomes in the name of communal survival?

To examine coordination, I begin with the simple case of shared agricultural labor in which farmers aid each other in times of need. While costs exist in working for neighbors, the costs are typically modest and the helper can request aid with an understanding of reciprocity. In much civil society, despite hierarchy and differential power, a belief in reciprocal rights and privileges is evident, creating a circuit of action in which all participate. My second example involves working jointly. Collective political projects reflect the power of group cultures as embedded in tiny publics. From the writings of Danielle Allen (2014) and Pauline Maier (1997), I describe how the Declaration of Independence was written collaboratively. This project stands for other moments of democratic writing in which negotiation among actors produces a lasting outcome. Conflict is managed despite different beliefs, but it begins with actors joining a project to which all are committed. The final case is that of the commons, a village communal system permitting neighbors to graze animals on shared land. Creating an interaction order in light of different interests is challenging, often leading to failure. In time, systemic failures (or at least belief in these failures) led to the enclosure of private fields, so that few open commons fields remain.[5] In this third case, a clear cost applies to independent, uncoordinated action, even if individuals benefit in the short run. The question is how an interaction order can support communal coordination over individual self-interest.

The second chapter, "Relations," asserts that social order depends on the reality that people know each other in ways that produce mutual concern. Community relies on emotional connections and patterns of interpersonal selection. Often this involves friendship but occasionally enmity as well. How do friendship and sociability create good citizens and, through them, the good society? How do hatred and resentment produce a politics of trouble? These relations allow for a nexus of public relationships, creating civil society. Of course, friendships also occur in undemocratic spaces, but, in such cases, they are often transacted outside a public sphere in secluded, hidden arbors such as kitchens and hearths (Goldfarb 2006; Scott 1998). Hatreds and betrayals can be more public in harsh political realms, but these are not my focus here.

I examine three friendship networks, different in their relationship to politics and power. I begin by describing mutual aid within a working-class African American community, as documented by Carol Stack (1973) in her classic analysis of social support, *All Our Kin*. These neighbors, despite their rich group cultures, think of themselves as outside a consciously considered politics, but the existence of expected routines—of help networks—contributes to making the neighborhood livable. I then address Katherine Cramer Walsh's (2004) account of a morning coffee klatch of middle-class men, meeting regularly in a local café, examining how, through interaction, groups engage with political issues. Even if unaffiliated, they constitute a tiny public that discusses issues of the day. Finally, I describe an elite group of associates, the "Georgetown set," a gathering of American politicians, journalists, academics, and bureaucrats, residing in a tony neighborhood in the District of Columbia, whose shared perspectives shaped American foreign policy and national security debates in the post–World War II era. Although tiny, the group reveals how influential publics operate. While the group was never dominant, their influence was extensive and flowed from their mutual friendships and linkages with leading state actors.

The salience of Tocqueville's claims about the organization of American life is underscored in chapter 3, "Associations." Friendship is often organized and flourishes through recognizable structures. This is the virtue of associations. While associations exist in all sizes, I focus on those that constitute small groups in which participants recognize each other. While no precise limit exists for the optimal size of a group, once routine contacts—a shared and knowing culture— dissipate, the organization becomes bureaucratic. While large associations also depend on groups—boards of directors, committees, cells, or chapters—each of these interactional units becomes, in effect, an association with its own interaction order and group culture. As Kathleen Blee (2012) argues in her ethnographic census of social movement activism in Pittsburgh, there are social movement organizations and social movement groups, segmented by size and by the forms of democratic deliberation. This permits different types of social relations and encourages distinct social arrangements. Of course, small decision-making groups control large organizations, even if these groups are at some distance from rank-and-file supporters or dues-paying members. Extended associations operate through leadership circles and establish subsidiary groups, such as committees, that provide input for the decision-making process. When an extended association holds a mass meeting, a rally, or a demonstration, groups are found among both organizers and attendees.

My first case is Blee's (2012) census of small social movement organizations. She explores how movement groups are tiny publics and asks how these diffuse groups develop associational cultures and how these cultures contribute to (or undercut) movement goals. I then describe Nina Eliasoph's (1998) comparison of two groups pushing a local antidrug agenda. Eliasoph focuses on distinctive group styles— cultures—in shaping the practices of volunteers. When does civic engagement outweigh sociability in local associations? My final case is the growth of nineteenth-century fraternal organizations, such as the Masons, Knights of Columbus, or Shriners. Despite their success in creating community through sociability and their linkages to larger forms of social engagement, these fraternities as publics stratify society and erect barriers to egalitarian participation, warning us of an overly rosy picture of civic belongingness (Kaufman 2002; Skocpol 2003).

Chapter 4, "Place," analyzes how engaged communities depend on the affordances of public and private spaces. While one's associates matter greatly, places shape interaction and culture, producing action fields. Some locales demand privacy. In contrast, public spaces are, at least in principle, open to all. The expectations of the interaction order result from understood proprieties in particular sites.

I begin by describing that classic site of community political action, the town meeting (Bryan 2004), now remaining only in northern New England. Here is a democratic institution where, theoretically, all adult citizens can participate. It is the archetype of a tiny public. Of course, spaces are never as open as they claim, but the commitment to the form of the gathering presumes an ideological openness, whatever limits prevent full participation in practice. The space is treated as secular (even if, at other moments, it serves as a church). Such is democratic engagement. The second case provides a dramatic contrast. The Bohemian Club, described by G. William Domhoff (1974), is a private club of prominent men in business, politics, and the arts. Every summer for two weeks these men stage an encampment in the woods of northern California, a site known as Bohemian Grove. Events at the camp include lectures, concerts, theatrical productions, sporting events, masculine high jinks, and ritual ceremonies. Members pride themselves on their robust group culture. The site, away from the "cares of the world," permits a jokey camaraderie, but one that continues after the end of the encampment through the power of networking. In his account, Domhoff suggests that their networking creates a political upper class, a hidden, if distressingly effective, community. In contrast to town meetings, Bohemian Grove is deliberately exclusive, set apart from the larger civic realm. The third case compares traditions of sociability in eighteenth-century Paris and London. Stylish conversation was widely admired among elites in both cities, but the locations of discourse differed. By the early eighteenth century, London had numerous public coffeehouses in which educated citizens gathered to discuss the issues of the day. Anyone could enter and participate. Paris, in contrast, operated through invited weekly salons, organized largely by aristocratic women in private homes.

The French system relied on a structured, bounded interaction order, while the British model permitted a more open-ended public sphere, a cause and a result of political organization.

The fifth chapter, "Conflict," corrects the impression that communities invariably produce consensual group cultures and an interaction order to which all are equally welcome. While tiny publics often share commitments, they may also be riven by division and conflict. Sometimes the conflict is lasting, causing ruptures, and, at other times, conflict merely results in temporary breaches and divergent perspectives. Accord is not inevitable and circuits of action are not always smooth, particularly when interests and resources diverge. Groups that endure, despite internal differences, must manage dissent.

I begin with discord within a democratic structure as depicted in Andrew Deener's (2012) account of the management of vehement political arguments in Venice, California. Deener recounts clashes within this progressive seaside community, arguing that divergent interests produce both communal divisions and a challenge to maintain a single interaction order. I then turn to social breakdown and organizational turmoil as recounted by Tim Hallett (2010) in his account of unrest in the administration of a local elementary school and also as described by David Snow and colleagues (Snow et al. 1998) in their account of societal troubles that generated activism on behalf of the homeless. Who has the right to demand action—and how? Snow emphasizes the disruption of the routines of daily life in which publics lose a sense of control and in which forms of surveillance are altered. Finally, I examine accounts of the culture of the Mississippi Freedom Summer project (e.g., McAdam 1988), a crucial moment in the 1960s Civil Rights movement. McAdam reveals conflicts within movement groups and between the movement and oppositional forces. This complicates the understanding of conflict, suggesting that conflict can operate on multiple levels simultaneously, internally and in a wider social system.

Conflict and contention often lead to the desire by those confronted to react with surveillance and enforcement, the topic of chapter 6, "Control." How do challenged groups and threatened institutions respond? In systems of local authority, how is power deployed? How are options limited through the assertion of power on the local level? This constitutes a truncation of the interaction order.

I begin by comparing two instances of government decision-making, examining the internal dynamics of the meetings in which decisions were made. I examine the support of foreign policy advisors in the Kennedy Administration for the 1961 Bay of Pigs Invasion (Janis 1973) and contrast it with the response the following year to the Cuban missile crisis (Gibson 2011). These are occasions in which circuits of action within elite circles produce consequential outcomes. The policy choices reverberated through other military and policy groups in the United States, the Soviet Union, and Cuba. In the second instance, group dynamics produced a successful outcome, in contrast to the groupthink that characterized the first. Next, I examine a group that was targeted by government control and media pressure: the isolationist America First Committee, prominent in the years immediately prior to American involvement in the Second World War. The popularity of their beliefs and their influence led their opponents, the Roosevelt administration, British secret service, and interventionist supporters in the press to attack local chapters, using the presence of possibly disreputable actors to typify an organizational culture (Fine 2006). The America First Committee stands for other activist groups that take a position opposed by powerful others. Finally, I discuss ethnographies of police units. While I recognize the wider context of state control, I emphasize its operation in groups (Rubinstein 1973; Moskos 2008; Van Maanen 1988; Fassin 2012). How do local police cultures permit officers to control disorder? How does this culture permit or constrain the discretion that police see as integral to their work?

Despite the importance of local civic spaces, political systems operate in larger domains, especially given technological changes that sponsor new media. In chapter 7, "Extensions," I describe how a mesoanalysis might extend behind the local. In such circumstances, face-to-face interaction is altered, creating new circuits of action. This is particularly true given the prominence of social media and cyber-connection that challenge traditional face-to-face interaction, altering the meaning of "copresence" (Campos-Castillo and Hitlin 2013; Zhao 2003). New interaction orders are created as our understanding of what constitutes interaction has expanded. Social media require rethinking what it means to be together. Online communication, with its strands of "friends," exposes the significance of affiliative ties, even if these ties do not involve face-to-face interaction, once considered the sine qua non of social psychology. Are tiny publics truly tiny if anyone can join with a mouse click?

I begin by discussing the creation of terrorist cells by means of meetings that do not necessarily depend on face-to-face connection. Marc Sageman (2008) writes of "leaderless jihad," which can be constituted by neighboring youth but can also develop through online communication. Facebook produces communities—and they can be intense—but they have different contours than groups in shared physical space. This is the challenge of an interaction order freed from interaction as traditionally known. Then I address how social media organize mass movements. As is well established (Gerlach and Hine 1970), movements constitute themselves as tiny publics, relying on established communication channels, but how do cybermovements galvanize groups? What are the dynamics of coordination? The Arab Spring (Bayat 2013) demonstrated the activation potential of social media. Groups remain prominent, but the overarching structure consists of networks of groups. While such a reticulated structure can be effective, it is fragile as well. These mesolevel structures create the potential for a rapid increase in activity but, when interest wanes, an equally rapid decline. Finally, I examine a social movement explicitly tied to internet communication, only gathering on symbolic occasions to celebrate their own group culture. This is the Netroots movement (Kerbel 2009), a movement of progressive activists that meets annually but whose activism depends on creating an orderly online interaction space in which they coordinate their activities and recruit others.

The conclusion weaves together my themes and concepts, arguing for a mesolevel analysis drawing on culture, interaction, and structure. I hope that this provides a valuable and distinctive perspective on civil society through the core concepts of the interaction order, group culture, circuits of action, and tiny publics. Knitting civil society together through a set of locally based mesostructures holds promise, even if, inevitably, loose threads abound.

My Tiny Publics

I am grateful to the School of Social Science at the Institute for Advanced Study (IAS) in Princeton, New Jersey, for inviting me to spend a year as a member, participating in the "Egalitarianisms" workshop under the leadership of the wise Danielle Allen. This sabbatical exposed me to a wide range of philosophical topics and writings of social theorists, many of which appear in this volume. I am grateful to my colleagues at the IAS, particularly Danielle Allen, Peter Meyers, John Holmwood, Michael Walzer, Jill Locke, Didier Fassin, and Charles Payne. I appreciate the advice of other interlocutors, including Joshua Basseches, Ugo Corte, Jun Fang, Corey Fields, Tim Hallett, Brooke Harrington, Marcus Hunter, James Jasper, Lauren Langman, Kevin Loughran, Iddo Tavory, Hannah Wohl, and Bin Xu. Jerome Braun, Baptiste Brossard, Japonica Brown-Saracino, Andrew Deener, Michael DeLand, Judson Everitt, Danny Kaplan, Paul Lichterman, Jeffrey Parker, John Parker, David Trouille, and Jonathan Wynn commented on portions of an earlier version of the manuscript. These colleagues are my invisible college, my tiny public.

∿

This manuscript was completed on Christmas Day 2019. By the time copyediting was complete on Easter 2020, the world had changed. For how long or to what effect, we cannot know as I write these words at the end of Ramadan. But it was clear that something needs to be said, even while all of us are considering how we might engage with our tiny publics and whether interaction orders and group cultures will remain. I am grateful to my editor, Elizabeth Branch Dyson, for her permission to add a short afterword to this volume, even if we both realize that by Yom Kippur, I might have to atone for these speculations. The world can move rapidly; the publishing process less so.

1

COORDINATION

The Dynamics of Collaboration and Commitment

If we retain the natural attitude as men among other men, the existence of others is no more questionable to us than the existence of an outer world. We are simply born into a world of others, and as long as we stick to the natural attitude we have no doubt that intelligent fellow-men do exist.... As long as human beings are not concocted like homunculi in retorts but are born and brought up by mothers, the sphere of the "We" will be naively presupposed.

ALFRED SCHUTZ, *On Phenomenology and Social Relations*

The "tragedy of the commons," powerfully described by the American ecologist Garrett Hardin in an influential 1968 essay in *Science*, following the lead of the English economist William Forster Lloyd (1833), depicts the challenges of local groups acting in concert. Hardin writes,

> Picture a pasture open to all. It is to be expected that each herdsman will try to keep as many cattle as possible on the commons. Such an arrangement may work reasonably satisfactorily for centuries because low-level wars, poaching, and disease keep the numbers of both man and beast well below the carrying capacity of the land. Finally, however, comes the day of reckoning, that is, the day when the long-desired goal of social stability becomes a reality. At this point, the inherent logic of the commons remorselessly generates tragedy.

Can egoists live together? How? Millennia earlier the same dilemma had been raised by Aristotle in his *Politics* (bk. 2, chap. 3): "Everyone thinks chiefly of his own, hardly at all of the common interest." The assumption of self-interest suggests that everyone's property is no one's property (Gordon 1954). When will individuals commit to groups that shape their lives while not maximizing their own direct benefits? Recognizing the strain between self-interest and communal interest, how, when, and where does behavioral coordination occur, especially under circumstances in which the absence of coordination can produce undesirable outcomes for all? What is the role of inter-personal collaboration and group commitment in coordination?

Building on the vision of human nature propounded by Thomas Hobbes, Hardin saw humans as acting in ways that were dangerously individualistic and fundamentally selfish when not controlled. He argued that, left to their own choices, people would overwhelm the capacity of a shared environment. This perspective challenges a belief in the power of group organization, replacing it with what Hobbesian followers treat as a necessary, if baleful, balance between the greedy individual and the forceful state. Without a commitment to respectful sharing, one must rely on either state control or individual choices, as reflected in rights to private property in the enclosure of fields. In this view, to have order, control must be enforced by institutions or individuals, dismissing the influence of the voluntary group.

We should not assume that such choices are necessary. It is here that group cultures shape the conditions of the interaction order, leading to recursive and routinized circuits of action. Some groups have harmonious cultures. Even when they do not—as groups fight or split—the possibility for shared action through negotiation or coalition remains. This follows from the Tocquevillean perspective that suggests that citizens as individuals are weak, incapable of in-fluencing the course of events and would "sink into a state of impo-tence, if they do not learn to help each other voluntarily" (Tocqueville 2003: 597). Their traditions lead to styles of interaction (Eliasoph and Lichterman 2003). Coordination permits survival in a democratic system: not through top-down ordering but through horizontal engagement. Adjusting circuits of action is at the heart of politics (Somers 1993), allowing the individual citizen to navigate civil soci-ety successfully.

To understand how the Hinge operates, I work up from the ba-sic form of group development: the ability of individuals to sense a common purpose and to coordinate their actions. They adjust lines of action as part of a community. This produces a recognition that group members are continually considering the choices of others. Coordination is a basic form of interaction and, when recognized, helps explain how friendships and associations operate.

Political action and civic engagement provide a dramatic instance of the arts of coordination. Here the goal is to make local action run smoothly, often seen as an essential feature of the symbolic interaction perspective. In contrast to models that focus on how individuals shape their communities, I ask how groups motivate collaboration through commitment mechanisms. Individual energy, interests, and values shape action, but it is the recognition of group culture with its embraced traditions and common values that has deeper consequences for the community.

In contrast to Tocqueville's sunnier assumption of how communal action defined village life (at least in his traveler's view of American settlements), English villagers in this dreamscape did not privilege social coordination and its benefit—ecological balance—over self-interest and environmental catastrophe. The tragedy, in this telling, is that individuals, having access to a commons (often a grazing area) that all could use without formal restraint, were unwilling to limit personal use to preserve the meadow for the communal future.[1] This is what political scientist Elinor Ostrom (1990: 2) describes as the problem of common pool resources. The creation of private property on the meadow and in the fields, justifying the enclosure of the commons, provided for a state-backed system[2] that privileges the individual over the community (McCloskey 1975). The argument, linking the idea of the commons to the carrying capacity of environments, has had strong influence, shaping perspectives on development, ecological control, and population policy. The assumption is that the environment has a fixed and *knowable* carrying capacity, and requires external, compulsory controls for protection and preservation, whether through central planning or through the establishment of private property rights. For some, the real tragedy of the commons is that the powerful, with interests in controlling agricultural production, used the fear of overgrazing to create a regime of private property, denying the possibility of self-governing communities (Menzies 2014).

The image of the commons—and the possibility of voluntary coordination—is central to understanding collective action and its absence. The commons as a nexus for communal choice is vital not only for the relationship between the economy and the environment but also for the relationships within a community. For scholars like Ostrom who believe that the commons can be successfully governed, the challenge is to find systems of control that are enforceable and are recognized by participants as mutually beneficial. Research has emphasized "social dilemmas" through a set of resource games, such as the prisoner's dilemma game in which the intersecting decisions of several independent actors provide gains and losses for all parties (Yamagishi 1995).

As legal theorist Robert Ellickson posed it, the image of the commons raises the possibility of order without law. Is enforceable law inevitable? Perhaps this is an anarchist's question, but the discussion is valuable. Should we ask, selecting our literary metaphors carefully, whether a "romance of the commons" can compete with a "tragedy of the commons"? The two images depend on distinct views of human nature and on the feasibility of mesolevel social organization. A mesolevel analysis is one that economists rarely emphasize and which historians may not have the data to determine. A group culture—the existence of recognizable customs, traditions, and practices—constitutes a basis through which community members can, at times, work together in preserving a commons without relying on privatization or institutional control (Ostrom 1990: 8–13). By bolstering self-organization, culture potentially provides a system of self-governance without a Leviathan.

The idea of a commons—a community based on shared commitment and dependent on members who are willing not to maximize their own interests—raises important issues for the mesosociological understanding of civil society. When, where, and how do groups solve problems together, recognizing that an implicit and overarching question is why they choose to do so?

Journalist Sebastian Junger (2016: 91) suggests that this commitment is visible in warfare, where shared allegiance and a common threat create a "tribal" environment in which support for the community matters more—at least in this romantic telling—than individual success or survival. We can extend this analysis of the problem of coordinated action to the work that groups do for civil society, the limits of such work, and how, on occasion, groups undercut communal solidarity.

The commons is a site in which group coordination allocates limited resources. Even if pure common spaces rarely exist in the sense that there is land that belongs to all, societies find a commons whenever coordination is necessary to preserve resources that would otherwise be overused. Central to communal life, as imagined in accounts of bucolic villages, shared spaces are both an ideal and a threat, a possibility and a dilemma. Under the right circumstances, residents of small towns, rural communities, or urban neighborhoods work with and for each other. The exchange of labor is a recurrent feature of tight-knit communities. What seems to be personal altruism is but community order. Communal allegiance overcomes pressures for immediate self-interest, because of shared identification, informal surveillance, and social control. Once they identify with a group, actors are no longer purely *individuals* in their civic roles. Rather, communal members organize their rational selves and competitive interests to provide mutual support and regulate personal desires. Is it inevitable that a desire for common weal—a concern with the public good or local welfare—leads to tragedy in light of private interests that override group affiliation in the absence of state-based systems of social control?

The tragedy of the commons, especially Hardin's (1968) account, has been highly influential in the literature on law and economics, suggesting that private property bolsters social order in specifying rights and their limits (but see Bollier 2014; Linebaugh 2014). Further, the state preserves a property regime to check rivalrous competition, to promote resource accumulation, and to reward innovation. The enclosure of fields in England, fully enforced by the nineteenth century, marked a salient change in how the society organized itself, moving from the centrality of local groups to the primacy of individuals and their families, backed by state power.

Yet establishing this property regime does not necessarily eliminate all forms of the commons. Despite ownership rights, private property need not exclude interdependency, especially at the boundaries of adjoining properties or when title is ambiguous. Cooperation does not require an open and unenclosed meadow. Building and maintaining roads and other forms of infrastructure can raise collective action problems that demand communal adjustments to overcome the free-rider problem in which members wish to use common resources without contributing. How can there be order without law?

Coordination and Commitment

Every collaborative project demands coordination. The centrality of the group stems from the argument in phenomenology that the "we"

comes before the "I" (Schutz 1967), emphasizing the intersubjectivity of everyday life (Scheler 1954). In this tradition, community is a
phenomenological given. When parties agree on the processes that
underlie group life, collaboration creates comfortable social order.
We need no all-powerful Leviathan if we embrace a shared duty to
stability.

The commitment to maintaining interaction recognizes the centrality of negotiation (Strauss 1978) and the power of informality in
personal relations that motivates agreement despite different preferences (Stinchcombe 2001).[3] Awareness of a group's traditions and
practices and of members' commitment to them permit disagreements to be managed or, in the worst case, treated as inevitable.

Drawing on the analyses of philosophers of social action, I define
coordination as interaction in which individuals shape their own actions in response to others with the intention of carrying out a collective plan (Gilbert 1997, 2009; Bratman 1992, 1993; Tuomela 2007).
In contrast to those analyses of social dilemmas that focus on choices
arising from potentially conflictual resource distribution (Schelling
1960), here I focus on a desire for smooth interaction (disruption will
be discussed in chap. 5).

Coordination requires verbal and nonverbal signaling, commitments and intentions, and scripts and negotiation, a central theme of
both symbolic interaction (Blumer 1969; Scott and Lyman 1968) and
microlinguistic conversation analysis (Sacks 1995; Schegloff 2007).
Put another way, mutual understandings of an interaction order permit participants to engage together in response to forces that might
disrupt them. This highlights the interactional flexibility that provides
the mesolevel mechanisms that establish order.

Given that much collective action is performed routinely and without challenge, this reveals the power of circuits of action. These collective meanings have an ethnomethodological penumbra: implicit
et cetera rules (Garfinkel 1967) permit those copresent to adjust their
behaviors to facilitate smooth interaction and create mutual entrainment (Campos-Castillo and Hitlin 2012; Collins 2004). The recognition that a complete set of rules can never be specified permits both
desired flexibility as well as the possibility of misunderstanding, a
form of rough interaction that can be productive (Tavory and Fine
2020). Copresence permits the synchronization of attention, emotion, and behavior, even while also constituting the basis for conflict.

In most circumstances, adjustment is the desired default, whereas behavioral breakdown, even if mild and temporary, requires repair and accounts. Although collective meaning aids coordination by justifying action, these long-standing mutual understandings are not a necessary condition, as coordination only requires individuals to recognize that they have a shared goal and to direct their actions toward that end.

The optimistic claim that groups inevitably arrive at beneficent outcomes cannot be empirically supported. This is incorrect because participants acting in concert may generate costs that do not benefit all involved, but also because tiny publics as civic players may generate public outcomes that benefit some at the expense of others. In either case, this can be a destabilizing form of civic egocentrism.

Affiliative Practices

With affiliation as a guiding principle of collective life, respect often is more effective than discipline. *Soft communities*—spaces that accept all those who commit to core traditions and values—operate as effectively as hard domains that demand tight behavioral conformity (Fine 2015). Coordination organizes social systems through local practices and through broader authority that bridges local worlds, establishing translocal order. While complex structural coordination is essential for state governance, interaction routines are found at each level.

In a different sense from that of Benedict Anderson (1991), I write of "imagined communities." Anderson examines state systems, focusing on the effects of national literatures and common languages. However, microcommunities are imagined as well, perhaps with greater identity consequences. While Anderson assesses the role of the imagined community in linking individuals to systems of governance, imagined commitments are potent because citizens see other citizens as being *like them*. Affiliation is most powerful when neighbors serve as stand-ins for all citizens. Publicly performed rituals such as ceremonies, pageants, or parades (Warner 1953; Lane 1981; Glassberg 1990) create local cultures that are treated as national, just as organizers of degradation ceremonies use ritual performances of symbolic separation from a community to legitimate a shared political order (Garfinkel 1956).

Tiny publics depend on shared emotional entrainment to make

political order possible. Systems that rely on voluntary action are especially sensitive to emotional linkages among participants. Likewise, if tiny publics encourage apathy when their practices distance sociability from direct engagement, that apathy exists because members believe that their role as citizens demands only sociability and no more (Eliasoph 1998, 2012). Many publics disavow the political, distancing their group from public engagement with potential opponents (Baiocchi et al. 2014: 40). A person lacking connections—the stranger, the hermit, or the alienated—rejects deep participation in any of the available tiny publics that shape civil society.

Further, naming one's interaction partners supports belonging. The salience of identity work harkens back to Émile Durkheim's (1912) emphasis on collective representations as crucial to communal participation. This reflects Michel Maffesoli's (1996) belief in the importance of tribes in contrast to individual actors. Whether we accept that a group instinct creates tribal affiliation (Chua 2018), the desire to belong to a community larger than oneself, but smaller than everyone, is powerful. Junger (2016: 2–4) argues that the emphasis on the emotional component of a mesolevel bond explains part of the appeal of Native American culture. He notes that Euro-Americans occasionally drift into indigenous societies, but rarely the reverse, reflecting a comforting—if incomplete—belief that caring is characteristic of the tribe. The salience of identity-defining groups is evident in research by the Iowa symbolic interactionist school (Kuhn and McPartland 1954) that developed the Twenty Statements [Who Am I?] Test, emphasizing that individuals define themselves through participatory groups: families, clubs, or workplaces. We recognize ourselves not only through Charles Horton Cooley's (1902) "looking-glass selves" but through "looking-glass communities." One does not simply *have* an identity but instead *acquires* an identity through embracing a bounded public (Snow and Anderson 1987).

Self or Others

Despite discussing the theory of the commons, my concern is not the limited, if essential, debate about balancing public goods with private interests, but how coordination provides for the self-organization of small communities. Research on what has been labeled "nowtopianism" directs attention to institutions such as community gardens, soup kitchens, or cooperatives that create solidarity through hands-on action. In the words of Chris Carlsson and Francesca Manning (2012: 933), these constitute "emergent convivial 'nowtopian' communities" in which cohesion depends on unpaid, communal labor. This collaboration is separate from a narrow conception of self-interest and challenges the "extreme atomization of modern life."

This mesolevel focus causes us to question the often implicit assumption of microtheorists that individual choices do not depend on the primacy of colleagues. Much analysis of social order depends on the belief that by optimizing individual outcomes, an efficient market will develop, benefiting society at large, even if it does not benefit all equally. Yet rational choice theory is compelling only in a world of isolated actors who conceptualize their personal outcome as the most desirable option for all. This approach, in its pure form, assumes that people make decisions without concern for others in their social surround: a theory of monad morality. However, in a world of concerned citizens, this claim is both theoretically and empirically naive. We rarely find individuals maximizing their desires; rather we find embedded actors, part of nested and networked groups that take priority.

Models of rational action typically exclude the interactive middle—the site of group cultures—and then bolster their theoretical conclusions through methodological choices that shape that conclusion. Much rational choice research relies on experiments, but this methodology has the effect of supporting the theory with an experimental setting that creates a world of isolated actors. Experiments force subjects to respond to social dilemmas, but they ignore the conditions under which these choices are made in practice. In these studies, individuals are unmoored from their social environments and are forced to decide in isolation (Bernard and Barclay 2014). Given the complexity of any interaction order, this is implausible. Without the presence of others, subjects select strategies that emphasize personal benefits. The methodological structure by which researchers control extraneous variables, determining what is included as relevant and what is excluded as peripheral, shapes the findings. The problem is not the methodology of behavioral economics, rational choice, and experimental studies of social dilemmas as such, but rather the theory of *relevances*—the exclusion of the social—that stands behind these methods. Experimental methodology simulates a model of decision-making, but what happens when the simulation as structured misses the presence of family, friends, and neighbors?

Identity and Affiliation

A mesolevel approach to civic life starts with commitment and the coordination that being embedded within a tiny public entails. Put another way, identity is built on joint activity, not only personal belief. Coordination depends not only on the presence of interaction but assumes a commitment to interaction. Civic engagement stems from an interaction order that presumes the legitimacy and the necessity of negotiation, stemming from a recognition of shared morality and common identity (Greene 2013). A belief that interactants participate in the same normative world permits those adjustments on which stability depends. As Douglas Harper (2001) notes, examining farming communities in upstate New York, farmers routinely aid each other (even today, despite a growing service economy), rejecting payment in the expectation that reciprocal help will be freely given. As one North Country farmer explained, "If we got done [harvesting] first, we'd go help somebody else finish. Or if they got done, they'd come and help us. It was all worked back and forth. There was no money involved. Of course, nobody had any money!" (Harper 2001: 89). Harper refers to these social relations of mutual aid as constituting a "neighborhood system." Each farmer lacks sufficient labor for immediate tasks, but a system of trading labor benefits each farmstead and the local economy.

When community defines social relations, help given and received is treated as essential and natural. For Richard Sennett (2012: 263), cooperation builds society, preventing shocks to the system. However, as Sennett emphasizes, cooperation is not inevitable but a skill to which people must be socialized, threatened by individualism and market economies. Building community is a vocation. Morale, so central to evaluating group success, refers to the willingness to cooperate without coercion, and not to a mere state of happiness. Morale, thus, is interpersonal. In other words, "favor banks" depend on patterns of microcredit.

In this view, identity becomes social, tied to commitment to systems in which we are embedded. These linkages encourage consistency between our self-image and the imagined self-images of those around us. We come to see ourselves as the kind of people who will gladly aid others in our social surround.[4] Boundaries of the community, defined by local institutions such as churches or schools, bolster this belief and provide reputational benefits when aid flows. Informal exchanges are evident in ethnic self-help organizations in which individuals or families contribute to a fund loaned as needed, creating webs of support (Mitchell 1978; Nee and Nee 1973).

This system has been institutionalized through microcredit associations, transformed from communal-help fellowships into banks that provide small loans. While the money lent by these banks is from outside of the community, often provided by supportive nongovernmental organizations (NGOs), banks in rural communities or in impoverished urban neighborhoods may establish gatherings of borrowers to provide support as a condition of financial provision (Sanyal 2009). These are truly tiny publics in the sense that these gatherings are developed in order to contribute to civil society. Such groupings, based in strong local cultures, may encourage women's entrepreneurial development or challenge gendered attacks (Chakravarty and Chaudhuri 2012).

This provisioning of resources depends on the *charity of small numbers*, tied to a belief in reciprocity as a moral requirement, as an expectation of mutual exchange, and as a commitment to shared values. Groups transform collective concern into what E. P. Thompson (1971) described as a "moral economy," powerfully held and publicly acknowledged. Economic relations depend on ways of being and of living. These tiny publics mesh shared values and commitments into a system of support. Perhaps reciprocity originates in self-interest, but a devotion to group life rapidly takes priority. Affiliation becomes a virtue in itself.

In moments of dispute, allegiance tempers conflict, treating communal bonds as too valuable to breach. The dedication of the group to its continuation protects against rupture. Current negotiations build on past negotiations, creating an ongoing history of adjustments.

As I discuss in chapter 5, negotiations may fail and conflicts may arise when individuals draw on different views of the past, different logics of action, or different templates of mediation. These bases of rupture may include unresolved grievances, unreciprocated benefits, or competing practices of dispute resolution. In addition, relations are potentially unstable as actors leave and enter, especially when a new cohort enters the community together. Even without intending to do so, a cohort may alter norms of coordination.[5]

Three Joints

To describe the dynamics of coordination, I present three approaches by which community members jointly work together. A community can collaborate through joint recognition, joint action, or joint structures. The first, joint recognition, reflects the perception of a common world and a willingness to share that vision. Participants find that perception is not personal but communal (Friedman 2014). Consistent with the social constructionist perspective of Berger and Luckmann (1966), they construct a collective reality, evident through symbolic markers of consensus. This does not imply that people inevitably act in a collaborative fashion, but that they recognize the existence of similar interpretative schemas. What might otherwise constitute diverse modes of thinking are joined together, often through conversation in creating alignment.

A second form of coordination is joint action, often treated as central in describing why groups matter. Tocqueville's example (2003: 219) of a small group of neighbors joining together to remove a blockage in the road, an example to which I return in chapter 3, is an archetypal instance. This is more than neighbors independently recognizing that a problem exists but, rather, recognizing a superordinate goal and a common interest.

The third way in which communities come together is through joint structures. A structure is needed beyond common recognition and coordinated action. Some semipermanent social arrangement must provide for ongoing connections. Sometimes an outside agent may organize a group to achieve a desired goal. Alternatively, a set of individuals commit themselves to achieve goals that they consider mutually advantageous.

I return to Ellickson's (1991) neighborly disputes over the use of adjoining land. Some wish the land for grazing, while others worry about animals destroying agricultural fields. Some desire ponds stocked with fish, while others need that water for crops. Some demand the safety of a small-town traffic light, while others want to travel without delay.

In my tripartite division, the first communal sense involves joint recognition of a problem, the second calls for steps to solve the disagreement, creating a mutually agreeable solution, and the third recognizes that similar disputes might recur, requiring a forum tasked with addressing problems. This form of structuration—establishing an interactional arena for coordination—incorporates both joint recognition and joint action (Giddens 1984).

Because this model of concerted action does not presume that solutions originate from individual choice nor that they are externally structured, we must recognize both the layering and the networking of groups. Layering addresses the hierarchical arrangement of groups within a resource system and networking addresses the horizontal bridging of groups.

A mesolevel analysis asserts that there are "groups all the way up" and "groups all the way down." Local interaction systems connect with others with different amounts of power and authority to produce a hierarchy of coordination. The groups at the top of a hierarchy invariably depend on other groups to enforce policies down to the street corner or family circle.

Cooperative Worlds

Collaboration is central to creativity in artistic, industrial, and political domains (Sawyer 2007; Faulkner 2014), but it is also central in civic activity. Thinkers as diverse as Adam Smith and Karl Marx have understood cooperation as a "productive force," enhancing outcomes beyond the individual's personal needs. Just as innovation can result from collaboration, so can developing an innovative and productive interaction order.

I present three empirical cases. These examples address distinct forms of coordination: those in which benefits are to individuals (and their close associates), those that produce an outcome with benefits that extend beyond the group, and, consistent with the problem of the commons, those forms of coordination that assess immediate costs to individuals as well as long-term benefits to communities. This working together potentially advances collective interests as opposed to individual desires. Of course, while coordination has a harmonious tone, coordination may be pressured because other groups with more power force groups to collaborate in a conflictual world, as in the case of warfare.

First, I describe the practice of exchanging labor. This example involves mutual aid among farmers in rural communities, common when the labor market is thin and capital is in short supply. I present research that I conducted in southern Indiana exploring the value of intergroup contact under supportive circumstances. I also return to Douglas Harper's (2001) historical ethnography of agricultural cooperation in upstate New York.

Second, I consider political collaboration, a more structured form of coordination, examining the creation of civic documents. How do committees create a local interaction order (Schwartzman 1989; Haug 2013)? As scholars of meetings emphasize, gatherings are organized through the adjustment of time and space, creating agreement or dissention based on the pressures to complete tasks in light of constraints. Such collaboration is often sponsored by elites, whose impact results from their role as representatives of authoritative communities. Actors can represent others while representing themselves, and, as a result, external pressures impinge on free choice and compromise. This collaboration involves greater complexity than the simple labor exchange that characterizes farming communities but, like mutual aid, it also entails goal-directed coordination. I examine the composition of the Declaration of Independence in 1776 in Philadelphia by the Continental Congress, a process that political theorist Danielle Allen (2014) cites as an example of "democratic writing" or writing by committee. This constitutes a temporally limited—if inspired—form of coordination. Many constitutions are produced through similar strategies, as are other significant political documents such as the Magna Carta and the United Nations charter. Those selected for the task determine through mutual agreement the rules by which they will collaborate. While we may attribute a document to a single hand, it takes its final form through collective input.

Finally, I turn to the problem with which I began the chapter: the use of common spaces and the enclosure movement that limited these spaces in creating a regime of private property and state control. I draw on small-group theorist George Homans's (1941) iconic account of the everyday life of English villagers of the thirteenth century and the use of the pasture and other forms of rural collaboration, permitting local townsmen to graze their livestock on shared space. This system pre-dated the development of property enclosures and private property: what Karl Polanyi (1944) writes of as the Great Transformation in the European economy. These medieval practices raise the question of whether small communities can develop stable but informal resource distribution, given the preening power of individual interest.

CHANGING WORKS ACROSS THE COLOR LINE

Consider a simple instance of coordination—how farmers support each other in time of need—and how these routine transactions serve the interest of the community. Barn raisings are warmly satisfying markers of neighborliness. This mutual aid represents a communal ideal when residents define themselves as alike. However, even if differences are salient, support survives.

To describe agricultural sharing I rely on an oral history project I conducted in a corner of southern Indiana that explored how white and African American farmers built social relations that permitted mutual aid, despite the fraught race relations that have characterized the region. Many consider the area as an extension of Kentucky, part of the upper south. Abraham Lincoln's family, living in Kentucky at his birth, moved to southern Indiana a few years later. In 1903, a deadly race riot broke out in Evansville, Indiana, causing the death of twelve residents. During the 1920s, southern Indiana was a center of activity for the revitalized Ku Klux Klan. Racial harmony was the exception, not the rule.

How then during the period from 1857 until 1939—from before the Civil War until the Second World War—did members of a small African American community and their white neighbors live harmoniously together (Fine 1979b)? What features make group contact successful and shared space communal?

One way in which strains over resource competition and group rivalry are alleviated involves the creation of stable relationships. Under certain circumstances, social relations produce intergroup harmony, a finding—overly optimistic in some tellings—that proclaims that if only people could know each other, discrimination and prejudice would evaporate. The naive, "kumbaya version" is that simply by recognizing that others are human, icy hatred will melt. However, recognition of "universal brotherhood" is more the exception than the rule. Boundaries may include (in the best case) or exclude (in the worst). When does positive contact extend the circle of community?

This model, developed from research on race relations by social psychologist Gordon Allport, is known as the "contact hypothesis." The theory has been supported and specified by decades of research (Pettigrew and Tropp 2011). Allport (1954: 267) writes:

> Prejudices (unless deeply rooted in the character structure of the individual) may be reduced by equal status contact between majority and minority groups in the pursuit of common goals. The effect is greatly enhanced if the contact is sanctioned by institutional supports (i.e. by law, custom, or local atmosphere), and if it is of a sort that leads to the perception of common interests and common humanity between members of the two groups.

Merely placing members of distinct groups that have troubling histories in the same location with the possibility of interaction does not assure that they will collaborate or define themselves as part of a community. The history of American race relations reveals moments when contact elevates hostility. To specify the contact hypothesis, Allport points to four conditions that promote a positive outcome: the presence of equal status contact, involving common humanity, backed by institutional support, and with the perception of shared interests. Extending Allport's analysis, Yehuda Amir (1969) argues for the need for intimate, not superficial, contact. As a social psychological phenomenon, mutual contact is treated as individual contact. However, contact also shapes group relations. When do groups transcend divisions that they had once treated as defining?

As noted, the empirical basis of my case involves a community of farmers in Dubois County. This is a rural, largely German-Catholic county in southwestern Indiana, similar in topography but unlike much of the area demographically, as the broader region is dominated by Anglo-Protestants. The Pinkston community reveals how contact allows for coordination that contributes to local harmony. The connections and values of these farmers, black and white, produced harmonious group contact. While this is a satisfying story, an adequate interpretation must recognize the prejudicial policies of the state, the racism in the surrounding region, as well as unquestioned assumptions about racial hierarchy among the residents. Coordination and collaboration cannot erase white privilege, even in the face of neighborly goodwill and shared labor.

Around 1850 Emanuel Pinkston, a freeborn black man, married Millie, a slave, near Atlanta. Three children were born to them in Georgia, and Emanuel soon bought his wife and youngest son from slavery (Sounderman 1955). They subsequently moved to the free state of Indiana. Documents reveal that in 1857, a Manuel Pingston purchased forty acres of land in Dubois County for $365. According to oral histories and county documents, Emanuel Pinkston was at least as successful a farmer as his neighbors. By 1870 the population surrounding his farmstead had reached thirty (then increasing to fifty-eight according to the 1880 census). The settlement now included several farmsteads. By the late nineteenth century, a pattern of shared labor emerged among black and white farmers, reported in newspaper accounts and the memories of informants. During the 1870s, with the help of their white neighbors, the black community erected a building that would serve both as a Missionary Baptist church and a school (the Indiana Supreme Court had ruled in 1874 that public schools must be segregated). We shudder at the irony that the first recorded example of communal collaboration was the construction of a segregated school. Both black and white residents recalled ongoing mutual work tasks on local farms: thrashing grain, butchering pigs, and participating in communal quilting bees. Community members held social events, playing cards, singing, dancing, and celebrating birthdays. In 1904 Ida Hagan, one of the African American residents at the Pinkston settlement, was sworn in as assistant postmistress for the local Ferdinand Post Office and, despite some hostility from those in other parts of the county, served for eight years without incident. Outside the county, the attacks on the postmaster and his new assistant were vehement and explicitly racist. One wrote, "Of all the postmistresses under the skies/ There is none that I more despise." Reports indicated that Ms. Hagan was slandered in Jasper, the county seat, but accepted in her small community of Ferdinand (Fine 1979b: 234–35). While by no means definitive, the *Ferdinand News* noted, "The Negroes were highly respected by their white neighbors in the vicinity, being industrious and honest" (Fine 1979b: 237). Although one should not romanticize neighborly relations, evidence supports the existence of meaningful cross-racial cooperation.

This social relationship, as thin as it might be in the broader society, reveals the effect of positive contact in the creation of community feeling. Although rural, agricultural, and small-town life has often been thematized as tight-knit, leading to labor exchange, few studies have focused on how coordination of mutual interest can overcome racial or other boundaries. The case of the Pinkston settlement supports the importance of those conditions that Gordon Allport suggested produce positive social relations.

The Pinkston case involves groups that were, in the local context, of equal status. Land and tax records reveal that the Pinkstons and their neighbors the Hagans were as wealthy as their white neighbors were. Since they migrated to Dubois County at about the same time as their German-Catholic neighbors, they could not be claimed to have intruded. They did not acquire resources that others had previously held. They shared in activities found in farming communities. In Douglas Harper's (2001) terms, they were embedded within a "neighbor system" in which mutual aid benefited all parties in order to complete planting, butchering, thrashing, and harvesting. Harmony depended on blacks and whites not competing; the success of one benefited the other, as sharing could tide them over in times of scarcity. While institutional supports were not as clearly favorable given the established racial prejudice in the state, the reality that both African Americans and German Catholics were targets of discrimination allowed for recognizing common interests. While the Ku Klux Klan had no significant presence in Dubois County during its period of growth in the 1920s, both groups were potential targets as Klan activities in the region were widely publicized. The fact that several members of the Pinkston community converted to Catholicism surely bolstered these ties. Finally, the interaction must lead to the perception of common interests, producing an intimate linkage between groups. Over decades, the contacts were continuous and long lasting. In their cleanliness, religiosity, and acceptance of established authority, the two groups were similar, increasing the likelihood of coordinating actions. Of course, other factors, idiosyncratic to the situation, influenced comity, such as the personalities of the participants, similar group structures, and local cultures. Still, this case reveals that, given the proper background conditions, interaction orders can permit intergroup coordination to flower in what otherwise would be rocky soil.

DEMOCRATIC WRITING AND COLLECTIVE MANIFESTOS

While mutual aid appears natural, in other instances those in a community of interest must negotiate to produce a desired outcome. Consider a project in which political actors—a recognizable tiny public—must find common ground. With large organizations, such as the United States Congress, some system, formal or informal, is necessary to share information and to produce legislation. James Curry (2015) points to the control of information by Congressional elites (party leaders and committee chairs), themselves informal groups. The specific details of bills are tightly held and are negotiated by a few central actors who demand agreement before wide public discussion. This follows Nancy Pelosi's otherwise puzzling claim about the Affordable Care Act, "We have to pass the bill so that you can find out what's in it." Lobbyists, the offices of the Senate and House legislative council, and White House staffers wrote the bill through small group communication. Too much input would have made this legislation—and all complex legislation—unwieldy. Representatives rely on information that others—more active players—share. At other times, decisions arise through informal arrangements, outside of formal structures, revealing the power of group coordination. In recent years, the Gang of Eight (immigration), of Ten (energy policy), of Fourteen (filibuster rules), and two Gangs of Six (health care reform and public debt) have shaped Senate debates. Politicians strive for models of governance through close-knit groups, impossible in larger bodies. The ideal size for group action is generally claimed to be between five and eight (Bales 1954; Blenko, Mankins, and Rogers 2010; Hackman and Vidmar 1970). With this size, groups can coordinate decisions that produce an outcome that all will support, even though it represents none of their views perfectly. This is the challenge of civic compromise, but it permits a larger community to find the outcome acceptable.

We can conceptualize political communities as metaphorically akin to a small town. In this sense, these are truly tiny publics—minute civic worlds. Drawing on his Congressional Fellowship, William Freudenburg (1986: 321–22) emphasizes the importance of personal relationships, the salience of interpersonal chemistry, the emphasis on friendliness, and the prominence of gossip in establishing relations. Others speak of legislatures as akin to a college dorm or clan with each committee having its own group culture (Weatherford

1985: 178). A study of British government reveals cultures based on gossip, joking, storytelling, and networking. These produce friendship, loyalty, and occasionally altruism (Rhodes 2011: 192–96). I return to these themes later, but here I emphasize that this research indicates that affiliation is crucial to the creation of legislation, an essential, if more technical, form of democratic writing. As Joshua Basseches (2015) argues, analyzing the passage of environmental law, informal social relations within a legislative body count as much as formal institutional procedures in generating statutory outcomes. Junior members may have their legislative priorities enacted because of positive relations with their caucus leaders.

The Continental Congress faced a huge challenge in its deliberations. Despite growing discontent by the colonials, how might its members justify a break with what many felt was the legitimate British government? The vast majority of the colonists believed that the king and Parliament were their rightful rulers. Revolution—or at least independence—must be justified. This was the great achievement of the "Committee of Five," tasked with writing the Declaration of Independence. While today's public believes that the document was solely the work of Thomas Jefferson, such was not the case, and a Jeffersonian Declaration would have looked quite different from the text that was birthed and embraced. This was an instance in which the small group served, in effect, as a performance team whose goal was to alter the perspective of the broader civil world, changing hearts and minds. The interpersonal coordination among the members of the committee provided the integration of a diverse set of perspectives that could shape public response. This emphasis on a joint process is consistent with the "art worlds" model of Howard Becker (1982) and the "collaborative circles" accounts of Michael Farrell (2001). These approaches downplay the role of isolated geniuses, recognizing that creativity flows from group support and inspiration and, further, that the incorporation of diverse inputs can prove persuasive and appealing to a broad audience.

In her account of the creation of the Declaration of Independence, political theorist Danielle Allen emphasizes group collaboration—what she labels "democratic writing"—demonstrating that the final product was the outcome of debate and negotiation. Thomas Jefferson was less of an independent genius—an auteur—and more of a member of a collaborative circle. As Allen (2014: 47) claims, "Group writing is not easy, but, when done well, it heads the ranks of human achievement. It stands even in front of works of individual genius, because it involves a far greater degree of difficulty."[6] Perhaps optimistically, at least from the jaundiced perspective of a social psychologist, Allen (2014: 47) asserts,

> We can see human intelligence as a collective force, a powerful instrument for grasping the world, effective because it pools the capacities of multitudes of people. The art of democratic writing entails understanding how to contribute to the collective mind.

As a scholar of group process, I find it more helpful to speak of strategies that organize social relations and interaction orders. These collective strategies rely on relationships of trust and influence. By the time that he arrived in Philadelphia in 1775, young Thomas Jefferson had already established a reputation as an effective, articulate, and radical writer, but the text was not Jefferson's alone. What finally emerged in "Jefferson's Draft" (Maier 1997) was shaped by ongoing conversations and letters on how to create new governments between John Adams of Massachusetts and Richard Henry Lee of Virginia. Based on their dialogues, Adams eventually published a pamphlet on independence, "Thoughts on Government." This text and other writings helped form the ideas in Jefferson's draft. Jefferson had to consider the concerns of Adams and Lee as well as of those less radical in their goals and rhetoric. As noted, the Congress appointed a committee of five — Jefferson, Adams, Franklin, Roger Sherman of Connecticut, and the New Yorker Robert Livingston—to prepare a declaration justifying independence of the colonies. (The Congress often appointed small committees of three or five members for various tasks, producing small knots of conversation [Allen 2014: 79]). Eventually Jefferson, less burdened by other business than his colleagues, wrote the first draft, but one that reflected the ideas in the Virginia Declaration of Rights, penned by George Mason. Together the committee, particularly Adams and Franklin, made editorial changes. After this work was completed, delegates to the Continental Congress further edited the document, which they shortened by nearly one-quarter. Unlike some instances of committee meddling, these changes produced an elegant final product (Maier 1997: 148). As Allen (2014: 80–81) demonstrates, the Declaration that we revere emerged through a multistage editorial process. She recognizes the role of Jefferson in producing a draft that survived intense committee debate but adds, "the authorship of the document belongs to all those who participated in the conversations leading up to the decision to declare independence and to all those who wrangled over the consensual statement of justification." Through negotiation and votes, the document is metaphorically an archeological site, where different layers of meaning, produced at different times, can be unearthed. This process of writing is comparable to the negotiation that one routinely finds in legislative work or perhaps on online wikis. People trade ideas and phrases, struggling to create a document that has the proper effect, even when later they can no longer defend its interpretation. Still, the deliberative process reminds us of the salience of group action in coordinated governance.

THE COMMONS AND SCARCE RESOURCES

If a tragedy surrounds the ultimate historical failure of the commons, a romance envelops it as well. These alternate images assume the possibility of interpersonal harmony, a harmony taking priority over the amassing of resources. It references a beloved time when herders and tillers held land in common: a socialist imaginary. Yet the system of commons and its enclosure began to disappear as early as the thirteenth century (Homans 1941) and had largely vanished after the General Enclosure Act of 1845 in England (open fields lasted longer in the Scottish highlands [Menzies 2014]). As a result, one must rely on historical documents that often lack a social psychology and rarely address the details of cooperation or competition. The open field system for growing crops in what the English termed "champion country" operated in conjunction with common, or open, grazing land for cattle and sheep.

As George Homans (1941) describes English villages of the thirteenth century, agricultural fields, other than those of the lord of the manor, were often divided into strips, each controlled by a family. Farmers helped each other complete their work, jointly plowing fields and borrowing tools (Homans 1941: 78, 82). This is another example of shared agricultural labor.

However, common meadows and fields—grazing land—posed different challenges, especially when the land might be overutilized if all relied on it as much as desired. Further, changes in agricultural practices were slowed because of the need for group decision-making. Innovators could be frustrated by those who were more skeptical of experimentation. In both custom and change, communities had to determine the allocation of this scarce resource. The control of "greedy neighbors," using too much of the collective resources, was at issue. Good character was essential for a congenial community. The village as a social group depended on the willingness of individual farmers and their kin to define themselves in common cause and act accordingly, sacrificing for a larger group benefit. Enclosures helped to solve this problem (as well as providing windbreaks and firewood), but at the cost of community and by creating hierarchy and *private* property.

As thirteenth-century farmers knew the value of fallow fields, they could use those fields for feeding cattle and, in the process, fertilize the fields for the following spring. Neighbors objected when farmers used part of the fallow field for their own crops. Even so there was a danger of overgrazing, and, as a result, communities sometimes limited the number of livestock each farmer could graze (Homans 1941: 60). Some villages hired shepherds, swineherds, and neatherds (for cattle) to protect the stock of each family, with each assessed proportionally. The wide streets served as a collective pen for cattle. While many rules for the use of the commons were based on custom, at times explicit coordination was necessary, adjusting to weather conditions, deciding which hedges were closed or open, selecting the herdsmen, and regulating the common herd. These restrictions, which prevented overgrazing, meant that the commons were "stinted," restricting the number and kinds of animals permitted to be pastured (Allen 1992: 26). Beginning a tradition of town meetings, villagers met as a collective body to establish bylaws coordinating village husbandry and enforcing these rules when violations occurred, often by fines or the forfeiture of animals (Homans 1941: 101–4). Each community created a system of order with forms of discipline and officers to organize their common spaces: a "miniature parliament" of a "self-governing village community" (Tate 1967: 31; Menzies 2014: 53).

This system thrived because of a commitment to the primacy of group life. As decisions built on communal routines, a circuit of action organized village life. As George Homans (1941: 106), himself a small-group researcher, understood well, social comity depended on continuing associations:

Villagers worked together successfully in carrying on the various affairs of their community, and people work together not usually because they recognize that it is to their advantage that there be such cooperation, but because they feel certain active sentiments which make them able and willing to cooperate with their fellows.... Villagers even had a name for these sentiments: they called them *neighborhood*. Of course, in any particular village, neighborhood might break down into mutual distrust. Perhaps it was always in danger of breaking down, and perhaps when it did so the bitterness was all the greater because of the closeness of the contacts between men. But if we can judge by farming communities in modern times, the traditions of cooperation were probably so well established that they could survive a great deal of petty bickering. Neighbors groused at one another but worked together just the same.... A village formed a community chiefly because all its members were brought up to consent and act together as a group ... actively considering how to make provision for a successful future.

The commons provides a strong case of how communal coordination operates when individuals depend on and are committed to each other, creating beneficial private and public outcomes (as well as possibly negative outcomes). Although it had many causes, the decline of the commons suggests that coordination is difficult to achieve as a social system that continues over time and is resistant to claims of individuals and of larger institutions. Perhaps the decline in the commons proved economically beneficial. Indeed, many agricultural historians suggest that enclosure ("the yeoman's revolution" [Allen 1992: 21]) led to increased agricultural productivity and national prosperity. Still, in ways that are smaller and more transient, under the commons, community members could set aside personal desires to achieve collective aims. Interpersonal harmony became a goal, producing coordination. The commons, no longer found within agricultural communities, remains a model for civil society sometimes found in other arenas (notably technical and digital domains as well as food co-ops and industrial cooperatives (e.g., Whyte and Whyte 1991; Haedicke 2012).[7] In these settings individual desires for maximum gain potentially place a heavy burden on the carrying capacity of a system unless local actors are able to moderate personal interest.

Common Dreams

I draw on three cases to support my claim that shared commitments and joint action produce coordination and productive outcomes through the development of interaction orders that rely on group cultures. Circuits of action, building on these understood routines, create a stable community in which members see themselves as linked in common cause, believing that their relations will continue in a predictable and orderly fashion. Communal help, collaboration, and co-ordination trump individual self-interest.

These three cases reveal the possibilities of group coordination and suggest potential benefits of people working in concert. In each, action is sustained by a collective "we-feeling," which is self-reinforcing. However, differences separate the cases: we find benefits to individuals, benefits that extend beyond individual actors to larger social spheres, and individuals' willingness to incur immediate costs in the expectation of long-term benefits. Further, we find distinct time-based organization: are individuals focused on immediate or long-term outcomes? Collaborative projects have different temporal horizons (Tavory and Eliasoph 2013).

The Tocquevillean concern with shared action and common cause must be central in considering the public good.[8] The "civil" component of civil society suggests that meaning depends on social relations within an interaction order. Although I do not insist on "civility" as essential, given the battles that can be fought in the name of justice, discourse rarely degenerates into a fearsome Hobbesian war of all against all. However, the recognition that collaboration is an ongoing project in a democratic system means that circuits of action can both be stable and open to alteration as the need arises.

Civil society is ultimately built on routines, understandings, and negotiations that groups embrace. Capacities and skills, critical for organizing a social system, are taught and are learned within communities. Individuals make commitments, affecting what joint action is permitted. Likewise, a model of commitment and coordination must account for the reality that social relations occur within a structure in which external forces and controlling groups have great influence. We fight for our beliefs from our niche within a wider world. Recognizing the value of examining individual choices and external constraints, we find something vital when we consider projects that are bigger and more complex than what an individual could achieve. These are too closely linked to community considerations to be merely the detritus of state decisions, but develop on a local stage. Imagining—and *knowing*—that others are part of the same realm of meaning creates tiny publics that together do the work that constitutes society.

2

RELATIONS

Friendship and the Politics of Sociability

*Every real Friendship is a sort of secession, even a rebellion. It may be
a rebellion of serious thinkers against accepted claptrap or of faddists
against accepted good sense; of real artists against popular ugliness or
of charlatans against civilized taste; of good men against the badness
of society or of bad men against its goodness. Whichever it is, it will be
unwelcome to Top People. In each knot of Friends there is a sectional
"public opinion" which fortifies its members against the public opinion
of the community in general. Each therefore is a pocket of potential
resistance. Men who have real Friends are less easy to manage or "get at";
harder for good Authorities to correct or for bad Authorities to corrupt.
Hence if our masters, by force or by propaganda about "Togetherness"
or by unobtrusively making privacy and unplanned leisure impossible,
ever succeed in producing a world where all are Companions and none
are Friends, they will have removed certain dangers, and will also have
taken from us what is almost our strongest safeguard against complete
servitude.*

C. S. Lewis, *The Four Loves*

Although we may conceive of civil society as dependent on the coordination of beliefs and behaviors, shaped by those who fill institutional roles, social relations are at the center. Relations matter as
much as institutions or selves (Emirbayer 1997). As a result, civil societies and national cultures are shaped by friendships, both through
groups and in networks.[1] Much modern social theory, not grounded
in relational politics, treats personal ties as either apolitical or even
as antipolitical. If, however, as the ancients taught us, citizenship depends on affective engagement, friendship has a prominent place in
the relationship between the citizen and the state. As Aristotle wrote
in the *Nicomachean Ethics* (NE 1155a2224),

Friendship (*philia*) seems to hold states together, and lawgivers to
care more for it than for justice. For when men are friends they have

no need of justice, while when they are just they need friendship as
well, and the truest form of justice is thought to be a friendly quality.

Flourishing societies require an energetic "culture of friendship":
a collective promotion of connection and mutual engagement. This
culture provides order to interaction and commitment to the group
cultures. Intimate ties inspire personal creativity, but the friendship
group and affiliative network generate a civic creativity that is based
on trust. However, the question is how friendships matter and how
this results from the social location and the resources of participants.

Both the ideology and the practice of togetherness constitute society as built on gemeinschaft relations, not gesellschaft structures.
This requires a recognition of forms of interaction: exchange, debate,
or influence. We need to invite "friendship back in" (Kaplan 2018). To
contribute to a larger community depends on recognizing oneself as
embedded in a set of meaningful idiocultures that involve embracing
a domain (the nation, the citizenry) that extends outside one's circle
of friends. The sociality of group life depends on generalizing beyond
the local. Civic friendships potentially can build the good society: a
patchwork network of trust (Bellah et al. 1991: 116). We become committed to participating in circuits of action in which our past relationships justify our current and intended future choices. The ability
to talk with others in productive and trusting ways builds political
capacity among colleagues (Allen 2004; Honohan 2001).[2]

Despite the appeal of the romance of friendship, we must not assume that these relations always bring freedom, equality, and harmony in their wake. Even if we recognize that positive affective ties *in
general* are desirable, they may also exclude, oppress, or harm. Even
terrorists have chums. However, it is not only the friendships of outsiders that can damage a vibrant civil society. As Jo Freeman (1972–
73) points out, friendship ties and an absence of transparency can lead
to elite control, a recognition that the "Georgetown set," discussed
later in this chapter, reveals. Friendships can promote preferential
treatment. This is, after all, why many worry about interlocks among
corporate boards and among privileged male, white, and Ivied colleagues in a gendered and racially divided world. It is significant that
the small group of Supreme Court justices all have Harvard and Yale
pedigrees. While we should not dismiss Aristotle's belief in the virtues

of friendship or C. S. Lewis's belief that intimate ties prevent malignant control, we must not erase the vices of closeness.

In conceptualizing friendships in light of tiny publics and minute communities, we recognize that bundles of friends, burning brightly, can cool or split, and that groups can define themselves in opposition to others. The existence of a thousand rings of intimates does not presume a single cohesive community. Politics in America today with its multiple divisions and derangements surely demonstrates this all too clearly.

Politics and Poker

Political activists depend on the power of relations in shaping collective action through their emotional attachments and patterns of discourse (Gurbuz 2015: 1; Shepard 2015). This is what Michel Foucault (1981), speaking of gay culture, described as "friendship as a way of life."[3] For Foucault, the history of friendship constitutes the basis of a challenge to widely held norms. In these circumstances, generating firm and lasting friendships becomes integral to a personal commitment to others and to shared goals, allowing for the gathering of resources (McCarter 2017). Powerful relations—fraternization in Jacques Derrida's (1991: viii, xi) terms—provide the basis of a strong but hidden solidarity that stands athwart convention (Shepard 2015: 21). Claims of the value of friendship are hardly new; the argument that friendship is the platform on which a just society rests reaches back to the Greco-Roman claims of Plato, Aristotle, Cicero, Seneca, and Plutarch (Devere 2013). This argument suggests that civic friendship determines the possibility and the limits of democratic freedom and equality (Schwarzenbach 2009; Mallory 2012). It has this power because of the robust group cultures created. These cultures provide a basis for communal engagement and those routinely accepted patterns that I have described as circuits of action.

Despite the appeal of the "romance of the friend," friendships can also lead to violence or oppression toward those outside the bond (and, sadly, as in the case of romance, sometimes of those within). Friendships are civic in that they model larger social relations—creating the tiny publics that contribute to civic order. However, civic orders are neither always virtuous nor always civil.

The salience of social relations in creating a just society is captured in one meaning of the phrase, "the personal is political."[4] Although the phrase sometimes suggests that what some consider personal issues (childcare, maternity leave, abortion) should be treated as matters of state concern, it also suggests that personal relations (and networks of like-minded, supportive colleagues) provide the basis of political processes, the point originally made by activist Carol Hanisch, its author. Those with a shared commitment are most likely to create vibrant group cultures that then can be utilized for civic ends.

Mark Granovetter (1973) argues that both strong and weak ties provide communal organization in distinct ways. Weak ties build local extensions (described in chap. 7) that span interactional gaps, while strong ties establish the support that builds allegiance to civil society. The salience of connections led to the "relational turn" in social theory (Crossley 2011; Donati 2011; Donati and Archer 2015). Ties among those who have authority or who respond to control shape structures. Power is relational, but so is justice.

Friendships stabilize community, and, for this reason, sociability is central in public life. This recognition must transcend the Simmelian view of interaction devoid of instrumental purpose (Simmel 1950) but rather embrace Erving Goffman's perspective that affective interaction creates commitments. This permits those with a wide network to gain influence. Although friendships are dyadic, dyads build on each other, expanding outward to establish cliques or communities. In creating friendship nodes, tiny publics constitute a mesolevel civil politics. As Hannah Arendt phrased it, "Friendship is so eminent a republican virtue," suggesting that the practical truth of statecraft is a politics of friendship. For Arendt, friends are "partners in a common world—that they together constitute a community" (Gebhardt 2008: 335–36). While we must not treat interactional connection as inevitably producing caring or shared fate, when that caring or recognition of fate occurs, we find the virtues of acquaintanceship.

This approach explains how small groups have become essential forms of support in helping individuals address personal problems, including spirituality or addiction. Robert Wuthnow (1994) suggests that these relational arrangements are characteristic of American society. The "small-group movement" provides the social capital that scholars such as Robert Putnam fear is lost, given the declining membership in once vibrant formal associations. For Wuthnow, the copresence of those who face the same life challenges builds a commitment to civic action as well as personal growth. Like-minded others model democratic discourse and provide recognition that the larger civic community has legitimacy or, in contrast, can suggest the possibility of a shared desire for revolt. Even such seemingly mundane occasions as a coffee break (Stroebaek 2013) or snack time (Roy 1959–60) create a stage for a community of coping as well as providing a site for amused banter or heated discussions of current events. Although writing of a more resource-rich community, Martin Ruef (2010) describes the power of entrepreneurial groups, discounting the myth of the solo visionary. He describes business ventures in the context of relations and shared cultures. While homogeneity helps to establish the culture of an entrepreneurial organization, so do intimate working relations. The granular knowledge of each to each generates collaboration and coordination.

Although positive affect and personal obligations might seem far removed from political decisions, in classical political theory friendship was treated as central to the good society (Von Heyking and Avramenko 2008). In the Greek and Roman tradition, personal friendships could never be detached from political ones. Civic life is embedded life. Yet the modern emphasis on individual autonomy and personal interest has marginalized friendship in much political theory. The relationship among friends is now treated as fundamentally distinct from the relationship with the state (Dewey 1954), but at the cost of ignoring how the local ties of tiny publics model extended ties. In much contemporary political thought, friendship is treated as moving people *away from* the community, rather than bringing them *into* the community, perhaps because the dyad is assumed to be intimate, private, and closed. Dyadic ties are often treated as having priority over citizenship, separating the pair from others and rupturing civic commitment in the process (Brunkhorst 2005: 12).

Political actors often support the projects of close companions, perhaps as much because of the connection as because of the ideology. As a result, it is not surprising that citizens with civic experience are more likely to engage in political activities (Leighly 1991; Verba et al. 1995). Participation in civic groups has a political effect, even if that effect is not the reason for the group. An informal social arrangement, such as a neighborhood garden, not only provides a sense of belonging but, as significant, can open an opportunity to enact leadership, increasing confidence in democratic participation (Keohane 2014). The same is true for small groups that operate within a church setting. These groups provide opportunities for leadership with benefits for political engagement. As Paul Djupe and Christopher Gilbert (2009: 245) examine the political influence of churches and the groups that constitute "congregation life," they note that

> These small groups are the settings in which civic skills are nurtured, where church members meet new discussion partners and reinforce relations with old ones, where theological and political norms of the congregation are passed along and enforced, where clergy often have an opportunity to interact with individual members, and where recruitment into politics is most likely to take place.

Such sites are strong examples of the power of tiny publics. Interests are continually modified by a desire for harmony and a shared interaction order. This assumes a desire for interpersonal smoothness that motivates much negotiation.

FRIENDSHIP AND THE CITIZEN

While we desire the kindness of strangers, the kindness of friends is more secure. No matter where in the hierarchy of power we stand—in a military unit, a legislative committee, or a political cell—decisions are filtered through communal connections. The theory of politics must include camaraderie and sociability. No social system can long exist if we believe that we are independent egoistic agents, taking the Hobbesian view. As Aristotle put it, "Friendship would seem to hold cities together" (Brunkhorst 2005: 12). In Cicero's terms, in loving his friend, he loves his country (Brunkhorst 2005: 15).

Social ties are important not just because they create dyads (Shenk 2014) but because that dyad is incorporated in a more extensive "community of relations." Strong relationships provide the basis for order because they encourage group stability but also because stable groups build strong relationships. Friendships as building blocks of networks have a multiplier effect, permitting access to the friends of friends, and then to their friends as well.

A sense of justice derives from the centrality of communal friendship. Justice happens not because it is demanded but because it is what is owed to friends and acquaintances. The belief that others are our friends—and that we are theirs—builds cohesion and trust. In turn, shared political commitments draw people together. The relationship between affect and shared vision operates in both directions. From this perspective, friendship reflects a commitment to equality and a connection to the state. This model is particularly appealing for those who encourage participation by women in politics (Schwartzenbach 2009) as the nurturing of relationships is evident in female caring labor. However, even male models of fraternity, solidarity, or comradeship recognize group affiliation as the basis of a just political system (Rawls 1971: 105). Sociability matters not only for what it does in creating rewarding outcomes but also because it defines a community. The willingness to participate in an equal-status social system, coupled with a desire to share resources, creates what Sibyl Schwartzenbach (2009: 54) speaks of as "civic friendships," social relationships that operate through the state's social and political institutions. This is necessary, Schwartzenbach claims, for true justice and political health.

To be sure, one might wonder about the extent to which societies that are less just also rely on friendship. Preferential treatment and patron-client relationships reveal the effects of friendship ties. In highly stratified societies (such as France's ancien régime [Horowitz 2013: 21]), friendship was a tool to access power. Even though patron-client relations are grounded in the exchange of resources, deference, and loyalty, they also suggest positive affect. Perhaps in one circumstance the patron dominates, and perhaps in another—because of familial or neighborly relations—the client or the client's kin will have power. These forms of inequality depend on friendship but do not lead to egalitarian relations. In totalitarian regimes, a tight-knit set of relationships may be present, as the ability to work with those one trusts may be especially salient when condemnation can lead to severe consequences.

These relations constitute what Robert Vargas (2016a) has termed "cultures of camaraderie." Friendship can provide entry into systems of governance for those with limited resources. We see this, for example, in the pragmatic significance of personalistic relations in accessing bureaucracy (Herzfeld 1993). As Vargas describes, governments may hire outreach workers whose responsibility is to build relations to clients so that they feel they will be treated fairly in that these workers perform the role of friends.[5]

The cultural ideal of a governing authority within a democratic state assumes that those selected as leaders are people with whom one could become friends or at least have positive social relations. As a result, politicians work at grooming ties with their constituents at breakfasts, open houses, and coffees (Fenno 1978), returning to their legislatures and departments to participate in other small groups composed of more lasting political friends and with distinctly different cultures. Many of our presidential candidates—of both parties—offer opportunities for comradeship: a steak dinner with President Trump, pizza with Mayor Pete, or coffee with Senator Warren. These are surely thin relations, but the fact that they work as fund-raising devices bolsters the claim that these are "friendship-worthy" people. The successful politician, like the competent ethnographer, should be skilled at recalling names and personal details. Although stronger in democracies, the idea of the leader as friend occurs even in pseudo-democracies, such as dictatorships that claim the support of the public. This explains why both Hitler and Stalin had themselves pictured with young children. If they were the kind of leader who loved—and was loved by—children, they must be likable and worthy of support. They claim qualities that make them desirable public citizens: someone with whom to share a beer.

One of the crucial points for those who study political and economic elites is that the powerful are themselves linked by the existence of friendships. These are relations to which those with less authority or privilege (perhaps because of class, race, or gender) have limited access (Mills 1956). This grooming of elites begins early on (Khan 2012). While friendships as a generic form contain much virtue, they are always situated in webs of power or in their absence.

SOCIABILITY AND THE CITIZEN

Friendships are an instance of a broader issue: the social ties among citizens and the creation of tiny publics.[6] Here I look beyond specific relationships to general principles of relations among civic actors, treating an engaged sociability in the context of an ideology of friendship. This emphasizes friendliness more than friendship; it involves the ability to maintain an open performance style.

I address the dynamics of conflict in chapter 5, asking whether disruption between or within groups may serve valid civic purposes and create affiliation for those who share ideals, but smooth interaction has virtues in producing affiliation and negotiation. This emphasis on the virtues of cordial disagreements stands in contrast with the current discussions of politics in Washington. Although some friendships cross the aisle in Congress, as in bureaucratic and journalistic Washington, there seems to be a thickening of partisan divides that may produce sharpened personal divisions as well as an unwillingness to negotiate. The reality that external audiences see personal friendships as undercutting political beliefs may weaken the *display* of camaraderie among rivals. Further, to the extent that politics is treated as an indicator of moral virtue, these ideological divisions may weaken the likelihood of a communal culture. The belief that partisans should be treated "as if" they are not split by irreconcilable differences is hard to maintain when disagreements are treated as ethical claims.

Societies differ in the emphasis that they place on sociability, at least rhetorically. Ancient Greece, early eighteenth-century England, Revolutionary France, and post–World War II Germany are sites where social connections were emphasized as the basis of civic virtue. The ideology of fraternity, brotherhood, or comradeship became a marker of a strong community. The flowering of tiny publics was treated as a blessing.

Post–World War II Germany is a case in point, at least in part because German intellectuals were explicit in desiring a sociable society. Jakob Norberg (2014), examining the ideology of sociability there, emphasizes that, in a society in which civic structures needed to be rebuilt, interpersonal connections were vital. Citizens recognized that this reestablishment had to include those with different perspectives, backgrounds, and attitudes to the Nazi regime (although not those who were directly implicated in its cruelties). Norberg (2014: 5) writes of the postwar era,

> New or old acquaintances greeted each other, invited others into their drawing room for a light lunch or tea and cake, and began to articulate their very own personal opinions on the state of the world while being (somewhat) mindful of what could blatantly offend their interlocutors.

These meetings constituted a "conscious effort to return to or symbolically enact the resumption of a genuinely civil life." The desire to resurrect "bourgeois sociability" became, for some thinkers, the path to a new Germany, a cross between therapeutic practice and political tolerance. In arguing for a public sphere as a training ground for institutionalized democracy, theorists such as Jürgen Habermas emphasized the value of this form of interaction. As Norberg (2014: 6) writes,

> Intellectuals and engaged theorists looked to how sociability draws together and coordinates individuals in shared activities that could be presented as civil rather than martial, voluntary rather than coercive, sustained by self-monitoring individuals rather than imposed by an external agency, tied to quiet and peaceful circumstances rather than emergency and war, and based on reciprocity rather than narrow self-interested pursuits.

This produced the desire to create small social circles—tiny publics—symbolically capturing the golden age of Goethe (Norberg 2014: 15). If the Nazi regime depended on the silence of citizens, postwar Germany welcomed a culture of talk. One might consider this desire as a more explicitly political version of the other-directed man as postulated by David Riesman (1950) during the same period. After the trauma of war and state violence, for many Germans friendly gatherings represented a treasured form of normalcy.

Sociability provides a model of friendship in that it both overcomes political divides and generates a transcendent view of community based on the veneration of locally constituted groupings that support government legitimacy. In other words, these tiny publics are the basis on which a state builds civic loyalty by permitting citizens to create conditions for the sharing of political virtues and the belief that others act from similar honorable principles.

THE ACTIVATION OF FRIENDSHIP

Friendship—and the sociability that flows from affective ties—constitutes a resource for successful action, often labeled social capital. While social capital need not imply the positive emotions inherent in friendship, it assumes the presence of supportive acquaintanceships: perhaps as much a transactional model as one based on affect. One can utilize friendships in one's civic role using the metaphor of a favor bank. Yet, we err if we conceptualize social capital as merely the number of friends one has or the number of groups joined. More significant is that recognized relationships permit claims to be made on others (Lichterman 2006).

Although the social capital approach has a lengthy genealogy, its contemporary prominence developed from the insight of James Coleman (1990), who treated social capital as a strategy by which individuals maximized their interests, building community by creating dense networks. Less tied to rational choice arguments but equally influential in emphasizing a mesolevel analysis, Robert Putnam (2000) has doggedly asserted that a robust civil sphere depends on the prevalence of strong relations and supportive institutions.

Although social capital provides a compelling image of the value of friendship, the metaphor, part of the neoliberal monetization of sociality, is not without challenge. However, rather than defend or attack this now widely discussed concept, I utilize it in light of the concepts that motivate my analysis: interaction orders, group cultures, tiny publics, and circuits of action, putting aside the economistic imagery. A system of action that incorporates the activation of friendships with their rights and responsibilities—the heart of the idea of social capital—provides a set of understandings through which relations become the basis of structure. This was the fundamental insight of Erving Goffman, who understood that interaction orders depend on shared recognition of allowable and expected actions. These understandings—local and transient as they originate—serve, in effect, as structures that guide performance. Routine and regular interaction partners—what we term groups—create ideas of what is right and proper. As these ideas are given solidity through shared memories of particular occasions and their display in action, they constitute group cultures that provide a content-laden commitment to the interaction order.

Social capital is currently a favored metaphor, but different groups emphasize different forms of "capital," each of which can be deployed in light of the group circumstance: in wealthy suburbs or inner-city barrios (Small 2004). However, in both locations connections and the resources that result are powerful. Group norms of coordination may matter more than the simple fact that members can request favors from those in their circle.[7]

How do friendships and acquaintanceships affect civil society?

Why, in the face of interests and resources, do connections matter? In this, a tiny public—a group committed to communal participation—provides a platform for civil society. As a result, we can explain the value of relations through concepts developed in psychology (identification), sociology (allegiance), or political science (loyalty).

While civil society can be treated simply as a network of meaningful relationships, it operates through the dynamic engagement of participants whose actions depend on their recognition of their relationships. Put another way, social capital assumes skills of sociability (Portes 1998). Networks do not only provide information, they produce a wish to engage with others. They create a desire to heed local norms and bend to social pressure and, as a result, shape political behavior, encouraging involvement in the democratic process (Sinclair 2012: xii). This is true even though social relationships, often homogeneous, are rarely formed solely based on political attitudes. However, those friendship ties and the culture that they produce encourage involvement, particularly during periods of focused political activity, such as campaigns or social movements. "Politics"—an active consideration of policy and policy makers—never occurs in isolation but as part of an embedded community. It requires a cadre of *social* citizens, activated by family and friends.[8]

Intersecting groups have the potential to develop expansive networks, creating the possibility of organizational recruitment through whom one knows and how one knows them. As David Snow and his colleagues describe for the Nichiren Shoshu Buddhist movement, a school of Japanese Buddhism, American adherents recruit through their connections, building on established relations and differential association (Snow et al. 1980). As individuals are embedded in multiple networks with crosscutting pressures, this increases the extent of potential recruitment (McAdam and Paulsen 1993: 640).

Of course, some relations constrain participation in collective activities. Relations can be greedy, preventing those involved from extending their network or sharing activities (Tavory 2016). Marriage is a notably greedy institution in this sense, limiting outside engagements (Coser 1974). To suggest that social ties inevitably create new social commitments neglects the cultural content and the emotional intensity of dyads. Personal relations with their local cultures must be consistent with preferred identities to create new affiliations, and these change depending on circumstance. Thus, at a given moment a person without alternative commitments might find a friend's influence to be powerful, while on another occasion, the guidance will be ignored. Friends do not inevitably matter. Further, multiple ties—ties with a preestablished group of friends—are more compelling than the ties of a single friend in motivating commitment.

Only later does mass media bolster personal recruitment. Movements thrive with close-knit supporters, even if these groups have only occasional linkages with those of greater power or institutional centrality. Groups are motivated through collaborations, producing a strong group culture that generates commitment to costly action (Della Porta 1988) and overcoming the collective action problem (Olson 1965). Marc Sageman (2008) speaks of a leaderless jihad in the post-9/11 era, arguing that terrorism consists of "informal local groups ... conceiving and executing from the bottom up." Who needs Bin Laden in a world of Facebook and hookah bars? Any clique can be a violent cell. To be sure, not only terrorist cells are at issue. Many revolutions and insurrections depend on partisan bands no larger than a small group. These groups have conviction, the ability to move swiftly, and, because of their tight boundaries, can resist state surveillance.

Through their social relations, small-scale networks build solidarity through grievance frames that larger units cannot easily generate, overcoming fears of retribution by state actors (Gould 1995; Pfaff 1996; Gamson, Fireman and Rytina 1982). Commitment to the group may be so powerful that failure does not produce disillusionment (Summers-Effler 2010).

Group efficacy does not occur only among elites but at all social levels. This is supported by the neighborhood-effects literature in which researchers of urban poverty, otherwise at some remove from the examination of small-group cultures, find that characteristics of local communities determine how social systems are organized through collective efficacy. The contextual features of an urban interaction order are crucial for analyzing the organization of inequality (Sampson, Morenoff, and Gannon-Rowley 2002; Quillian and Pager 2001). Robert Sampson and his colleagues claim that broad structural forces are mediated through the lifeworlds of particular communities with their distinctive cultures, linked to local institutions that encourage or retard the development of collective action and social control (Sampson, Morenoff, and Earls 1999; Sampson and Raudenbush 1999). This research challenges the view that all poor neighborhoods are alike because of their structural similarities and recognizes that community feeling can buffer external threats.

While the focus on local effects is important, such projects must recognize how historical processes affect neighborhoods. Japonica Brown-Saracino's (2009) ethnography of Chicago gentrification emphasizes that this dynamic depends on the communal backstory—both real and imagined—of the neighborhood that is being transformed. While the microstructural perspective on neighborhood effects is insightful in recognizing the diversity of community, the "processual how" of these effects may be lost. In other words, the neighborhood-effects literature requires an urban ethnography to demonstrate how efficacy operates not only in principle but in practice. As David Harding (2010) points out, the dynamics of collective efficacy can produce within-group control, preserving social relations, or can create preemptive violence among groups, grounded on the defense of turf. Ultimately, the patterning of interpersonal relations builds capacities that create power within group contexts, whether used for community building or for disengagement and disruption.

Civic Friendships

The salience of relationships in civil society becomes clear through three cases that vary in their linkage to power and to overt participation in politics. Friendships are connected to civic engagement, from neighborly aid to breakfasts with friends to dinners of elites. I begin with the simplest case: a network of social relations that provides personal support. I draw on Carol Stack's (1973) impressive urban ethnography, *All Our Kin: Strategies for Survival in a Black Community.* Stack describes how mutual assistance moderates—but does not eliminate—the poverty that characterized the Flats, a midwestern African American community. This is a point consistent with many subsequent urban ethnographies that find robust interaction orders in impoverished neighborhoods. Whether this involves limiting gang activity, help to those facing eviction, or sharing childcare, local cultures prevent the breakdown of a normative order (Desmond 2016; Duck 2015; Pattillo-McCoy 1998; Venkatesh 1997). In contrast to the routine expectation of help in farming communities, Stack describes how friendships matter. While these communities appear unstable to the outsider, the trope of a "disorganized neighborhood" is misleading. Although impoverished neighbors are not often directly involved with wider civic engagements, their real friendships, collective help, and shared concern transform the neighborhood into a site of protection, despite the dangers that remain. Stack's detailed observations emphasize that communities are solidified through friendships that generate reciprocity, even if these relations are fragile or disposable (Desmond 2012). Friendship is essential but is found within a status quo that disadvantages the community that lacks a tradition of activism. In other cases, distinct from the ostensibly apolitical Flats, friendships may establish recognizable communal boundaries as in the case of defended neighborhoods (Suttles 1968; Rieder 1985).

More political in content, if not political in action, is the group of friends that Katherine Cramer Walsh (2004) describes in her account of informal meetings of a group of middle-class men, gathering regularly at a café in Ann Arbor, Michigan. These men, longtime friends, enjoy discussing current events. Although they rarely participate in political activities apart from voting, their relationships solidify their commitment to a progressive community in which their conservative views are marginal.

In contrast, some sets of friendships have wider consequences. Friends who see themselves as part of communities of influence can be powerful, whether elites (Goodwin 2013) or those in revolt (McCarter 2017). Elite connections can be transformed into relationships of patronage (McLean 2007). In all circumstances—in democracies and under dictatorships—government policies are set by those with personal commitments to colleagues and to policies. To understand this process I describe the political engagements of a group of associates who hoped to shape American foreign policy. Members of the Georgetown set (Herken 2014) included American politicians, intellectuals, journalists, academics, and bureaucrats, most residing in Washington's posh Georgetown neighborhood. The group never fully dominated American foreign policy, but their influence was extensive and flowed from their ability to activate their deep and lasting friendships.

COMMUNITY AS KIN

When Carol Stack first visited the Flats, an impoverished African American community located near the rail line between Chicago and

New Orleans, she discovered a community that appeared anomic, apparently lacking a productive interaction order. However, as she came to know the residents, she learned of its tensile strength, its resilience, and its organization. This community, like many lacking resources, was not politically engaged, but residents created relations of support, trust, and interpersonal responsibility.

Familial structure, linked through bloodlines, is not the only means through which tight-knit commitments are built. Families can be biological or social. In either case, mutual obligation is powerful. In locations that appear to be dangerous—what has been labeled "dysfunctional"—alternate forms of social relations are possible. A network of friendships develops norms of social exchange. Stack (1974: 57) writes,

> Men and women in The Flats know that the minimal funds they receive from low-paying jobs on welfare do not cover their monthly necessities of life: rent, food, and clothing.... They place their hopes in the scene of their life and action: in the closed community, in the people around them, in kin and friends, and in the new friends they will make to get along. Friendships between lovers and between friends are based upon a precarious balance of trust and profit.

These ties build a tight yet changing array of group cultures. A relationship grounded in trust assumes that through shared effort participants will recognize a common past and envision an extended future. Friendship is treated as integral to neighborliness. As Magnolia explained,

> Some people don't understand friendship. Friendship means a lot: that is if you can trust a friend. If you have a friend, you should learn to trust them and share everything that you have. When I have a friend and I need something, I don't ask, they just automatically tell me that they going to give it to me.... If a friend ain't giving me anything in return for what I'm giving her, shit, she can't get nothing else.... You can't care for no one that don't give a damn for you. (Stack 1974: 57)

She depends on a model of friend-based reciprocity as constituting civic relationships. This relational model is particularly evident in "social families." One finds the construction of extended families, often involving the care of children. Some in the personal network are treated as aunts and uncles and have authority to discipline children that are not theirs biologically. For the state that takes formal biological ties as the basis of authority, this system is challenging, but friendship networks accept the reality of social families, creating a set of safe spaces in which those lacking privilege can find security (Collins 2000). Stack describes instances in which non-kin raise a child with whom they have no biological connection, such as Oliver Lucas, who is raising his ex-girlfriend's daughter, while he lives with his mother and her kin:

> My girl friend had six children when I started going with her, but her baby daughter was really something else. I got so attached to that baby over about two years that when my girl friend and I quit, I asked if she would give the baby to me. She said fine, and my "daughter" has been living with me, my mother, my grandmother, my sisters and brothers ever since. (Stack 1974: 66)

At other times, children are shared with members of extended kin networks; unlike borrowing money or equipment, taking a child is consequential. In contrast to clans that are larger than nuclear families but are still based on blood, social kinship allows relationships to be reconfigured flexibly. These ties are shaped by acts of kindness or anger and evaluated through gossip (Stack 1974: 58). Other studies of impoverished communities, as in the Canadian north, reveal similar patterns (Van den Scott 2015), leading to a belief that the constricted nuclear family results from resource luxury, even while limiting commitment to children. What is important in these local relationships is that some families are seen as trustworthy agents, and so the Old Head, elder, or respectable person (Anderson 1998; Duneier 1992) is part of the structure of a community that might otherwise be poorly networked. Even street corner groups (Anderson 1979) or those in bars or taverns (Bell 1983; May 2001) translate friendship ties into a recognizable community. We should not be so romantic as to suggest that these relations equal the advantages of resource-rich communities or communities in which a strong value-consensus exists, but networks based on trust and group affiliation create stability in the face of change, unpredictability, and threat. The Flats constitute a set of interlocking group cultures, which, if relationships are fragile and political discussions are rare, are still a friendship-based civic space.

TALKING WITH FRIENDS

One reason that talking to strangers is so difficult is that talking with friends is so easy. Talking with friends assumes a shared culture, an understanding of interaction norms, and an extended commitment to continuity. As a result, disagreements can be treated as engaging entertainment. Friends are second selves to their fellows (Allen 2004: 132–40). Comradely talking establishes a space between the home and the state, creating an open civic life by means of an intimate public. Acquaintances find their remarks understood in supportive ways, ignoring potential pejorative interpretations. In conversations among friends, judgments of opinions are shaped by social relations, rather than through the content of the talk alone. Among acquaintances, but not strangers, the speaker's civic virtue is assumed, even if these intimate ties may demand deeper exchanges, sometimes more stressful.[9] Danielle Allen (2014b) writes of a connected society, grounded in democratic knowledge. These citizens enjoy the bonds of solidarity as they establish bridging ties with diverse communities, recognizing and transcending differences. This ability constitutes the art of affiliation.

In contrast to the friendship-based exchange relationships in the Flats, some groups engage explicitly in political discourse. This talk arises from social relations in settings where, given operating norms and expectations, free-flowing discussion is encouraged. Politics makes for entertaining discourse. As Allen (2015: 184) points out, both ceremonial expressions and mundane talk maintain communal norms and contain disputes. Friendship knots are true tiny publics: intimate and observant of the surrounding world and willing to engage with it. Yet their boundaries, while creating affiliation, also constitute the "dark side of social capital" through exclusion (Walsh 2004: 181).[10]

To observe a tiny public is to confront how politics is cultural, even outside of explicit activism. As people develop political beliefs from personal experience, they rely on the narrated beliefs of others. This leads to Katherine Cramer Walsh's (2004: 4) observations of a group that she refers to as the Old Timers: "a group of retired, white, middle-class to upper-middle-class (objectively defined) men who meet every morning over coffee in a neighborhood corner store in Ann Arbor, Michigan." The group consists of about thirty-five regulars, although daily attendance is lower. As Walsh describes them, the men are politically conservative, although similar dynamics of consensus-building are found among ongoing progressive groups as well. Some groups are more cohesive than others (the Old Timers are tight-knit with many ties from their school days), but all these groups desire a sociable politics. Consider a discussion Walsh monitored in which inflation, class structure, economic inequality, and racial position merged in a seamless way. Disagreement is evident, but so is the commitment to maintain the conversation and the relationship. In these tight-knit groups, people agree to disagree and enjoy the disagreement:

> Dave: I was in the mood for English muffins last night. I like English Muffins. Went to the store to get some. We were out. The wife usually has them around the house. So I went to the store for them. You know how much they cost? $2.49!
> Stu: How many were in there?
> Dave: Six, I think.... I don't know how people do it these days. I don't know how some families survive.
> Stu: Well, they're making a lot more now than we used to, Dave.
> Harold: Yeah, but some of them don't make very much and they have two or three kids to feed. That's hard.
> Dave: The problem is the divide between those on top and those on the bottom is growing.
> Stu: I don't know about that . . .
> Harold: It is getting bigger.
> Dave: Disappearing middle class. More and more people on the top and on the bottom.
> Stu: I would disagree. I think the middle class is growing, getting larger, more prosperous.
> Harold: I would agree with that. I think the problem is that the ones on the bottom are getting worse off—that part is growing. The heavies are getting better off, but so is the middle class. It's the ones on the bottom that are hurting.
> Stu: I don't know. They aren't all that bad off. I volunteer at the Peace Neighborhood Center.... The families that are down and out now don't have it nearly as bad as the families that were down and out twenty-five years ago. (Walsh 2004: 34)

Walsh also observed a group of blue-collar workers, a group of elderly women, and a group of homeless people who met at a breakfast
program, indicating the diversity of groups, even if not a wide diversity of expressed opinions within groups. Revealing the prevalence of
tiny publics, the Citizen Participation study (Verba et al. 1990) finds
that approximately half the adult population was part of a group that
discussed politics. Steady acquaintances may gather in factory break-
rooms, in faculty lounges, in library seminars, or in church fellowship
halls. Crucial is that participants treat the discussion as a place for
comradely affection, never too invested in winning a point. If debate
becomes too heated, unleavened with respect and humor, the group is
likely to dissipate or politics to be treated as off-limits. The challenge for
those who wish to involve a wider array of citizens is to create situations
in which talking to strangers is transformed into talking with friends.

ELITES AT TALK

Whatever the ideological underpinning of democratic debate, friendship counts. People who work together often like each other, and
those who like each other work together. Building on chapter 1, contact can moderate the weaponized divides in contemporary politics.
Communities of political actors are akin to small towns with their
commitments, affections, and disputes.

I select the case of the American foreign policy establishment in the
period from the end of the Second World War until the Vietnam era,
examining a generation of journalists, academics, and policy makers
who together helped shape a muscular anti-Communist foreign policy, generally aligned with the Democratic Party. Significant figures
such as Joseph Alsop, George Kennan, Paul Nitze, Ben Bradlee, Chip
Bohlen, Katherine Graham, Allen Dulles, and Richard Helms participated in this group. These figures constituted beau monde Washington as well as the foreign policy establishment. Senator—and later
President—John Kennedy was close to several members of the group
and discussed sensitive foreign policy challenges with his friends,
including Khrushchev's ultimatum to the United States to evacuate
Berlin. While these men did not fully shape American foreign policy,
they and their allies were highly influential. George Herken (2014:
13) describes this group as the "Georgetown set," because of the resi-

dences of key members in a privileged neighborhood of Washington, a political village with all of the intimacies and divisions that the term "village" implies. Herken (2014: vii) quotes Henry Kissinger, part of the broader community, as remarking (perhaps playfully, perhaps derisively), "The hand that mixes the Georgetown martini is time and again the hand that guides the destiny of the Western world." With a similar implication, Herken (2014: 7) describes the Georgetown set as "one of the most extraordinary clubs the world has known ... a natural aristocracy." These friendships were intense and highly political. From college many of these (mostly) men knew each other through tight social networks. The strong culture of the group protected its members from scandal as well as providing opportunities. While civility and sociability do not inevitably serve benign civic purposes, they prevent thorny contention and bitter exclusion, such as was evident in the extreme rhetoric of the McCarthy era.

Ultimately, a political clique tends to become a social group. While the Georgetown set was never the only game in town, it was particularly influential. Dinner parties, liberally lubricated by alcohol and Joseph Alsop's terrapin soup, became known as the "Sunday Night Drunk." As Philip Graham, the publisher of the *Washington Post*, exaggerated,

> In other cities, people go to parties primarily to have fun. In Georgetown, people who have fun at parties probably aren't getting much work done. That's because parties in Georgetown aren't really parties in the true sense of the word. They're business after hours. ...
> It's fair to say that more political decisions get made at Georgetown suppers than anywhere else in the nation's capital, including the Oval Office. (Herken 2014: 62)

These festive gatherings were sites of debate that eventually influenced cabinet meetings. This was a powerful and self-conscious tiny public: tiny in membership and large in effect. As problematic as friendships can be in the shaping of policies that support friends, when affection becomes enmity, the desire to damage a reputation through policy disagreements can become potent. These networks reflected a personalization of policy as the character of the sponsor became the basis of evaluation.

Influential tiny elites are evident elsewhere as with the Cliveden set, British aristocrats who argued for appeasement of Hitler. Examinations of the culture of Washington (Pearson, 1944; Leibovich 2013) reveal the long-standing prominence of networks of friends.

These relationships create barriers for those from other backgrounds to break into elite social circles (Rivera 2012). A power elite is often a cultural elite as well (Mills 1956). Often American political leaders graduated from the same Ivy League universities. This is "a form of government by invitation" (Herken 2014: 7). Members were awarded the title of "wise men." What was important was not their wisdom—if wisdom they had—but their social connections and the use of these connections to provide patronage and to guide others into those influential circles.

Gazing at post–World War II Washington, one virtue of Joseph McCarthy's crusade against the State Department with his staff of ethnic Catholics and Jews was to demonstrate how insulated were these elites. This cultural closure permitted subversives with the right backgrounds to gain influence and patriots with the wrong credentials to be excluded (Beim and Fine 2007). Despite their strong anticommunist stance and their concern with America's failed China policy, most of the Georgetown set were implacably hostile to the enterprise of Senator McCarthy, in part because of his déclassé standing, in part because he targeted their friends, and in part because of his "disagreeable" tactics (Herken 2014: 114–26).

In contrast to the impoverished residents of the Flats and the middlebrow Old-Timers, the Georgetown set had national impact that continued over time and shaped the choices of others. This ambition to extend a group's reach is important in establishing a public sphere that shapes other spheres. As with many coherent intellectual groups (Mullins 1974; Collins 1998), each depends on a social and intellectual structure and access to sympathetic media. They constitute a collaborative circle (Farrell 2001): a group that works together-but-separately with a shared sensibility. The Georgetown set was remarkably well placed to shape policy, especially during the period before internal disagreements became prominent. Eventually, the war in Vietnam upended the close conviviality of the Georgetown set. In politics, the reality that issues emerge and evolve underlines the fragility of social relations.

Sociable Citizens

In chapter 1, I described how actors collaborate for desired outcomes, detailing the coordination of action. However, politics depends on more than simply working together; those who work together must find their relationships meaningful, pleasurable, and lasting. But how does this occur? Friendship does not move citizens from the political arena but inserts them into it, constituting a salient hinge between the citizen and the state. As a result, friendship and sociability are essential features in an approach that emphasizes the relational and situated quality of politics. Examining focus group discussions among five distinct types of civic organizations, including religious, labor, and business groups, Andrew Perrin (2005) proposes the existence of political microcultures, sites of discourse that vary according to group context and culture. The particular contexts make political engagement more or less likely, encouraging or discouraging political talk. Social relations produce distinct moral, ideological, self-interested, or pragmatic logics because of shared framing (Gamson 1992). The narration of politics among friends is crucial to a mesolevel political engagement (Polletta 2006). The reality that these groups consist of participants who have worked and talked together generates a civil logic.

Those who hope to generate affiliation beyond the local must use group relations for their benefit. As political scientist Richard Fenno (1978) emphasizes, successful politicians are skilled in cultivating friendships, real or imagined. This approach underlines the relational components on which consent of the governed depends. The local constitution of affect is essential for civil society. Mutual care contributes to civic virtue.

However, as these examples demonstrate, the forms of friendship and their relation to politics differ widely. The first case indicates that communities depend on relational connections. Citizens, even without extensive material resources, rely on each other to share, and they expect reciprocity. They produce a system of rights, responsibilities, and castigation. I extend the "rural support" example of chapter 1 with attention to the social relations that generate mutual aid.

The second example connects a friendship network with political discourse. While the case of the Old-Timers involves regular gatherings, groups of friends often discuss politics. Ongoing discussions can be filled with savory and controversial commentary and vast disagreements. It is not that participants agree, but rather they assume that the group and its continuity matters more than the topic. The desire to belong overrides winning an argument or persuading a colleague.

The final example ties friendship to the shaping of policy. Powerful sets of colleagues often surround government, providing the basis for a penumbra of policy. Political actors do not merely have positions, they also have friends. Some of these publics are highly influential, reflecting a set of aspirations and a set of beliefs. When working within cultural domains, such as art and science, these take the form of collaborative circles (Parker and Corte 2018). When oppositional, they constitute "critical communities" (Rochon 1998). In both cases the groups wish more than amiable discussions; they want influence. Farrell (2001) describes the common purpose of the early feminists, the circle surrounding Elizabeth Cady Stanton and Susan B. Anthony. However, the Georgetown set, less a social movement than a foreign policy faction, has much the same structure. A set of actors develops ties, meets congenially, and uses their connections to promote an agenda at least for a time. By the late 1960s, the Georgetown set had lost their early influence: a group that had been seen as the best and brightest was now interpreted by many—other groups in other worlds—as responsible for misguided and even disastrous foreign policy.

These cases, despite their different lineages and linkages to power and resources, underscore the multiple ways that social relations provide the basis for commitment to civil society, denying that friendships are either apolitical or antipolitical. Whether dyadic friendships cement or separate individuals and communities, affective engagement cannot be removed from conceptions of the social. Even absent a formal structure—and sometimes due to that absence—friendly ties can serve similar ends as associations, perhaps with greater flexibility. The recognition of friendship can persuade participants that they belong together and, as a result, claims of citizenship are part of group culture.

Friends run in packs, providing network connections for civil involvement. In this, relations provide a context that permits ongoing circuits of action: a stable connection with (relatively) clear boundaries that permits routines and practices to be treated as legitimate and necessary.

3

ASSOCIATION

Bonding, Banding, and Bridging

> *The ingenuity of Americans in creating organizations knows no*
> *bounds . . . from the Aaron Burr Society to the Zionist Organization of*
> *America, one discovers such intriguing bodies as the Grand United Order*
> *of Antelopes, the Elvis Presley Burning Love Fan Club, the Polish Army*
> *Veterans Association of America, the Southern Appalachian Dulcimer*
> *Association, and the National Association for Outlaw and Lawman*
> *History. Some of these groups may be the organizational equivalent of*
> *vanity press publications, but surveys of American communities over*
> *the decades have uncovered an impressive organizational vitality at the*
> *grassroots level.*
>
> ROBERT PUTNAM, *Bowling Alone: The Collapse*
> *and Revival of American Community*

Emphasizing the significance of local associations, Alexis de Tocqueville (2003: 220) in *Democracy in America* provided a possibly apocryphal example,

> Should an obstacle appear on the public highway and the passage
> of traffic is halted, neighbors at once form a group to consider the
> matter; from this improvised assembly an executive authority appears to remedy the inconvenience before anyone has thought of
> the possibility of some other authority already in existence before
> the one they have just formed.

Thus begins the romance of associational theory with the role of tiny publics as central to civic harmony. Progress depends on the organization of the local. This vision extends the ideal of friendship as the bulwark of working together and assumes that associations are not only instrumental entities but are expressive ones (Mallory 2012). Democracy depends on citizens collaborating to achieve an end that no *one* could produce alone. The association provides a context in which circuits of action—the routines of the civil—are possible, even essential.

Between the informal coordination of mutually aware actors and the formal, institutionalized bureaucracy stands the association, crucial for establishing local engagement. By association I refer to an ongoing group that develops from a shared interest or from a common sense of purpose in which members believe that belonging is a meaningful marker of identity. As the term is generally understood, many associations are bureaucracies that may or may not have local chapters, but I limit my discussion to modest-size groups or chapters of a larger group in which the chapter is an action unit.

As a structure for mesolevel politics, associations allow participants to address common concerns with shared ideas of what is proper. The concerns of participants may be explicitly political, as with social movements, or they may tie solidarity to a desire to improve a community as with Tocqueville's road repairs. Associations work best when they "act locally," whether or not they "think globally." These groups allow members to have local impact, while valuing each other's company.

The magic of grouping has often been linked to American exceptionalism. Whether empirically justified or simply a cultural template that reflects American desires (Swidler 2001), the belief has been powerful in treating associations as a form of robust Americanism. Yet because of this cultural centrality, some fret over what they see as the decay of associations. The number of associations and the frequency of participation is taken as a measure of democracy, a canary in the coalmine of freedom. More and larger associations are seen as bolstering a civic, participatory culture (Putnam 2000). My goal is not to compare societies but to examine the cultures of associations. Further, I do not claim that active associations are necessarily virtuous, but that, moral or malign, they contribute to the group basis of public life.

Associations operate at all levels, from national organizations that require only a financial contribution to groups that rely wholly on neighborhood volunteers. In the theory of American pluralism, democracy depends on the presence of multiple associations, each with specialized knowledge and interests. However, these associations do more than push policies; they also commit individuals to a civic system. As political scientist Robert Dahl (1961: 100) argues, "Participation generates new rewards. Because an association provides opportunities for conviviality, it can come to fill a normal human need for friendliness, comradeship, respect, and social intercourse."

Many lasting voluntary associations connect local chapters, state councils, and a national organization (Skocpol 2003). This provides for a hinge in which local networks and national elites are integrated. While some organizations are purely local and others are fully national, many operate on multiple levels. In addition, the voluntary sphere is rarely entirely separated from the sphere of government (Lichterman and Eliasoph 2014).

Although informal coordination, social capital, and friendships embed individuals in social systems, the recognition of a group culture as motivation for action is essential for coordination and commitment. However, group culture is not merely people affiliating but, rather, congregating under conditions in which they see the gathering as meaningful and identity-laden. A group culture transforms common interest into an ongoing, identifiable pattern of social relations. This is what community organizer Ernest Cortes speaks of as "relational power" (Stout 2010: 149). As Paul Lichterman (2006) suggests, observing groups of midwestern volunteers, group style may be more consequential than personal social capital. Put simply, what is crucial in civic engagement is not the personal characteristics of actors but the practices that support common goals and establish bridging relationships with similar-minded groups. This builds organizational capacity, internal allegiance, and programmatic activity (Andrews et al. 2010). Associations can produce intense bonding among members, but the danger is that they will be isolated bands, separated from others, lacking the desire or ability to bridge to other groups. To understand how associations work, we need to examine the degree to which they generate bonding, banding, and bridging.

In the local model of democratic theory, groups presume that all participants have a right, if not always an equal right, to shape decisions. In chapter 2, I described how friendship and affiliation support group action; here I focus on solidified groups that build civic praxis. Civil society is a web of groups, nodes in a network of tiny publics (Cohen and Arato 1992: 252).

An association is not merely a structure through which tasks are completed and pressures resisted, but one by which citizens feel attached to a continuing civic project (Arendt 1972; Back and Polisar

1983). By affiliating with a group, participants become part of a network. The culture of the local justifies a broader commitment. In examining the Kurdistan Workers' Party in Turkey, Mustafa Gurbuz (2015) emphasizes a process that he terms symbolic localization. The movement, affiliated with international Marxism, must appeal to local Islamicist practices. Leaders construct the culture and ideology of the chapter so that local communities feel that the broader movement is consistent with their beliefs and practices. In a different time and place, William Lloyd Garrison recognized in 1832 that knots of abolitionists were crucial for that movement. "Without the organization of abolitionists into societies," claimed Garrison, "the cause will be lost" (Stout 2010: 148). Other movements, such as radical labor groups like the Industrial Workers of the World (the "Wobblies"), used the events of particular labor disputes—and the songs that could be composed about them—to build local commitments then linked to broader demands (Dubofsky 1969).

The salience of tiny publics as integrative mechanisms is evident in that approximately 40 percent of Americans belong to a well-defined small group, including self-help groups, book clubs, movement cells, hobbyist associations, or religious retreats (Wuthnow 1994). In the words of historian Arthur Schlesinger (1944: 21), "every community large or small has assumed a cellular structure, with these subdivisions of humanity intricately interlaced and overlapping." In associations, citizens develop sociable public structures outside government, outside the clique, and outside the family. Whether they are communal help groups, addressing a local problem, or movements that hope to alter an attitude, institution, or policy, associations treat interaction as a force for change. Even when associations become translocal, recruiting widely spread members, supporters, or sympathizers, many still depend on chapters. Groups gain influence from the bottom-up and from the top-down. Associations have a long history, including house churches in the early Christian era and secret societies in ancient Athens (Meeks 2003; Stone 1988; Ober 1989: 258). The desire for a lasting group of one's own is fundamental to human societies, even if foes condemn their secrecy and their exclusivity. The widespread antagonism toward Masonic orders reveals its importance for creating community as well as its perceived dangers (Marcus 1999).

The challenge is to insure that the association remains at the heart of democratic decision-making, rather than becoming marginalized by those who seek a large-state solution (Arendt 1963: 242–43). Associations are desirable, but their power often provokes mistrust by the state. Hannah Arendt writes about the embrace and distance of the commitment to local governance in the French Revolution:

> The famous forty-eight sections of the Parisian Commune ... constituted themselves immediately as self-governing bodies.... To Robespierre, speaking in September 1791 before the National Assembly, to prevent the delegates from curtailing the political power of clubs and societies, this public spirit was identical with the revolutionary spirit.... He insisted, the clubs and societies were the only places in the country where this freedom could actually show itself and be exercised by the citizens. Hence, they were the true 'pillars of the constitution.'... However, no sooner had Robespierre risen to power and become the political head of the new revolutionary government ... that he reversed his position completely.

The creation of a centralized group, constituted in the General Assembly under Robespierre, transferred his allegiance from an array of small groups to the authority of the legislative elite. This control limited the role of small decision-making gatherings, originally central to the Revolution. Councils, much praised by Arendt (1963: 265) and others, including Proudhun, Bakunin, Rousseau, and Jefferson, each believing in the revolutionary quality of localism, are frequently challenged in complex societies, where associational decision-making has often been formalized through representative government (Arendt 1963: 252). Jeffersonian little republics—temporary structures emerging from revolutionary necessity or from emergent pressure groups—could potentially connect groups of citizens, organizing diffuse decision-making: *e pluribus unum*. Arendt (1963: 253) suggests that a local council system could be "an entirely new form of government, with a new public space for freedom." This sounds optimistic—perhaps romantic—but whether local governance will inevitably be democratic is doubtful as associations split and power is struggled over.

Exceptional Republic, Exceptional Associations

Not all societies have the same ecology of associations, even if all political activity depends on the existence of an interaction order and group presence. I focus on the American republic with its emphasis on associational life, a claim strengthened by the absence of officially sanctioned secondary institutions such as a royal court or state church. While I do not address why some nations have a denser ecology of associations, this is an area in which "American exceptionalism" has been prized and Americans are said to excel. Arthur Schlesinger (1944) wrote that Americans are a nation of joiners. This is surprising given that Americans are also known as robust individualists. As early as the 1820s, citizens of Massachusetts were forming nearly seventy new voluntary associations each year, including occupational associations, societies promoting good morals, educational and cultural organizations, charities, and civic groups (Brown 1974: 38). These organizations were not state-sponsored but were crucial in regulating community morality. As Max Weber pointed out in "The Protestant Sects and the Spirit of Capitalism," belonging to and participating in a religious group (a sect in Weber's terms) marked one's financial reliability.[1] Secret and selective societies created a diverse urban matrix. Spatial propinquity as a defining characteristic of community was replaced by reputation, social relations, and shared interest.

Perhaps because of the less intrusive American state, citizens feel that they have the power and the responsibility to solve problems.[2] This leads to the belief among conservatives, libertarians, and those on the syndicalist left that tiny publics are a bulwark against an overarching state. Recalling Edmund Burke, these "little platoons" battle the government's big battalions. This metaphor is apt for neighborhood associations and social movements, even if, as Theda Skocpol (2003: 10) emphasizes, not all American civic associations are separated from government. Many associations, especially those that define themselves as more than transitory and as translocal, are hybrid, dependent on a state-civic partnership (Lichterman and Eliasoph 2014: 799).

The value of a dense associational life is widely believed to be central to civic republicanism (Warren 2001: 9; Dewey 1927: 148; Sandel 1996: 208). Of course, associations can have a "dark side" and may support totalitarian ideologies, as in Weimar Germany (Koshar 1986) or Fascist Italy (Berezin 1997). Civic groups do not inevitably imply a liberal mindset or progressive community as a robust civic culture may support authoritarianism (Riley 2010). However, in general, mediating organizations are crucial to republican life. Communitarianism and the interactional practices that are implied are not always socially desirable in that they can undercut a commitment to equality, even while promoting stability (Kaufman 1999).

If it is true that large and formal associations have withered, as with the decline of PTAs, bowling leagues, and the Masons, informal and transitory fellowships thrive. As I describe in chapter 7, internet communication has contributed to the flowering of casual associations that now transcend geography and include specialized (or stigmatized) interests that might make more formal organizations difficult.

This diversity of flexible, nonbureaucratic groups offers significant advantages for civil society, particularly when citizens participate in several. As a result, associations provide participants with multiple, and often crosscutting, affiliations. Such groups expose individuals to diverse experiences, people, and perspectives (Sunstein 2000, 2001). This works against the balkanizing pull of "amoral familism" as well as bureaucratized associations (Portes and Sensenbrenner 1993; Banfield 1958).

Despite substantial evidence that associations benefit civil society, benefits focus on increased commitment and not necessarily consensus. We should not assume that the more groups, the more placid the society. Associations, particularly when constituted as movements that desire institutional change, may prove contentious. For Thomas Rochon (1998: 22), these constitute "critical communities": close-knit assemblies with the goal of altering the conceptual frameworks of others. In their activism, social movements potentially alter the moral or political consciousness of the community by challenging unconsidered beliefs and practices, as with those that pushed for the abolition of slavery or for marriage equality. While these are dramatic examples of altering civic consciousness, most movements desire new social arrangements.

Challengers require fortitude. Pollyannas cannot halt tanks if soldiers keep driving. Militant groups, because of their willingness to give or receive suffering, are often more successful than those more docile. In societies with sharp value divisions or divergent policy perspectives, organized civic engagement may provoke conflict, which, while democratic, may prevent elites from enforcing their will (Mouffe 2005). Groups with heated passions, firm ideologies, and willingness to incur and inflict costs divide as well as bridge.

While this organized and democratic tension welcomes power

from the bottom and the sides, it is not necessarily beneficial in the absence of an overarching commitment to civil society. James Madison worried in *Federalist #10* about the growth of factions whose interests may conflict with the perception of a general good. In other words, groups may promote "civic vice" as well as "civic virtue." Various groups—gendered, racial, occupational, or class-based—believe that segregating and benefiting themselves or excluding and disadvantaging others through enforcing boundaries is virtuous. While this cuts against an ideology of inclusion and equality, virtues and vices are locally and historically situated, not absolute or universal.

Some organizations desire inter-group conflict (see chap. 5), treating that conflict as justifying the organization, as with anarchist groups or iterations of the Ku Klux Klan. Conflict can be either a defining feature of interaction or a by-product. Some associations hold beliefs that, while solidifying the existing community, prevent the inclusion of a diverse membership. The flourishing of groups can create either networks of shared affiliation or islands of discord.

Associations provide ongoing structures with the potential to support collective action. Again quoting Tocqueville (2003: 598–99), "The only way opinions and ideas can be renewed, hearts enlarged, and human minds developed is through the reciprocal influence of men upon each other.... In democratic nations, associations must take the place of those powerful individuals who have been swept away by the equality of social conditions." While coordination is found wherever individuals gather, the solidity and continuity of associations gives them influence. Tocqueville suggests that what is crucial is not that individuals spontaneously gather but that they form a decision-making body to solve problems. How this body is structured shapes its culture and its rules. In this view it is not the individual or the society that matters, but the group, which is treated as a source of identity.

As noted, associations are of many sizes, contents, and structures. A local environmental band or a small-town civic association develops from the idea that engaged interaction matters. In contrast, bureaucratic organizations such as the expansive American Association of Retired People (AARP), the National Rifle Association (NRA), or the National Association for the Advancement of Colored People (NAACP) depend on a centralized office (a group at headquarters), recruiting contributors by creating a mass organization. As a result, there is little in the way of interaction within their diffuse memberships, even if employees in the central office provide tropes that shape the beliefs of members.

Despite the sway of these extended bureaucratic organizations, my focus on local associations and the face-to-face components of mass associations addresses how these knots of actors fit into civil society. A characteristic of smaller units is that many participants know each other personally or by reputation. As civic participants, they operate as tiny publics, energized by internal obligations while facing outward.

No matter how minute, every group develops shared, mutually understood references—culture—without which interaction would have no continuing value. This has been a central feature of my research on restaurants, government offices, sports teams, and clubs, and, as this chapter demonstrates, is true for activist movements, sociable groups, and fraternal chapters. We belong together because we share local memory: a group is a site for shared recall (McFeat 1974). This provides a basis from which ideas can spread outward.

Despite the importance of collective recall, reminiscences and traditions are not forever, even in strong groups. These common allusions have a "referential afterlife" (Goffman 1981: 46): the period of time—long or brief—that the reference will be understood and can be mentioned meaningfully. How long will we remember the nicknames, jokes, or miscues that demonstrate that members belong together and care about each other (Fine and Desoucey 2005)? The end of a season or a school year can be a time of forgetting, as updating will occur once the group forms again (Yerkovich 1977).

Local memories emerge from the opening moments of group life as participants attempt to gauge with whom they are dealing. Cohorts of graduate students or start-up political campaigns are examples. Names, scraps of biographical background, and forms of speech each set the tone for later cohesion, and then these memory bits become revised as appropriate, further solidifying social relations. Participants, believing that they will remain in their association, recognize that they share experiences that can be referred to in the expectation that they will be understood and will establish a common reality. As a result, group experience is historicized. Tradition, mutual references, and customs are integral to the identity and cohesion of any association. This depends on performances that routinize interaction, creating a recognizable style (Eliasoph and Lichterman 2003). Rules of discourse are not only selected from personal experience but are linked to expectations of how colleagues should behave. Those dialogues and practices determine collective action, propriety, and political views (Kretsedemas 2000: 639; Cramer 2016). As Lawler, Thye, and Yoon (2008) argue, recognizable structures produce distinctive "micro-social orders," each with their own routines.

Any analysis of group cultures must incorporate the presence of extralocal, environmental relations. Abstractions like "national culture," "cultural myths," or "institutional logics," even though they originate externally, influence group activity (Nagim and Ocasio 2010). Associations exist in an institutional surround, shaped by forces that are macrocultural.

This context, combined with the backgrounds of participants and based in the norms and expectations of group interaction, shapes the local meaning system. Idiocultures are found in small groups in all institutional domains. These cultures are a means by which individuals coordinate collective pasts and plan shared futures (Katovich and Couch 1992). Groups that share—and recognize that they share—goals, expectations, or values are likely to coordinate their activity. Similarly, when the local hierarchy is stable and understood, groups are less likely to be riven by dissent or to dissolve (Kaplan 2018).

When members appreciate their shared history, group affiliation is bolstered. These associations, more so than thin populations of solitary actors, can respond to, challenge, and alter the extended social system. Further, these cultures are a boundary and means whereby groups treat themselves as distinctive, even when part of more expansive associational networks.

Ultimately, culture is a form of group practice, joined to a belief in civic order and to those shared perspectives that stand between individual agency and the constraints of institutions. This civic culture orders social life by recognizing joint pasts and prospective futures. Lasting groups treat tradition as central to their relations, displaying those connections in action and discourse. Part of what makes associations powerful is the bonding of participants whose mutual interests can be leveraged into something more solid and more permanent, given available resources.

Diverse Associations

The three examples of associations described here demonstrate how organizations are the pivot for action and order. Associations are sites that depend on both a recognized interaction order and an acknowledged group culture, and, as a result, they allow for the routine circuits of action that are at the heart of a local sociology. I select these cases to address distinct features of associational life.

I begin by describing the flowering of associations as each attempts to create an appealing culture and a public presence that potentially achieve social change within a competitive organizational marketplace. Each organization strives to develop a compelling idioculture and a set of strategies that cement participants and prove worthy of wider public attention. To examine the diversity of local movements and the outcomes that group cultures permit given the organizational ecology, I draw on Kathleen Blee's ethnographic survey of small social movements in metropolitan Pittsburgh. Blee describes how group cultures permit them to recruit a set of potential activists (see Baiocchi et al. 2014: 101–10). Not all groups are successful—far from it—but in thinking about their organizations and how they fit in with others, Blee reveals how the meanings held by members constitute the group and how these meanings can create a space for influence. Group culture is "sited," recognizing that the movement environment is a market in which committed bands of committed individuals confront other groups, including those with more resources and more expansive cultures.

I then turn to how certain associations can limit civic engagement by establishing sociability—not civic politics—as their goal, believing that members lack adequate expertise within the public sphere to have major policy influence. These civic associations have only an ambivalent relationship with explicit political engagement. Not all associations are active within the public sphere. This relies on a creative examination of the social production of apathy by Nina Eliasoph (1998), who examines the group style of two associations that adopt an antidrug agenda. Eliasoph asks how associations choose to limit their impact, retreating from politics although still shaping the feeling that they have a civic role to play. Members' perceptions of external institutions and their idealized concept of citizen responsibilities truncate the association's culture.

The linkage between local cultures and the perception of their *collective* responsibilities is the hinge that connects them to larger structures, even while as individuals their members have personal opinions. This study helps explain why those who do not engage feel entitled to complain. These groups might have a stronger and more consequential impact within their community, but they believe that sociability is their primary mission and that political controversies would undercut this goal and can be more effectively handled by others with more legitimate authority. Eliasoph emphasizes, perhaps surprisingly, that individuals often take stronger stands than groups, despite the support that group membership and resources could offer. In this case, we find *weakness in numbers*.

Finally I examine how associations, given their tight bonding, may build barriers to a more inclusive and open community. This relies on research on fraternal organizations by Jason Kaufman (2002) and Theda Skocpol (2003), addressing how bonding and boundary-making contribute to each other. Frequently the tighter the group, the stronger the borders.

Fraternal (and, occasionally, sororal) associations have often been taken as the heart of American communal engagement. Although Americans did not invent lodges such as the Masons or the Odd Fellows, for a century these brotherhoods were integral to the national fabric. Much can be said in their favor as providing social support, personal belonging, commitment to common dreams, and allegiance to community life. However, support of widows, orphans, and the luckless assumed that only some groups of people were worthy and deserved aid.

Although fraternal life is alluring, this enthusiasm must be judged critically. Many such organizations gaze inward. The localism of chapters is linked to the creation of a national fraternal sensibility, but this sensibility can divide as well as heal. Theda Skocpol emphasizes that although these associations depended on vibrant chapters, many maintained a translocal component. Further, as Jason Kaufman demonstrates, the existence of an association, no matter how much good-hearted sociability, does not prove that it generates broad community feeling. The opposite effect is possible, creating resentments among organizations representing divided social segments: ethnicity, class, occupation, religion, race, and gender. These rivalries prevent bridging. Desired bonding can too easily become banding against outsiders.

THE GARDEN OF MOVEMENT CULTURES

A social movement is a dramatic instance of an association in that its desire for change is explicitly part of its mission. A group recognizes an injustice and organizes to alleviate it. However, as Ziad Munson (2008) explains, social relations often precede ideology, particularly at life transitions when individuals search for community. Thick groups attract those with thin beliefs. As historian Robin D. G. Kelley (2002: 9) explains, activism can do "what great poetry always does: transport us to another place, compel us to relive horrors and, more importantly, enable us to imagine a new society." Still, this civic poetry depends on poets and audiences. We are transported together and we hope to persuade others that our poesy of the world has merit and is worth the effort.

While movements can have many sympathizers, their groupness retains members and overcomes risks in participation. Whatever their core, movements hope for relational ties that incorporate many. Movements work best when they are organized as a set of network nodes connected through interlocking groups, cells, or chapters (Lofland and Jamison 1984; Gerlach and Hine 1970). Further, the groups that together constitute a movement may be quite distinct, as evident in cells of the Communist Party of America, Tea Party branches, or chapters of Mothers Against Drunk Driving. Differences may result from relational styles, regional traditions, demographic backgrounds, or the places in which the group meets. As a result, numerous groups form and operate within an associational ecology in which groups are both allies and rivals, partners and competitors.

The desire of activist associations for internal cohesion and external impact is crucial to their impact on politics. Associations act out their beliefs, ideologies, and demands on members and on external publics, performing private and public identities that serve to differentiate them from others, leading to growth, contraction, or organizational death (Blee and McDowell 2012; Ghaziani 2011; Fuist 2014: 428).

Kathleen Blee (2012: 3) explores an ecology of associations that populate a cityscape. She searches for social-psychological and micro-organizational processes through which sixty grassroots Pittsburgh-area social movements establish idiocultures. In the process, she tracks group-level development and dissolution. Many groups form in any dense urban environment, but few have staying power in their internal stability and external impact. While each handles these challenges in a distinctive fashion, a result of local practices based on membership, resources, and surveillance, the choices determine effectiveness and continuity.

Often the origin of groups is hazy. Many movements lack an explicit moment of formation, seeming to slide into structure. Over time and with the need to confront those outside their boundaries—friends or foes—an amorphous set of relations is transformed into solid patterns of practices, linked to an appealing origin story (Clark 1972). Blee (2012: 16) recognizes the salience of an interactional frame,

> Activists disagreed about when their group started, hinting at deeper divisions on what constitutes activism. When asked to describe their group's beginning, some activists pointed to personal ties. For them, the group began when people started interacting, even long before it had a common political focus or goal. An anti-drug activist [explained], "when we started out, most of the people were just friends. We've expanded since then." For these activists, activism is rooted in interaction and personal ties. In contrast, other activists traced their group to a time when people started learning together. For them, personal ties are merely social; a group of people does not become an activist group until the members start to have common understandings.

Whichever perspective is preferred, both treat the mesolevel as constituting the basis of political action. As Blee (2012: 15) emphasizes, "the salient context of grassroots activism is local." Benjamin Shepard (2015: 3) explicitly treats associations as an expression of friendship,

> From anarchism to gay liberation, from the settlement houses to the Beats, from the AIDS Coalition to Unleash Power (ACT UP) to Occupy Wall Street, from public space to environmental justice— one can trace a story of friendships coming together.

But which group of friends to choose? People begin to gather in common purpose to promote change, although they may later split through disagreements over goals, because of personal animosity, or because of the presence of other more appealing or successful groups (Shepard 2015: 181–82).

For movements, a name serves as an identity marker that helps commit an individual to a community ("I am a member of X"). Simultaneously the name displays the group as a distinctive entity to those outside, advertising activism, even if, at times, freezing the group with an outdated set of positions (Blee 2012: 13). Yet, despite traditions that solidify group culture, movements sometimes shift focus. (Larger groups are less nimble as changes to accepted practices must overcome stasis.) Blee (2012: 13) reports,

> Activist groups continually modify themselves. They form coalitions and alliances or fracture internally. They reorient from local to national efforts and back again. People drift in and out, turning a group of young professionals into one of economically marginal students or reforming a youth-dominated group into one of middle-aged activists. Boundaries blur as groups dissolve into each other and activists migrate from one to another.

As goals, membership, or the organizational environment changes, movements must decide whether to retain their identity. Groups may appear stable from the outside while their internal culture has shifted in ways that alter the expectations and the experience of belonging. Blee (2012: 13–14) points to animal rights activists who over time changed their focus to issues of war and peace. Their former identity proved a burden, unable to motivate potential supporters. Another group changed their name from "Death by Heroin" to "People Opposing Drugs," allowing them access to more influential networks and better advertising their activist agenda.

To understand how associations develop, Blee emphasizes culture, paths, and turning points. She relies on the case of an animal rights organization that she names the Animal Liberation League (ALL). As Blee details, part of what transforms individual actors into an association is a collective understanding that they are accountable for their norms, values, stories, and customs. Their virtue is on the line if they fail to live up to professed beliefs.[3] As Erika Summers-Effler (2010) demonstrates in her ethnography of the Catholic Workers movement houses, participants make each other accountable for their professed norms and justify their actions through narratives that address their failures. Routine practices—those circuits of action that define the group—are path-dependent, channeled by internal and external cultures but not fully determined by them. Actions provoke responses, creating a cascade of events that shape culture, influence interaction, and refine identity. When consequential, the group may define the action as a turning point: a moment when the group recognizes that it has been fundamentally altered. For the Animal Liberation League, after searching for an issue on which they could gain public attention, the group chose to pressure restaurants to stop serving foie gras. Blee (2012: 41–4) argues that each step in making and publicizing this choice shaped the group culture as well as being responsive to it:

> ALL's campaign began when they decided to force restaurants to stop selling the appetizer foie gras on the grounds that geese are harmed in its production. It ended when Pennsylvania passed an "eco-terrorism" bill that ALL interpreted as outlawing its protests. Three distinct sub-sequences define this campaign. The sub-sequences overlapped in time but had different chains of causes and effects. Sequence A commenced with ALL's decision to campaign against foie gras, a move accompanied by a radical shift in the group's sense of itself. Sequence B began as ALL shifted tactics, with a new definition of what it faced in the campaign [becoming more confrontational]. Sequence C was marked by a shift in the group's emotion and affective nature as ALL reconsidered the nature of its allies and enemies [becoming more critical of their opponents].

For ALL, first the group shifted its sense of self, then it shifted its tactics in light of this new self, and eventually it altered its map of the cultural field, shifting supporters and opponents. If participants were unwilling to accept these confrontational tactics, they failed to live up to the group's goals. They held themselves accountable to changing communal practices. Each event reverberated so that the association shifted its sense of self, understanding of tactical opportunities, and cartography of other organizations.

SOCIABILITY AND THE PROBLEM OF POLITICS

Despite the belief that small associations advance public agendas through mutual support, such is not always accurate. Many associations proclaim their civic virtue, but they do not define their actions as interest-group politics. Participants are often less political than association theorists imagine. One reason is that adversarial democracy can be socially upsetting, unlike the comforting image of a Quaker meetinghouse. Many would trade their own personal beliefs, even if strongly held, for placid consensus. This perspective has virtue. Without it, jury deliberations might crumble if holdouts refused to bend. Even in the social movement space, groups that begin with a public agenda find collective commitment weakened from individuals' desire to get along.

We see this rejection of conflictual civic engagement in the fact that some groups—particularly those focusing on recovery or personal support—establish rules that ban political talk in their moderated meetings. Even though politics might be tied to structural conditions that lead to addiction or illness, the group culture privileges a focus on therapeutic work and an avoidance of any form of conflict. Some groups (such as Alcoholics Anonymous) even prohibit cross talk, not permitting members to respond to other members. While members converse as they wish in informal settings, within the group context debate is outlawed. Banning arguments from the idioculture is one means of avoiding the problem of politics, although not the only one.

To explore the absence of political engagement, Nina Eliasoph (1998) describes how shared apathy grows from sociability in her impressive multiple ethnography of volunteer-based community groups. Specifically she examined two antidrug groups, "Vote B for Substance Free" and "Just Say No Team." Both are small groups, composed of volunteers, one with approximately twenty participants and the other with just eight. She also participated in the Parent League, a dozen parents who volunteered in their children's high school. She describes her puzzle, "Volunteers shared faith in this ideal of civic participation, but in practice, paradoxically, maintaining this hope and faith meant curtailing political discussion: members sounded less publicly minded and less politically creative in groups than they sounded individually." Politics vanish.

Eliasoph found that her informants desired to present concrete solutions to what they viewed as an overwhelmingly large problem. Participants searched for goals that they and their friends could achieve: an approach that has advantages, even while limiting the range of possible action. As Eliasoph (1998: 32) describes,

In one meeting, Just Say No members talked about starting a collection drive for foster children who were turning eighteen. A member said 18-year-olds were not supported by the state, so many were simply turned out of foster care to fend for themselves. One volunteer said, "Those kids wouldn't have *anything* of their own." The first volunteer had a solution. "*One* thing that 18-year-olds would surely need would be *blankets*," so they were planning a drive to gather blankets. Emphasizing the word "one," the volunteers left tacit their doubts about the other things homeless teenagers might need—toothbrushes, clothes, beds, homes, jobs, education, love: thinking about all that would be overwhelming. The volunteers wanted to believe that regular citizens can solve local problems, but the perceived, implied political structures make it difficult to do.

Something similar applied to discussions at the League of Women Voters in which participants discussed the strategies of politicians but not the substance of their programs (Eliasoph 1998: 27). This finding was consistent with my research on political volunteers who worked diligently on campaigns, addressing and stuffing envelopes, distributing yard signs, and making phone calls, but only discussing political issues on ritual occasions (Fine 2012: 141). Such observations contrast with the view that mutual presence inevitably generates deeper political engagement. For groups that valued sociability in a society in which complex problems were assigned to experts, the opposite is often the case.

Eliasoph's topic is not what one might call "macroapathy": the unwillingness to vote or indifference about large public issues, a disavowal of the political. In contrast, her concern is how groups avoid direct political engagement on the mesolevel. As Kathleen Blee emphasizes, this does not imply that groups will never be politically engaged or will avoid increasing the likelihood of confrontation, but rather that there is a push to minimize conflict. When political engagement is suggested, members of (some) volunteer groups are skeptical:

The longest reflective conversation I heard in a volunteer group was one that a teacher practically forced on the Parent League. Wearing a cotton blend plaid shirt and sporting a crew cut, this teacher did not appear to be a hippie with wild ideas. Handing out a sheet entitled "Prom Madness," he argued for putting a limit on spending on the prom, so that students would not be forced to work too many hours to pay for prom expenses. The problem was there was nothing but fast-food restaurants there; the students wanted a more stylish prom than could be held at Pizza Hut or Taco Bell, and spent vast sums to travel by limousine to get it. Danielle passed me a doodled note half-way through the discussion with an apostrophe-eyed smiley face on it, quizzically asking, "Are we having fun yet?" with the obvious answer being, "No." Everyone looked bored. (Eliasoph 1998: 33)

The challenges were more than the group had bargained for (although perhaps they privately endorsed the idea of elaborate proms). This was not a topic that they felt compelled to address. I found something similar in my research on mushroom collectors (Fine 1998). Here was a group that might have defined environmental activism as the basis of organizing. However, although concerns about acid rain, pollution, and development were raised, they were never considered topics on which the group should take a stand, much less protest. The group organized displays of mushroom specimens at local museums, but the display raised no political challenge. Getting along in the group and with those who surrounded the group was a desideratum. The Minnesota Mycological Society was first and foremost a sociable organization (Aldrich 1971); members insisted on this shared purpose. In dividing adversarial democracy from unitary democracy, members often prefer the latter (Mansbridge 1980; Hartz 1955; Varenne 1977).

Despite recognizing dangers—from drug use, racism, or environmental degradation—Eliasoph's volunteer groups imagine that their ability to shift policy is limited. However, they are comfortable with this limit because of a belief in their lack of expertise and resources. These volunteers define their activities as personal and close-to-home, and they resolutely reject the label of political. Participants treat volunteering as separate from the engagement of explicitly activist groups. In this, they focus on issues with personal impact. As Eliasoph (1998: 25) put it,

These extravagant assertions of self-interest helped volunteers feel empowered within a small circle of concern: they could tell themselves that they did not care about problems they felt powerless to fix. The assertions aided the cycle of political evaporation, by preventing volunteers from voicing clear concerns, even to themselves.

The boundary of what is perceived as a group's responsibility leaves problems to other groups with greater institutional authority and reservoirs of knowledge. As a result, Eliasoph claims that volunteering demonstrates how associations build community in establishing affective ties in an otherwise diffuse metropolis, even absent activism. The implicit norms defining which groups can legitimately speak may produce different forms of action from that envisioned by Tocqueville and other associational theorists.

FRATERNITY AND BOUNDARIES

With spatial barriers less salient in urban and suburban regions, neighborhood no longer is the primary basis through which individuals create a social world. Residence is replaced by class, interest, or occupation. This is not entirely new. By the eighteenth century, city clubs and salons were places where men could meet others of their social class and background, creating a private and dense network. The same is true as nineteenth-century workplace communities became separated from class-based neighborhoods (Gould 1993). As Barbara Black (2012: 27) writes of British male club culture, participating reflected a "fundamental human desire to join like-minded comrades as a way of forging community beyond blood ties." Participation in clubs provided autonomy but simultaneously built cohesion and conformity (Ringmar 1998: 541–42). These clubs depended on the desire for public intimacy, status based on exclusion, and congenial discussion. Trust and identity contributed to broader civic virtue and political allegiance (Capdeville 2016).[4]

In the United States, scholars treat the period between the Civil War and World War I as the golden age of fraternal organizations (Harwood 1897; Putnam 2000: 388; Skocpol 2003). This was a time in which fraternal organizations were numerous and influential. Unlike informal gathering spaces, such as taverns, coffeehouses, and beauty salons (see chap. 4), these associations provided solidified "third places" where the like-minded shared firm comradeship (Oldenburg 1989). Members engaged in rituals—drinking, revelry, and social service—in the company of "brothers." A group of actors, searching for a place to imbibe on Sundays, founded the Benevolent Protective Order of Elks. Their search for sociability transformed into an organization when they began collecting donations for sick and unemployed members (Kaufman 2002: 22).

Beyond sociability and mutual support, fraternal associations allowed members to control their relations by admitting—and, as important, excluding—potential members. As late as 1972, the United States Supreme Court ruled that a lodge could refuse to serve the black guest of a white member since it was a "private club," outside the reach of the state. The Moose Lodge of Harrisburg, Pennsylvania, could also legally require that members must be "Male persons of the Caucasian or White race above the age of twenty-one years, and not married to someone of any other than the Caucasian or White race, who are of good moral character, physically and mentally normal, who shall profess a belief in a Supreme Being" (Kaufman 2002: 18). Such associations were agents of self-segregation.

Examining a late nineteenth-century city directory discloses a diverse array of social and civic associations. Each served as a tiny public within the civic space. Some are social, some religious, and some political, but each appeals to a target audience and each requires sufficient resources. Given the existence and the recognition of distinct groupings, this results in a process that Kaufman refers to as "competitive voluntarism." Within an organizational ecology, groups fill empty or unused niches, appealing to underserved populations. Kaufman notes the formation of the Knights of Luther in Des Moines, Iowa, in 1912, a Protestant secret society, aiming to compete with the well-established Catholic Knights of Columbus. By "competitive voluntarism," Kaufman (2002: 7) refers to "a general social process whereby the number of voluntary, or nonprofit, organizations in a given society rapidly increases, thus fueling competition among them for members, money, institutional legitimacy, and political power." The Odd Fellows, a national organization, maintained six separate branches in Boston: two for African-Americans (one of these could be integrated), two for women, and two for white males. While internally homogenous, the diversity of clubs segmented society. Each group provided insurance, burial benefits, and other forms of support, decreasing the demand for governmental welfare programs. Kaufman (2002: 31) argues that "by recasting ordinary citizens as Catholics, whites, Germans, and so on, American associations heightened the various ethnic, religious, and racial lines that divide the country." Self-segregation creates a politics of group interest in contrast to common interest: banding, not bridging. However, given language differences, residential segregation, and religious rivalry, how much blame for societal division can be placed on voluntary associations?

As a result of membership criteria (revealed in elections and in blackballing), groups are likely to be homogeneous, challenging the possibility of full integration. Perhaps the eventual decline of civic organizations resulted in part from increased acceptance of diversity. For Kaufman (2002: 9–10), banding represents the dark side of fraternity:

> The costs of the "golden age" greatly outweigh the benefits. Its most lasting legacies have been those very problems most lamented in America today: a long-standing tradition of racial prejudice and interethnic hostility; a pernicious political system dominated by special-interest groups; an ominous love for guns, accompanied by a menacing fear of government; a weak and subservient labor movement; and a half-hearted tradition of public social service provision, capped by the repeated failure to pass even the most rudimentary universal health insurance legislation.

Perhaps Kaufman's most salient argument is less about prejudice and division but about a belief—whether for good or ill—that associations provide for the public good while actually providing for private welfare. These tiny publics may be too exclusive for a generous and comprehensive civil society. Kaufman notes the irony that the problem that neo-Tocquevillian associational theorists attempt to solve of the diminishment of the common good is precisely a result of the kinds of associations that they promote. Whether we examine the sunny or dark side of associations, and it is essential that we do both, the desire for grouping shapes the availability of resources.

The Mesolevel of Associations

Just as social relations create conditions in which we coordinate our actions and commit ourselves to civil society, so do continuing associations. Associations have the potential to establish a sphere apart from government, whether separating from state control in the form of social movements, rejecting participation in direct political processes, or dividing the public square into multiple tiny publics. While often treated as larger-scale bureaucratic organizations, many associations are communally based or depend on local chapters. A large membership and extensive financial resources, such as evident in the NRA, the AARP, or the NAACP, can provide influence in that dues-paying members often accept organizational endorsements. However, the power of associations to create commitment derives from interaction and a common culture. The AARP may influence legislation through lobbying or letter-writing campaigns, but it demands little of its thirty-eight million members and does not establish deep social networks (Campbell 2003). It relies on groups, but these are groups located in the Washington headquarters. In contrast, other associations have rituals of belonging and require that commitment be tied to action. It is a strain to be a free rider among friends.

I first described the flowering of small, locally based social movements and their attempts to create group cultures that cement members into continued participation and to speak to wider publics (Blee 2012). Informal groups can become associations through a process of solidification; associations can split into competing groups. Frequently movements change tactics or formal structure when internally challenged, when the environment shifts, or when external forces influence internal practices. The creation of a movement idioculture that mediates inside and outside is crucial for political effectiveness. Local associations gain power by the willingness of participants to commit to shared goals in the face of external pressures. But, in this, each group is in competition with other groups that also exert their own pull in a market of associations, each promoting its own culture and agenda.

In addition, as Nina Eliasoph (1998) emphasizes, small associations, despite civic concerns, do not always contribute to the political process. They may view participation as outside their realm of expertise. Perhaps this is not quite the production of apathy—after all, these volunteers do believe in civic betterment and they care about each other—but it exposes a boundary between the civic and the political.

Finally, fraternal associations are integral to civic life, even if not always in a positive vein. In contrast to the rosy visions of Alexis de Tocqueville and Robert Putman, Jason Kaufman (2002) points to a discomforting reality of bounded interaction. These associations rarely bridge social divides, seeing their separation from uninitiated outsiders as crucial to their identity. They create bands of brothers, not only brotherly bonds. In providing resources for members, associations may reject broader government programs, excluding those who do not or cannot join a voluntary society.

Associations are critical building blocks for mesolevel communities. While people cooperate in spontaneous and informal community, they act jointly within solidified group cultures. Whether or not associations are key to a good, generous, and gracious society, they permit individuals to feel that they are a part of something that is larger than themselves and to recognize that this something is likely to exist for more than a passing moment. Participation in associations reveals the semiautonomous hinge that links the individual and the institutional.

4

PLACE

Performance and Solidarity

The elegant Part of Mankind, who are not immers'd in the animal Life, but employ themselves in the Operations of the Mind, may be divided into the learned *and* conversible. *The Learned are such as have chosen for their Portion the higher and more difficult Operations of the Mind, which require Leisure and Solitude, and cannot be brought to Perfection, without long Preparation and severe Labour. The conversible World join to a sociable Disposition, and a Taste of Pleasure, an Inclination to the easier and more gentle Exercises of the Understanding, to obvious Reflections on human Affairs, and the Duties of common Life, and to the Observation of the Blemishes or Perfections of the particular Objects, that surround them. Such Subjects of Thought furnish not sufficient Employment in Solitude, but require the Company and Conversation of our Fellow-Creatures, to render them a proper Exercise for the Mind: And this brings Mankind together in Society, where every one displays his Thoughts and Observations in the best Manner he is able, and mutually gives and receives Information, as well as Pleasure.*

DAVID HUME, *Essays: Moral, Political, and Literary*

With spaces everywhere, institutions take root, group cultures co-alesce, and actors perform. As the French sociologist Henri Lefebvre (1991: 44) writes, "What would remain of the Church if there were no churches?" Could congregations survive without the routines of congregating? Spatial access — the places where people gather — sets the conditions for public and private action. These constitute action arenas, "designated physical places where decisions are made" and where spatial constraints determine outcomes (Jasper and Volpi 2018: 15–16). To speak of arenas or places assumes boundaries: What bit of space is a *place*? Under the right conditions, space is transformed into place (Tuan 1977), a marker of communal identity (Jacobson 2001). The affiliation with place establishes a group, separating them from those who are merely present. Such spaces can be counted, in some instances, as "safe spaces" in which protective norms hold, and in other cases as more dangerous in which those with differing norms, values, and interests intersect, sometimes with contention or even with an aggressive intent.

Meaningful places provide for local politics, and, as such, civil society is spatially organized. As Ari Adut (2012: 238) argues, every public sphere has a spatial core. Public spheres must be visible; they are sites of publicity and of public notice (Adut 2018: 43). They are places in which culture becomes revealed, both for members and for those observing. A shared space provides for the continuing and reflexive routines that constitute circuits of action, a stage for performance (Allen 2015: 178, 181; Adut 2012: 244).

Following Richard Sennett in examining the fall (or rise) of "public man," I consider citizens together and apart. The group, the crowd, and the hermit depend on spatial presence (and absence). Civic space transforms action to acting when the performance is available to an audience.

Spatial meaning inevitably is transformed into a normative order. Public life is theater (Sennett 1977: 64), both scripted and improvisational, but always emplaced. This is what the Russian dramatist Nicolas Evreinoff (1927: 98–112), writing in *The Theatre in Life*, decades prior to Erving Goffman's (1959) dramaturgical theory, described as the "stage management of life." Set designers and directors matter as do playwrights. Evreinoff suggested that an impulse to drama and the performance of self was endemic to sociality. Interaction is always localized—staged—and this localization is not something that "just is," but rather is something that must be shown and interpreted. How can it not be? In those spaces in which deliberative democracy occurs, practices shape the forms of talk that are considered to be legitimate (Button and Mattson 1999), and an interaction order is shared. The same is true in places where contentious politics play out.

However, just as spaces facilitate collective action and organized debate, they also permit combative rivalry. This recognition cautions us against treating thorny patches as rose arbors. Copresence may reveal divisions and encourage conflict within and between groups. James Jasper (2004: 13) speaks of the "band of brothers" dilemma, the recognition that affiliation that is too tight in threatening spaces— seemingly a virtue—may be exclusionary, raising the question of whom group action protects: the in-group or all present.

Still, spatial copresence in civil society is essential. Consider the ethnographic trope of the "corner" as the stage of community (Anderson 1979; Liebow 1967; Whyte 1943): a place where people are known and are expected and where practices are well established. Villages or even kibbutzim serve much the same purpose in that there is a pressure for routine interaction to be treated as friendly and secure—though admittedly that is not always achieved. In a sense, spaces, more than minds, create moral orders, and as a result we can speak of safe spaces. Religious spaces serve as a case in point. Sites of worship need to be comforting places of community (Hart 2001: 35). Lacking a place for congregants to gather for devotional practices, could religious belief express identity? As Iddo Tavory (2016: 64) argues, synagogues are clubs, providing the possibility of "synagogue life." For religious congregations, believers are not only orthodox (sharing beliefs) but orthoprax (worshipping together), and these shared commitments shape identity rather than only following from it. Jeffrey Guhin (2016) argues that some religions—Islam, for example—emphasize the shared performance of ritual (doing faith together). In other religions, such as conservative Protestantism, public discourse bolstering orthodoxy (talking together) may bolster affiliation as well. Whether by ritual as action or talk as action, it is being together, primed for a religious identity and aware of appropriate practices, that reveals the power of a shared mesolevel culture and, thus, bonds of faith.

To defend an interactional order, some groups guard spaces or privatize public space (Duneier 1999). The large event known as Burning Man, composed of a network of small friendship groups and emergent organization, consists of such public-private space in the midst of the Nevada desert (Chen 2009). As Marcus Britton (2008: 442) explains, groups may claim "regular spots," and those locations shape identity and permit private (or even deviant) behaviors in public. One group reveals greater racial consciousness on a street corner, owning the space as black men, than they do in a soup kitchen that lacks racial identification. Likewise, groups may be accessible to outsiders in certain spots (e.g., Pagans in the Park or Pagans in the Pub), while having closed meetings elsewhere for those most committed (Coco and Woodward 2007). The power of bounded spaces is evident in scientific discovery groups. The place itself may lack significance until group presence gives it some. John Parker and Edward Hackett (2012)

speak of such "hot spots and hot moments." In gathering those with
shared interests to work on collective problems, they become magnet
places (Farrell 2001) or truth spots (Gieryn 2002). The place is the
location in which group history is recalled and performed.

The most basic ecological reality is that spatial structure encourages (or discourages) gatherings that generate collective action. The
mingling of people, shaped by the obdurate structures of urban architecture, can build coordination. When friends and acquaintances
meet, civic engagement can result. Dingxin Zhao (2001: 147) reports
of the 1989 Tiananmen Square protest, "I found many [interviews
and memoirs] in the form 'I walked down the road and saw X ... and
then I decided to do Z.'" While he considers this to be unplanned and
spontaneous protest, it emphasizes the importance of meeting places
(DeLand 2018). Spatial contexts and constraints permit spontaneous
protest (Snow and Moss 2014: 1146). The proximity of Beijing's universities, the walled separation of these universities from the city, and
the densely located dormitories encouraged risky collective action.
Central campus locations—such as Beijing University's Triangle—are
sites at which groups can spontaneously gather.

People go where they know: where they understand the demands
of the interaction order. These are microworlds that Ray Oldenberg
(1989) terms "third places": sites of voluntary, communal belonging,
apart from the more formal structures of work and home. The ecological features of neighborhoods affect the social relations and local
cultures that develop within. Streets, cul-de-sacs, parks, and plazas
make gatherings more or less likely (Grannis 2009). Along similar
lines, Christopher Browning and his colleagues (Browning et al.
2017) discovered that neighborhoods in which residents interact
more frequently—dense econetworks—show greater levels of local
efficacy. However, these networks, often involving structural segregation, produce a belief in the similarity of residents that, in turn,
creates a neighborhood identity and an imagined comity.[1] The idea of
neighborhood depends on a recognition of the right to belong.

As the examination of neighborhoods suggests, some spaces are
treated as sites for civic action (e.g., Speaker's Corner in London's
Hyde Park). Others are politically neutral (parks, cafés), although under certain circumstances they can become locales from which collective actions emerge.[2]

Group cultures provide "dramaturgical times" that permit the public display of commitment and connection and, by generalizing the local and demanding attention, establish belonging. Groups struggle if they lack places that, in practice, they come to own: civic engagement demands it. As Hank Johnston (2006) notes, small resistant episodes, found where surveillance is unlikely, are crucial to contestation in repressive societies. Privacy helps to generate "actor constitution": the willing participation in groups that counter repression. The hush arbors of African American slave religion in which resistance could be spoken reveal how space can be utilized for undercutting authority (Scott 1989). The sociology of small things depends on a sociology of small places. Here the kitchen table, whether it be that of anticommunist labor resisters, such as Lech Walesa, or early feminists, such as Elizabeth Cady Stanton, becomes the font of political life. For Jeffrey Goldfarb, the interaction order of places creates shared perspectives and common purposes. Goldfarb (2006: 15) argues that the hearth is a stage, asserting, "When friends and relatives met in their kitchens, they presented themselves to each other in such a way that they defined the situation in terms of an independent frame rather than that of officialdom." The home became central to the resistance to Eastern European authoritarianism and the kitchen table became an arena for deliberative democracy (Button and Mattson 1999: 620). As Hank Johnston (2006: 198) explains,

> Away from surveillance by authorities, oppositional speech can occur almost anywhere: the kitchen, the coffee shop, barhopping at night, informal discussions at a book club or a cinema society, and those small circles of friends that linger for hours after the proceedings of more formally structured groups and organizations.... Politicized kitchen talk has been frequently commented upon.... Yet, its widespread nature suggests that something important is going on, namely, in the context of repressive states, opposition speech represents the first steps of actor constitution.

However, if resistant talk occurs in public/private spaces such as coffeehouses (Tallinn's Unicorn Café) or public parks (Grozny's central park in Chechnya), governments may tolerate them precisely because they permit easy surveillance of ostensibly backstage communication.

Theorists have described these gathering points in the creation of the modern public sphere, but their importance has not always been emphasized as operating within an "interaction regime," providing expressive sites of provisional intimacy. If, as Craig Calhoun (2001) argues, civil society relies on the self-organization of social relations, then the ability of members of embedded small groups to gather is central, no matter whether used for the expression of elite discourse (Habermas 1989) or working-class grievance (Weber 1976). Could a vibrant public sphere exist without the coffeehouse (Back and Polisar 1983), the café (Haine 1996; Davetian 2009), the lodge (Koselleck 1988: 70–92; Levtzion 2002), the club (Agulhon 1982: 124–50, Amann 1975: 33–77; Cousin and Chauvin 2014), the saloon (May 2001; LeMasters 1975; Bell 1983), or the salon (Giesen 2001: 223–24; Romani 2007)? Each site of liquid camaraderie has been used to reveal the local features of civil society.

If such gathering points constitute what Balzac referred to as the "parliament of the people," what is the effect on a once democratic society in which these little assemblies have declined (Putnam 2000)? Perhaps, as Mario Small (2009: v) suggests, urban daycare centers provide parents with knowledge to achieve goals that their limited resources do not permit, but are these entrances sufficient to create a robust public?

Spaces in which tiny publics discuss and debate the issues of the day provide for a civil culture, as was evident for the Old-Timers gabbing in a coffee shop, discussed in chapter 2. Political discourse is encouraged in locales where passionate argument is legitimate, even welcomed (Emirbayer and Sheller 1999: 150; Mische and White 1998: 706; Ikegami 2000). Ann Mische's research on Brazilian youth politics demonstrates that it is not grievance or ideology that creates action but the ability of locally based groups to establish a network. Spaces in which individuals gather, either through focused interaction (Collins 1981) or through circulating discussions (the archetypal cocktail party) (Riesman, Potter, and Watson 1960), generate recognition of community. These places can be narrow as in rooms or expansive as in towns.

Craig Calhoun's analysis of the development of radicalism and revolt in nineteenth-century British artisan communities facing the strains of the Industrial Revolution demonstrates the value of treating mesolevel spaces as the basis of collective action. The village with its opportunities for routine interaction permits engagement that leads to a radical perspective and joint action. Calhoun (1982: 149–50) finds that a close-knit community can generate a sense of injustice and awareness of techniques of resistance. As he writes,

> These movements were largely based on the social foundations of local communities. The people they mobilized were knit together through personal bonds within these communities much more than class unified them. As such movements attempted to go beyond local communities in their mobilization or objects, they foundered.

In place of class consciousness, Calhoun asserts the centrality of place consciousness. Being close-knit suggests not only a warm emotional register but that these relations are continually activated. Radicalism depended on preserving and engaging traditional social relations. The ability to generate oppositional movements depends on shared awareness of oppression in spaces in which collective action is possible (Chua 2012).

People organize themselves with regard to particular places within broader economic structures. For Roger Gould (1995), examining the events leading up to the Paris Commune of 1870, the transition from housing surrounding craft-based workplaces to neighborhoods distant from work led to novel forms of revolutionary collective action, not focused on conditions of labor but communal economic conditions. A heterogeneous neighborhood (with residents similar in social class) replaced the workplace as the site of protest.

Repertoires of action, of which the weapons of the weak (Scott 1985) form a central part, are not merely abstract techniques of resistance but emerge from action spaces. Yet while theorists refer to groups, chains, relations, or clusters, they rarely explore the micro-cultures that lead to the perception of common interests and, like Charles Tilly (2006: 156), retreat from the interaction order to emphasize durable categories of actors, less grounded in place.

Civil society operates not just in spaces that are explicitly political but also in ostensibly apolitical locations. Well known is "Slim's Table," made famous by Mitchell Duneier. At a table in Chicago's Hyde Park neighborhood's Valois Cafeteria, a group of black and white men talked about the issues of the day, transcending racial boundaries. As Duneier (1992: 159) reports, "In coming to a cafeteria in the integrated Hyde Park district, some of these men are expressing a desire to participate in the larger, more comprehensive society.... The wider society ... is a vehicle for them to express their own civility." The routines around Slim's table and the communal recognition of those routines allows for a circuit of action that transforms these marginal actors into citizens, but it was the ability to "own" a table that permitted these routines. More explicitly political, but no less social, is Katherine Walsh's (2004) observation of the daily discourse among a group of Old Timers in a small café, described in chapter 2. The café provided a long table at which these men could sit, enjoying a slow and talky breakfast. The willingness of the owner to allow the space to be filled with these men served a civic purpose. In a similar vein, Karla Erickson (2009), describing a neighborhood restaurant, discovered that, despite it being a place of business, it was also a place of caring and civil, civic discourse.[3] These and many other locations are potent sites for mutual camaraderie, and, as Eric Klinenberg (2018) emphasizes, the proliferation of such social infrastructure, when supported by enlightened governments, can moderate alienation and inequality. When discourse involves more than pleasantries, what appears from the outside to be apolitical can serve a public purpose. This, too, exemplifies Tocqueville's minute communities in which social order develops from common placement. Good neighborhoods provide places to gather, often repurposing empty spaces to create meeting points (Douglas 2014).[4]

The existence of shared space does not assure socially desirable action. As Sudhir Venkatesh (2008) describes, gangs also need places. Indeed, gangs may be the most spatially sensitive of all civic groups. Gang structure demands claimed territory, often in competition with claims of other gangs, attacking outsiders, either those with other group membership or "undesirable" racial or ethnic characteristics (Suttles 1968). Territoriality is so consequential that turf wars are common as gangs expand their spaces of control. In addition, gang members are aware of points of surveillance to avoid the police gaze, just as the police target spaces in which trouble might arise. Spatial violence proves so significant that some residents of public housing refuse to move if, as a result, they would live in territory claimed by a hostile gang, a severe problem for those raising teens. Their cognitive map includes gang violence, recognizing the control of local places (Rymond-Richmond 2006; Pattillo-McCoy 1998). Physical danger and psychological belonging are salient in the choices of residents, despite the benefits of improved housing. In these cases, absent the presence of supportive publics, one's communal location may be a matter of life and death.

Acting on Stages

Once we gather, what to do? We perform as actors and witness as audience. A mesotheory of group culture is not in the mind but on the stage: set in scenes. An approach that emphasizes the interaction order is, as might be expected from a Goffmanian analysis, fundamentally dramaturgical and, thus, spatial. This perspective builds on the sociological tradition of valuing action as the basis of social organization, treating skilled performers and knowing audiences as central to the reproduction of social relations (Giddens 1984; Fligstein 2001; Martin 2011). While recognizing the influence of logics and affect, both gain meaning through action and especially interaction (Hallett and Ventresca 2006). An interaction order is a realm of rituals, rhetoric, and responses, not mere reflex or reflection. As a result, a civic group develops a performance style that can be distinguished from other groups (Hart 2001: 3). This is a means through which a group reveals its moral basis and civic imagination (Baiocchi et al. 2014: 25). Culture is praxis, found not only in heads and hearts. Groups engage in "civic action," revealed in a behavioral, rather than cognitive, space (Lichterman and Eliasoph 2014: 794).

Within democratic systems, it is not that all must agree. In fact, respectful rivalry is often more valuable. Civil society depends on the public sharing of distinct perspectives and different values. Healthy political systems depend on groups that perceive themselves in long-standing opposition. Structured contention—an interaction order that permits disagreements—is integral to democratic decision-making. Finding places that allow, or encourage, contained disagreement— town meetings, legislative halls, or candidate debates—contributes to civil society. When ordered dispute breaks down, communal identification is endangered. Citizens must regularly and publicly reaffirm their belongingness. While mass rituals are often organized by states, such mass events are powerful because they are observed and discussed and are found in open civic spaces. Further, they gain impact because small groups travel together, part of a mass composed of other groups. Large rituals that seemingly create an expansive public are, in fact, created by the assembling of knots of colleagues. Singles attend rallies, marches, protests, and events, but more often are found with friends and acquaintances who provide support and sociability (Aveni 1977). Crowds are not undifferentiated collections of persons, their individuality erased, but involve the assembling of established groups (McPhail 1991). These groups may appear a mass, while remaining a collection of tiny publics. The crowded space is comprised of a grid of groups.

Further, the mass, when well organized, can disassemble in an orderly fashion as well. Groups combine and then divide. In times of disaster, moments that depend on immediate response and the activation of individuals into groups, shared discussion is crucial and individuals merge into local sets (Shibutani 1966). As Bin Xu (2017) describes in examining the aftermath of the massive Sichuan earthquake of 2008, groups rapidly mobilized to aid the needy in devastated areas. These knots of action stood outside the official state response. They created an intimate culture as they delivered aid to overwhelmed locales: social relations provided support where the communal fabric was rent. At intense moments, people, sharing space, reveal, forge, and refine allegiances.

The salience of performance as a political act is evident in the mesoanalysis of social movements. While I discussed social movements as associations in chapter 3, here I note their sited performances. At times, a group can become, in effect, a troupe; actors gain confidence from their audiences (Fuist 2014). They perform on a public stage. These performances of commitment embolden high-risk activism as Jeff Goodwin (1997) describes in the case of the Huk rebellion in the Philippines. Consciousness-raising in women's groups in the 1970s served a similar end, providing a sympathetic audience for performances of grievance that might otherwise be ignored, rejected, or mocked (Cassell 1977). Even an act seemingly as personal as prayer is often performed jointly, if silently, in a sacred space to demonstrate commitment (Fuist 2015).

Staged high school drunk-driving tragedies by the organization "Every 15 Minutes" rely on a performance venue in which adolescent audiences can *feel* those dangers of which adults believe they should be aware (Miller 2012). As Émile Durkheim (1912) asserted, through demonstrating embodied and communal emotions, such moments generate collective effervescence. The challenge is to sustain this emotional attachment in the face of mundane routine and social control (Bartkowski 2000; Collins 2004).

The challenge of stoking emotion is especially evident in the rituals of oppositional groups. Although much social movement scholarship examines the relationship between the movement and the state, between the movement and the individual, or acquisition of resources by organizations, movements depend on the willingness of actors to perform opposition. Movements are effective tools of revolt and reform when they galvanize supporters to demonstrate their support through public actions (Freedman and Fraser 1966). Choosing a proper location for these demonstrations becomes crucial; the locale must gather an audience—sympathetic or hostile—to enter public discourse. The demonstration of political desire through action is influential when the performance garners publicity (Adut 2018).

For a movement to grow, become institutionally stable, and to cement allegiance, the public display of commitment and passion is essential. In this way, individuals form a community that then can generate public pressure. A display of solidarity helps groups transcend the free-rider problem by having the performance and reactions to it (and reactions to the reactions) bolster the actor's identity (Olson 1965).

Performance venues can be used by a powerful, even totalitarian, regime that attempts to shape identities in its own image. The People's Republic of China established small groups during the Cultural Revolution that used rituals and mutual criticism for indoctrination. These state-formed groups preempted autonomous primary groups operating outside the purview of the state (Whyte 1974: 10).

However, even in democracies, groups build a common culture and reveal shared purpose. Doug McAdam (1988) writes of "Freedom High" as an integral component of the civil rights movement. Freedom High was both performative and spatial. McAdam cites efforts by organizers of the Mississippi Freedom Summer project to build cohesion through spaces that allowed for classes, parties, and dialogues. In other domains, socialists and communists have sponsored camps and other sociable activities, distant from mundane locations, such as Unity House in the Catskill Mountains of upstate New York. The goal was to make Marxism a "way of life" and "a movement of families" (Mishler 1999: 2, 9). However, the way of life and the support for families depended on the availability of campgrounds and cottages. A stronger sensibility is evident in the Ku Klux Klan, whose fiery entertainments of cross burnings served to build cohesion

(Blee 1992: 167; Gordon 2017). These gatherings were held in rural fields; being present signaled belonging. Camps for survivalists similarly promote identity in locations that are set apart from the quotidian (Mitchell 2002).

Focused meetings and the narratives that emerge build organizations (Polletta 2002). As Jaida Sandra and Jon Spayde (2001) contend in promoting the political value of salons, conversation can turn people into activists by building a group culture. They write, "Passionate conversation often led to passionate action, to lives risked, and sometimes sacrificed in efforts to achieve social and political change." Organizations frequently debate the best location and how much privacy to ensure. Halls with a focal point—a lectern, podium, or dais—generate collective attention. The spatial ordering of authority can make a meeting more effective than an amorphous gathering. Place provides structure for discussion, debate, and decisions (Schwartzman 1989). David Gibson's (2011) exemplary case study of discussion during the American response to the Cuban missile crisis (see chap. 6) reveals the power of performance around a table in the White House situation room in the context of war or peace.

It is striking that in the peace talks to end the war in Vietnam, the precise shape of the table had enormous symbolic value in determining who was part of the decision-making and with what kind of authority. Agreeing on the right table, seemingly trivial, might have been the most contentious part of the process. Whether we examine powerful decision-makers or those who oppose them, the staging of action determines the outcomes.

Civic Places

Civic life can occur in places that are open or closed, available to all or shut to most, but each depends on ideas of the kind of interaction that is appropriate and each has its own history. For commitment, the size of the venue and the number of participants are crucial: these spaces promote group-based engagement.

When many Americans think of the spaces in which local politics are discussed, they often imagine an idealized New England town meeting, my first empirical case. However, this civic structure is no longer found often. There is no tradition of town meetings in the American South; it derives from the ideology of New England

Protestantism and the geography of small farms and tight-knit towns. As cities have flourished, towns have enlarged, and populations have diversified, town meetings have become rare, even in New England; those that still exist have their power truncated. Where they continue, managers and councils often make the routine decisions that affect local life. Increasingly town meetings are merely symbolic remnants, but the symbolism is important for those towns that continue the tradition. Just as working commons have vanished, becoming leisurely parks but still labeled the "commons," the town meeting has become a nostalgic vestige of an earlier age.

In contrast, some gatherings are spatially separated to exclude those who have not been invited. Closed meetings are common, surely more frequent than assemblies open to all. Klan get-togethers have this quality, but they are not unique in their exclusion. Tribal ceremonies or feminist music festivals often are bounded (Eder, Staggenborg, and Sudderth 1995). Emphasizing that places make us, Japonica Brown-Saracino (2017) describes how lesbian communities create spaces for community in accord with their local cultures. While white spaces and male spaces have advantages in resources and cultural privilege, they are not alone. Any place at which people meet, walled off from others, both demonstrates and builds cohesion. To understand place-based exclusion I discuss the Bohemian Grove, an encampment in the northern California woods, open to the members of San Francisco's Bohemian Club and their invited guests. Here male elites spend two weeks in forest lodges, networking and playing, and occasionally welcoming artists, politicians, and celebrities. As described by G. William Domhoff (1974), the camp solidifies a national upper class.

The third example compares the spatial organization of two historical moments: the proliferation of English coffeehouses in the early decades of the eighteenth century and the development of French salons in the late eighteenth century. These sites reveal a flourishing public sphere. The coffeehouse was a public site open to men with modest means but strong interest in political discourse.[5] In contrast, salons operated by invitation.[6] They were typically held once a week and presided over by admired hostesses. At both, talk was prized, although the French emphasis on polite, poetic discourse was not identical to the rougher and more diverse English coffeehouse. Despite their prominence, neither form became permanent. By the 1730s, the coffeehouse, so prominent a few decades earlier at the time of Joseph Addison and Richard Steele, was in decline. Revolutionary fervor upended French salons. If not directly tied to the royal court, salons attracted intellectuals and the wealthy and remind us of the congenial dinners of the Georgetown set of American foreign policy advisers. In time, other structures took their place. The French developed a world of cafés, close to British coffeehouses in their public availability, while British elites retreated into clubs, sealed off by requirements of membership (Capdeville 2016), a form of segregated elite sociability and cosmopolitanism that still exists (Cousin and Chauvin 2014). Cafés, like coffeehouses, permitted wider civic engagement that tempered the status-bound cultures of clubs, salons, and courts. They permitted wider, if not deeper, civic engagement and a more open public sphere (Davetian 2009).

However, for all of these sites of sociability, whether open to all or by invitation, the horizontal connections, acceptable performance, and shared cultures promoted civic engagement in contrast to public events that cater to a mass audience. Each could engender solidarity, whether in a more democratic, expansive public or a more limited, closed set of groups.[7]

THE TOWN MEETING AS CIVIC SITE

Political meetings are often treated as fonts of civic order. On those occasions, citizens engage in shared deliberation, at least in principle. Given their size and separation from larger governmental structures, townships and villages are sites where collective governance is possible, creating "an ardent civic spirit" (Gannett 2003: 1). A community meeting signifies a functioning political democracy. Political theorists, notably Hannah Arendt (1963: 165), discuss such occasions in these terms. In the local meeting hall residents pledge fealty to each other and to their community, not a higher power (Arendt 1963: 175–76; Gannett 2003: 13; Clark and Teachout 2012). Libertarians David Morris and Karl Hess (1975: 16) argue that "neighborhoods are tiny, underdeveloped nations": tiny publics that should be treated as self-governing units. As Robert Vargas (2016: 173) claims from his ethnography of a Chicago barrio, different blocks, based on their physical features, their social attributes, their cultural traditions, and their ties to external worlds, have distinctive characters. Some blocks emphasize active engagement in creating safe zones, while others are passive, frightened, dark locations. These latter are sites of gang violence.

Despite the allure of equality, groups do not always demand (or allow) participation and often not even total commitment. However, deliberations are only as valuable as the process through which talk leads to outcomes. Meetings have different power dynamics, hidden agreements, and do not inevitably generate satisfaction or a commitment to shared governance (Button and Mattson 1999: 633–34; Fishkin 2009). These dilemmas help explain why deliberative gatherings are not central to national politics and are often treated as experiments. While some meetings prevent alienation, encourage participation, and lead to stronger neighborhoods (Thomson 2001), the idea of group collaboration in setting policy is more often a promise than a reality.

The archetypal form of political deliberation, as routinized and formalized, is the New England town meeting, much beloved by Ralph Waldo Emerson and Henry David Thoreau but now largely limited to small-town Vermont. In the evocative phrase of David Bromwich,[8] "the town meeting is the grammar of democracy." Tocqueville (2003: 73) asserted that "town [meetings] are to freedom what primary schools are to knowledge; they bring it within people's reach, and give men the enjoyment and habit of using it for peaceful ends." Drawing on American colonial discourse, Hannah Arendt (1963: 238) speaks of the value of "public happiness," linking this joy to township politics. Neighbors meet and, in the best case, create consensual policies, even when facing adversaries (Mansbridge 1980: 39).

Frank Bryan (2004), the most indefatigable chronicler of the Vermont town meeting, notes the romanticism associated with these assemblies, an imaginary of a simpler and more harmonious time. With some skepticism, Bryan refers to the town meeting as exemplifying "real democracy," drawing a line from Athenian gatherings to those in Vermont's Northeast Kingdom. Bryan (2004: 83) writes, "real democracy works better in small places—dramatically better." Mirroring—but distant from—the timing of national elections, town meetings are typically set for the first Tuesday after the first Monday in March. In Vermont, this means that attendance is a function of meteorological conditions as well as the agenda, announced by "warning" notices sent to each resident. Melting ice, pelting sleet, or warm spring sun shapes attendance, the reality of which caucus attendees in Iowa are well aware. Today an increasing number of towns hold their meetings on the night before the first Tuesday or the prior Saturday to staunch the decline in attendance (Zimmerman 1999). The enthusiasm for democratic participation is supported by the spatial imagery of John Winthrop's city on a hill.

Meetings begin with a prayer and most outcomes are determined through a voice vote or show of hands. Public participation stands in sharp contrast to the secret (Australian) ballot, which some towns now use for potentially contentious issues. However, when the votes are public, not only does the citizen participate, but also a representative of the community is responsible for counting hands or judging competitive shouts. In contrast, secret ballots are a means by which adversarial democracy avoids personal enmity (Mansbridge 1980: 39). Open ballots, however, are an invitation and a goad to consensus, making conflict more costly when constituents know each other. Meetings end with some ritual of good fellowship, hoping to salve any ill will and assure the participants of their communal virtue.

Consider CBS reporter Charles Kuralt's visit to a town meeting:

> This one day, people in Vermont look not to their own welfare but to that of their town. It doesn't matter that it's been snowing since four o'clock this morning. They'll be in the meetinghouse. This is town meeting day. Every March for 175 years, the men and women of Strafford, Vermont, have trudged up this hill on the one day which is their holiday for democracy. They walk past a sign that says: The Old White Meeting House—Built in 1799 and consecrated as a place of Public worship for all denominations with no preference for one above another. Since 1801, it has also been in continuous use as a town hall.... There is pie, baked by the ladies of the PTA. There are baked beans and brown bread, served at town meeting by Celia Lane as long as anybody can remember ... When finally they did adjourn and walk out into the snow, it was with the feeling of having preserved something important, something more than their streetlights—their liberty. (Kuralt 1985: 288–91)

Equally nostalgic is that new residents may be impressed by colonial shabby chic, making democracy feel real, as in this account by a local student of a later meeting in the same town:

When I went to town meeting in Strafford this year, I sat behind and frequently conversed with a relative newcomer, Donna Bliss. Donna and her husband Stephen retired to Strafford from Boston about five years ago. They've built a gorgeous mansion atop a hill that overlooks much of South Strafford. [She was a journalist, he was a corporate CEO.] ... Donna hadn't been in the Town House before and was looking forward to seeing the interior of a building that she'd recognized from magazines when she first moved to Strafford. Donna found the Town House to be a charming place with its old wood stove and natural light. She was amazed that the Town House remains without plumbing, running water or electricity, and though a bit annoyed by having to walk next door to a neighboring house to use the bathroom, she tried not to show it. (Bryan 2004: 23)

These reports demonstrate the salience of the spatial configuration and decor of town meeting sites. The reality that citizens share a space, if only temporarily, is crucial. Democracy results from citizens in wooden chairs facing a raised platform. They transform well-recognized spaces, such as the town hall, village library, high school auditorium, gymnasium, or church basement into a realm of debate and decision, creating what Bryan (2004: 83) nicely terms an "architecture of governance." The diversity (and also the similarity) of the sites are striking:

The places where the people gather on town meeting day vary almost as much as the scratch and claw geography that surrounds them. In Brandon in 1987 the people met in the modern auditorium of Otter Valley Union High School. In Braintree they met in the West Braintree town hall.... They met in the elementary school gym in Cambridge in 1992. In Calais they met in a "quaint little church that had been converted to a town hall some time ago," in Ira in the cellar of the Ira Baptist Church, in Washington at "the small elementary school, that looked like a converted chicken barn," in Tinmouth at the Grange hall, and in Bolton at the fire station.... No matter where they were situated or in what kind of building the citizens met, all these meeting places shared one feature. They were too small — far too small — to hold all the registered voters of the town had these voters decided to attend. (Bryan 2004: 103)

The crucial misconception is that all citizens can fit in the space provided. Some writers assume that every resident participates in a town meeting or that they had done so in ancient Athens. The physical limitations of the spaces mean that universal participation is not feasible. As the English jurist John Selden (1689: 31) noted, a parliament is necessary, "because the Room will not hold all." The Grange Hall in Newfane, Vermont (Bryan 2004: xi), would not hold them; neither would the Athenian meeting place on the hill of Pnyx (Dahl 1989: 16; Ober 1989). Because of spatial constrains, communal democracy in moderately sized publics requires the willingness of some citizens to absent themselves, abstaining from debate (Zimmerman 1999). Direct democracy depends on apathy.

The larger the town, the smaller the proportion of engagement (Bryan 2004: 18). Although percentages vary, typically 20 percent of the eligible population participates. Critics consider this a specialized and unelected elite, lacking expertise and relying on neighborly cliques. Does true equality exist in these meetings directed by local leaders? Some residents may be less welcome or less encouraged to participate. Despite its happy image, exclusion can be implicit. Status seems well understood as residents array themselves in light of their standing with selectmen at front, active participants in the middle, and the less engaged at the back or sides. Location reveals a claim to authority; citizenship is spatial.

However, the town meeting, despite its limits, provides a mesopolitical model that demonstrates the possibilities of citizens gathering to achieve self-governance, whether or not the reality is as democratic as its imaginary. Still, the comforting and mundane spaces filled with neighbors means that cohesion is the desideratum. Meeting day is a time that all should walk from the site with their relationships intact, their culture embraced, and their tiny public burnished in the fulfillment of democracy.

HIGH JINKS IN THE WOODS

If a town meeting represents a space in which all citizens have the right—and perhaps the obligation—to gather, other sites are by invitation only, determined by rigorous procedures with patrolled boundaries. Clubs, gangs, cells, and lodges merge bonding and banding, and they gain appeal by exclusion. The secrecy of secret societies has appeal. Walls keep information within the group, limiting hearing and seeing. These access obstructions rely on the spatial structure of group gatherings. Whether the secrets are significant or not, physical barriers mark commitment.

I consider the Bohemian Grove, an encampment of elite men, affiliated with the Bohemian Club of San Francisco, established in 1878. For two weeks during the summer as many as three thousand corporate executives, lawyers, politicians, actors, and media barons travel to a site near Monte Rio, California. Although a rural and wooded area, the location is dotted with over a hundred elaborate "camps." As Domhoff (1974: 1) writes, referring to the encampment's Cremation of Care, a ritual designed to leave the outside world behind,

> Picture yourself comfortably seated in a beautiful open-air dining hall in the midst of twenty-seven hundred acres of giant California redwoods. It is early evening and the clear July air is still pleasantly warm. Dusk has descended, you have finished a sumptuous dinner, and you are sitting quietly with your drink and your cigar, listening to nostalgic welcoming speeches and enjoying the gentle light and the eerie shadows that are cast by the two-stemmed gaslights flickering softly at each of the several hundred outdoor banquet tables.

Domhoff demonstrates the presence of tight, elite networks—also found at Davos, Aspen, and similar locations—and he also captures the seductive allure of place in building community. The Bohemian Grove encampment promotes conviviality and sociability. As journalist Philip Weiss (1989) wrote about his experience,

> You know you are inside the Bohemian Grove when you come down a trail in the woods and hear piano music from amid a group of tents and then round a bend to see a man with a beer in one hand and his penis in the other, urinating into the bushes. This is the most gloried-in ritual of the encampment, the freedom of powerful men to pee wherever they like.

One spot is set aside for the lakeside talks, another for the formal drama, a third for the comic plays. Shaded nooks and hidden crannies hold meanings for the attendees. Place shapes the interaction order, and in this sense Bohemian Grove, despite the links to power, is not so different from urban street corners and honky-tonk bars.

Bohemian Grove is a special "third place." It exists separate from the routines of home and work, is limited in time, has guarded boundaries, and access depends on invitation. The encampment is an occasion, not simply an accessible space: time and space are joined (Wynn 2016). The motto is "Weaving Spiders Come Not Here." Away from immediate cares, occupational strategies, and the unwelcome (including women), members and their guests discuss politics, savor pleasure, and embrace power. Perhaps most significantly, participants establish friendships in a space that encourages an intimate, accepting camaraderie away from the "world." Its rhetorical welcome hides the reality that it contains tiny publics with vast civic power.

A CONVERSIBLE WORLD: COFFEE, COGNAC, AND THE PUBLIC SPHERE

Was the eighteenth century the golden age of discourse? This was a time when citizens were expected to talk about issues that mattered and about those that didn't, and to do both volubly and with panache.[9] In accord with David Hume (1758), this was a "conversible world," reflecting a belief that conversation produced political stability. Hume believed that political thought depends on the art of conversation (Miller 2006: 24). However, this was more than a matter of discursive norms. Community was not only conversible, it was a world. The commitment to talk required the availability of spaces that welcomed conversation.

The coffeehouse and the salon, while not the only sites for discourse in Western Europe, encouraged social engagement. The development of a coffeehouse culture and a culture of salons in England and France during the eighteenth century reminds us how influential sociable sites can be.[10] Nevertheless, they were fragile: flowering and withering. These locations were as temporary as teahouses, hookah bars, and working-class taverns; their numbers expanded and contracted as a function of fashion and economy.

Given their fragility, it is striking how central to modern civil society the structures of the eighteenth century have become. The coffeehouse and the salon stand for what Richard Sennett (1976) refers to as the locales of "public man." The decline of these spaces leads, perhaps, to the decline of the public person. This suggests that the outer-directed person—the social persona—has been overtaken by the inner-directed actor—the self-consumed. The latter cares less about the opinions of others. The public man mixing with other public men produced a culture apart from state control: a public sphere.

Much consideration of the development of the public sphere grew from the iconic essay of Jürgen Habermas, *The Structural Transformation of the Public Sphere*, originally published in 1962. Habermas (1989: 11) was particularly concerned with the development of public and private spheres. His essay grew from the debate in post–World War II Germany over the importance of sociability, but it also addressed which spaces most encourage civic sociability.

These two discursive sites—the coffeehouse and the salon—have significant structural differences. The English coffeehouse has been treated as the purest form of communal discourse, possibly, as David Hume appreciated, a result of the public discussions of governance and faith inspired by the Puritan Revolution (Miller 2006: 81). In retrospect, the democratic impulses of these institutions were perhaps exaggerated. As Sennett (1977: 81) remarks, "The coffeehouse is a romanticized and over-idealized institution: merry, civilized talk, bonhomie, and close friendship all over a cup of coffee." Yet the shining image remains. In this sentimental view, social ranks were forgotten as the communication of news and ideas trumped hierarchy. In the words of Stephen Miller (2006: 90), a coffeehouse was "an island of equality in a sea of class."[11] Or, according to the Abbé Prévost, "to see a lord, or two, a baronet, a shoemaker, a tailor, a wine-merchant, and a few others of the same stamp poring over the same newspapers. Truly the coffee houses ... are the seats of English liberty" (Miller 2006: 90). Downplaying the importance of status orders, Richard Sennett (1977: 81) suggests,

> In order for information to be as full as possible, distinctions of rank were temporarily suspended; anyone sitting in the coffeehouse had a right to talk to anyone else, to enter into any conversation, whether he knew the other people or not, whether he was bidden to speak or not.

Consistent with Habermas's (1989: 27) conception of the public sphere, these were places in which (mostly bourgeois) private people came together, claiming the space for themselves and asserting the right to discuss. As coffeehouses opened throughout England, totaling perhaps as many as three thousand during the first decade of the eighteenth century (Habermas 1989: 32), those who wished to read journals, such as Richard Steele's *Tatler* or Joseph Addison's *Spectator*, could visit one of these shops and not only read but deliberate current ideas in sharp discussions. The combination of exotic and modestly priced beverages and the expectation that one would meet acquaintances and strangers proved, for a time, a powerful draw. As venues increased in number and differentiated, each gathered its own tiny public, civic regulars who considered the location as theirs. Some London locations such as Will's or Button's were known for those habitués who led the discussions. These establishments differed in their politics, with some recognized for the dominance of Whigs (The St. James) and others for the presence of Tories (White's), creating distinct discursive communities, a separation evident today in the online silos of progressives and conservatives.

The problem, as Habermas noted, was that with the growth of coffeehouses, each with its own local culture, a means needed to be found to focus discourse, perhaps as trending topics do on Twitter. As Habermas (1989: 42) argues, journals served a critical role:

> The moral weeklies ... were still an immediate part of coffee-house discussions.... When Addison and Steele published the first issue of the *Tatler* in 1709, the coffee houses were already so numerous and the circles of their frequenters already so wide, that contact among these thousandfold circles could only be maintained through a journal.

The journals, each produced by a small group, became the basis for plentiful small discussions. Face-to-face discourse depended on the availability of an appealing topical agenda. To the extent that these groups connected through other ties and to the extent that the discussions shaped future debate, tiny publics built an expansive public.

The zenith of coffeehouses lasted from approximately 1660 until 1720 (Klein 1996) and then faded, perhaps due to the ebbing of their novelty. Sites of gathering can be evanescent, tinged with fashion or available technology. (Video game parlors, once urban fixtures, have disappeared.) The growth of private English clubs also contributed to the decline of the coffeehouse, perhaps creating a greater ease of interaction and increased status for members. The clubs provided a selective and selected network that generated deep sociability but circumscribed its breadth. The growth of coffeehouse culture emphasizes that there can be places for free discussion, but its decline suggests the fragility of these open spaces. By the mid-eighteenth century, the coffeehouse was no longer a central gathering place for political discussion.

The situation in Paris was strikingly different. Despite the existence of coffeehouses in Paris, they never had the same intellectual cachet as they had in London. Perhaps because of a more influential courtly system, invited salons were more salient than public shops, beginning with the regency of Louis XV and continuing until the Revolution. Paris in the mid-eighteenth century is recalled for its cultural and philosophical ferment. It is honored with the label of the Age of Enlightenment, but all such ages require revered texts and sites of talk. To become canonical, texts require places in which they are honored. Without social spaces—salons, clubs, seminar rooms, or literary societies—the translation from the written word to social argument is fraught. As Randall Collins (1998) suggests about philosophy, breakthroughs depend on social gatherings and dense networks.

Salons, weekly gatherings typically organized by women from wealthy French families, created an opening for sophisticated debate as well as a culture based on politeness and on the ability to converse with wit and style. The presence of well-known cultural figures drew guests. Public practices of social relations and the spaces in which these practices were enacted structured the political order (Arditi 1998).

In contrast to the coffeehouse and the club, the salon was open to men and women, and was as social as political. Daniel Gordon (1994: 191) describes the organization of the salon:

> The activity of organizing a salon involved considerable work and expense. Meals had to be provided for a dozen or more people on a regular basis. An effort had to be made to recruit talented and distinguished people. Gifts had to be distributed to the poorer artists and men of letters so they could maintain an appearance that would not

embarrass them in the presence of wealthier guests. Above all, the salon organizer faced the challenge of sustaining vibrant exchange, goodwill, and decorum within the assembly.

These gendered relations, while based in broad ideas about men and women, were expressed in the relations among particular men and women. As Dena Goodman (1994: 131) argues, explicating the beliefs of André Morellet, the presence of women recruited men. Although women were not in themselves central to the political sphere, they had the resources and glamour to sponsor occasions for male guests. Even if the debates did not explicitly address rebellion, they laid the groundwork for private discussions elsewhere. Because these salons had access boundaries that the coffeehouse lacked, the audience was sharply limited. The British scene, less tied to a curated group, permitted wider participation and a more explicitly political sensibility.

Cultural historians emphasize that the French salon was linked to the ideals of manners (Arditi 1998). Salons with their polite discourse could either be seen as creating an emergent public sphere or an impotent public. However, these conventions created a politics of sociability (Goodman 1994: 5). For Habermas (1989: 33, 35), even the apolitical focus of talk permitted a public sphere:

> In the salons, the nobility and the grande bourgeoisie of finance and administration assimilating itself to that nobility met with the "intellectuals" on an equal footing.... In the salons of the fashionable ladies, noble as well as bourgeois, sons of princes and counts associated with the sons of watchmakers and shopkeepers.... The decisive element was not so much the political equality of the members but their exclusiveness in relation to the political realm of absolutism as such: social equality was possible at first only as an equality outside the state.

Even if the range of participants was narrower than at the coffeehouse, the mixing still produced relations distinct from the court hierarchy. Despite limitations on what could be discussed under a monarchy, free-floating discourse in the salon allowed for a society egalitarian in its ideology. Both the coffeehouse and the salon provided spaces in which a public sphere developed.

Placement and Solidarity

Civil society depends on the existence of places of performance. Place legitimates certain actions, permitting citizens to join together. We can understand the mesolevel use of space in light of its obdurate reality, symbolic significance, and systems of control. This builds on beliefs about what constitutes a proper social "scape" for civic performances. While we may conceptualize "scapes" in light of the urban cityscape, all locations are scaped. A city that builds central squares, stadia, or parks has provided arenas in which some forms of public life can happen. The National Mall allows for demonstrations because of its size, symbolism, and proximity to sites of power. Such places are used both for state-sponsored patriotic events and for resistance rallies. However, gatherings do not require mass action. Cafés or taverns, kitchens or porches invite groupings and serve as a basis for civic action.

Places have more significance than from their physical structure alone. They can be controlled, colonized, or treated as symbolic. Physical locations are laminated with moral consequence. We speak of gang territories, gayborhoods, ghettos, skid rows, tony quarters, red-light districts, ethnic enclaves, gentrified districts, factory zones, and gated communities. As defined and known, an interaction order is embraced, enforced through surveillance, neighborhood watches, and police presence. Smaller sites, such as bars, libraries, hospitals, and churches, rely on standards of appropriate action. How areas are defined affects who is present and what is allowed. It is not only that Black Lives Matter, but that black lives matter in white spaces of privilege. Recent controversies about how African Americans are treated in quasi-public spaces such as Starbucks remind us that café cultures do not necessary include all. Some parts of the city are treated as more civil and civic than others. It is this comfort that Elijah Anderson (2011) refers to as the cosmopolitan canopy, spaces in which all are ostensibly given access, while recognizing tears in that canopy that let in the downpour above.

A physical stage permits structures of control. While the activities that citizens perform in public are often routine, at times gatherings can become contentious or oppositional. As a result, governments may choose surveillance, either in a benign fashion to judge public sentiment or in a more malignant desire for control. Open public spaces permit those who wish to observe group action to do so: places in which thoughts are presented in talk. Are there windows, points at which cameras can be installed, or unannounced watchers?

Ultimately, politics is not merely ideological but profoundly spatial. This is one reason that repressive regimes and those concerned about violence or disruption monitor space and time by creating curfews, containing demonstrations, and limiting the size of gatherings.

Individuals may act in isolation, but groups depend on meeting points. These constitute what Eric Klinenberg (2018) terms "social infrastructure," crucial to the preservation of civic life. Meanings bleed from spaces into activities. As a result, circuits of action, legitimate and expected behaviors based on cultural expectations, rely on physical arrangements. Civic spots, whether open to all or closed to many, create conditions for some citizens to discuss and to govern, but their boundaries—enforced explicitly or implicitly—define who are civic actors in civil society.

5

CONFLICT

Scratching Consensus's Veneer

Ordinarily the definitions of the situation projected by the several different participants are sufficiently attuned to one another so that open contradiction will not occur. I do not mean that there will be the kind of consensus that arises when each individual present candidly expresses what he really feels and honestly agrees with the expressed feelings of the others present. This kind of harmony is an optimistic ideal and in any case not necessary for the smooth working of society. Rather, each participant is expected to suppress his immediate heartfelt feelings, conveying a view of the situation which he feels the others will be able to find at least temporarily acceptable. The maintenance of this surface of agreement, this veneer of consensus, is facilitated by each participant concealing his own wants behind statements which assert values to which everyone present feels obliged to give lip service.

ERVING GOFFMAN, *The Presentation of Self in Everyday Life*

Is harmony the natural state of local politics, the default condition of social life? Is consensus a moral value, essential to group culture? Given communal engagement, under what circumstances will groups accept the legitimacy of challenge? Is smooth interaction within a tiny public more virtuous than spiky debate? If so, what is the effect on local politics of the desire for comity? When and where — and how — does conflict serve a civic purpose?

A frequent trope is that successful interaction orders depend on participants engaging in mutual coordination to achieve desired ends and to share role-taking, perspective-taking, and empathy (Davis and Love 2017). Given these preferences, under what circumstances does conflict serve as a hinge connecting the individual and the institutional?

From Erving Goffman's (1967) face-saving rituals of deference and demeanor through Randall Collins's (2004) interaction ritual chains, including conversation analysts' emphasis on repair (Schegloff 1992) and Anselm Strauss's (1978) highlighting the negotiated order, theorists treat interactional accord as the ideal of social relations. Yet, under some circumstances, conflict and contention provide tensile strength for local communities, birthing needed change. Goffman's "veneer of consensus" has been treated as both a basis and a goal of community, but is this so when considering the relationship among groups? By emphasizing the centrality of coordination and by focusing on collective action, accord has gained priority over dispute, but at what cost? Previous chapters focused on the commitment to agree, but here I discuss how conflict operates on the mesolevel.

Few deny that the willingness to compromise facilitates civic concord, reduces transaction costs, and encourages intersubjective understandings. Facing intense moral traffic, people search for exit ramps to avoid collisions. The desire for harmony is a powerful force that explains how shared dramaturgical practices signal the existence of a good society (Kuzmics 1991; Smith 2006: 25–26). While every interactional tradition recognizes disruption, it is often considered a failure of the social rather than as integral to it. These "conflicts of interpretation"—or "shipwrecks" (Reed 2006: 149, 156, citing Captain Cook's Hawaiian visits)—can lead to aggressive responses, temporary or continuing. These conflicts are not inherent but are one of the mechanisms by which groups formulate their relations with others.

Yet there is something unsatisfying in proclaiming conclaves as kumbaya or gatherings as Quaker meetings. My mesolevel model suggests that participants recognize the rhythms and rituals of action, even when they disagree on desired outcomes and fight for their beliefs (Stivers, Mondada, and Steensig 2011). Although the concept of circuits of actions depends on the existence of routines, understood by the parties, this does not assume that all embrace those actions. The focus on smooth relations precludes appreciating conflict as valuable for civic culture (Coser 1956). Contentious politics can produce desirable change; harmonious governance can be oppressive. Further, we need to think of conflict within groups as well as between groups, with the latter often perceived as conflicts between a group and what is conventionally known as "the larger society." Both of these forms of conflict will be described, especially in the context of the Civil Rights movement.

As discussed in chapter 3, associations oriented to change and confrontation—tiny movements—may instigate desirable challenges. By rethinking what had been treated as unproblematic, conflict allows for problem solving, even if it also opens the potential of social disintegration. Under proper conditions, contention can produce community. Although the continued harmonious functioning of a group through interpersonal strategies is a central skill in local communities (Fligstein 2001), disharmony also relies on interpersonal strategies. As Judith Butler (2006) emphasizes, dissensus and the recognition of troubles is performative and persuasive. When performance is provocation, groups can force collective rethinking that transcends individual preferences (Alexander 2017). In this sense, groups deploy confrontation to challenge powerful interests (Baiocchi et al. 2014: 70).

Interpersonal harmony is not an inevitable desideratum but a consequential choice in roiling an established social order. Instability, when it avoids epistemic turmoil, can prevent stasis. However, even if conflict *can* produce communal benefits, this does not mean that conflict, like consensus, inevitably strengthens communal life.

Harmony as Felicity's Condition

Treating harmony as an uncontested default ignores crucial connections between the interaction order and the relational network within which it is set. Group cultures are inevitably built on local interests, and local interests can differ both within groups and between them. A single-minded focus on consensus's veneer fails to solve the very problems that it was designed to address: how disagreements can be managed while still being respected. By embracing an assumption of consensus, groups achieve a measure of intersubjectivity. Still, participants confront an ongoing and existential suspicion that this veneer hides deep differences. This is evident in the strained politeness that is often evident in interracial discourse, as when structural bias is deflected in the name of civility (Whitehead 2009; Bonilla-Silva 2018). At times, we agree to let problematic claims pass (Anderson 1992; Perry 2017). On other occasions, conflict is overt. Instances when courtesy is challenged may strain community but are sometimes necessary (Anderson 2011). The apparent morality of local interaction (the veneer) can hide unspoken beliefs (the rot below).

The image of collective harmony as representing the felicity condition of civic society has a long history, linking politics and friendship as suggested earlier. Beyond enshrining sociality, the depiction of consensus as overcoming personal differences was deeply influenced by the pragmatist and reformist visions of early twentieth-century progressivism, as reflected in the civic commitments of members of the early Chicago school of sociology (Shalin 1988; Deegan 1990). For early interactionists such as W. I. Thomas and Dorothy Thomas (1928), the importance of a collaborative "definition of the situation" arose precisely through a recognition of the divergence between individual processes of assigning meaning and collective definitions, arising from joint acts that group members accept as revealing an "accepted reality" (Blumer 1969: 70). Given that the Thomases were explicitly examining social problems—in their case the "child problem" of the 1920s—joint understandings were inevitably linked to the perception of societal troubles.

An optimistic emphasis on recognizing a definition of the situation and a belief in the value of negotiated meanings has shaped much analysis of interpersonal (microlevel) and group (mesolevel) interactions. Anselm Strauss (1978) crystallized this view, arguing that negotiation, which presumes the adjustment of divergent perspectives, is the bedrock of social life. Strauss assumes the desirability of an order established through communal modifications. In this model, disruption is the threat that propels people toward negotiation.

The pragmatist stress on a shared definition of the situation locates smoothness at the heart of the mesolevel understanding of the communal engagements of tiny publics. This is evident in the early writings of Erving Goffman (1959), heavily influenced by his Durkheimian commitment to the necessity of ritual and emphasizing how shared representations lead to collective effervescence (Durkheim 1965 [1912]). In the Chicago tradition of Robert Park, Everett Hughes, W. I. Thomas, and W. Lloyd Warner, the interaction order generates rituals that permit circuits of action that in turn treat routines as revealing shared beliefs and leading to approved actions. Particularly influential for Goffman and other students of local ritual was W. Lloyd Warner's (1953) account of the power of communal culture in Yankee City in *The Living and the Dead*, which detailed civic commemoration in Newburyport, Massachusetts. Here a festival provided the occasion for communal commitment.

From this perspective, ritual helps community members unify in knitting together their lines of action. Whether by oscillating between frontstage and backstage, through tact, civil disattention, or in rituals of deference (Goffman 1967), we aim to preserve the smoothness of social relations. In this light, Randall Collins's (2004) analysis of interaction ritual chains emphasizes the emotional entrainment of people attempting to preserve a common perspective.

However, the ongoing collaboration of an active community does not preclude conflict. Harold Garfinkel (1967) is widely known for his ethnomethodological breaching experiments through which he exposed the existential dread that emerges when easy assumptions about shared understandings are upended. People must continually calculate which lines are essential and what happens when those lines are crossed. A divergence of meaning is inevitably part of social life and is valued when it preserves the fabric of collaborative understanding (Berger and Luckmann 1966).

The emphasis on coordinated interaction has been crucial in crystallizing a mesosociology of civic order and an emphasis on the power of local communities, but it is insufficient to explain the downplaying of conflict's role. Group cultures in which participants express dissent based on conflicting interests can energize local worlds as long as expectations regarding the proper form of exchange and respect for the participants are clear. Central is whether the members of a local community are aware of and respect the tacit rules of the interaction order. Successful interaction does not require identical beliefs or even a thin veneer of agreement. Desired outcomes may be altered under conditions of contained conflict, because of an acceptance of their rhythm, tenor, and moodiness (Silver 2011).

Disruption as Praxis

By focusing on the accomplishment or the disruption of local expectations, I present a mesolevel analysis of how conflict belongs to civic commitments. Discounting moral absolutes, communicating about difference is essential, supporting a dialogic approach to difference within rules of deference (Rawls 1987). This permits actors to commit to each other's self-presentation even if it harms their long-term projects.

Incorporating conflict into civic culture draws on two distinct approaches to social life. Each demonstrates how social life can be disrupted and conflict utilized in groups.[1] Consider Charles Tilly's

(1996: 589) discussion of the "invisible elbow." What Tilly means by his memorable phrase is that "social interaction entails incessant error followed by error-correction." For Tilly, interaction does not proceed smoothly but is a recursive and self-reflexive process. Rather than the efficient and invisible hand so beloved by classical economists, Tilly suggests that social life is filled with dead ends, clumsy attempts, and misdirection—elbows, not hands. We try to correct our inevitable errors as we make our way in the world. Bumps, of which there are many, demand a return to level engagement. Both the relational and the cultural patterning of the social world arise in the dynamic tension between conflict and coordination.

A second model that incorporates conflict into local culture is Victor Turner's (1969) analysis of the dramatic structure of ritual. Turner sees ritual as involving a sequential integration of breach, crisis, redressive action, and reintegration. Ritual within a community is characterized by a symbolic breach of the social order followed by a refashioning of that order by bringing in new identities and social positions. As in much performance, conflict is inherent in action within a social field (Reed 2006), but so is resolution, a domain in which ritual proves effective. By emphasizing the break in social order that ritual salves, we find the balance between coordination and conflict of Tilly's approach.

Daniel McFarland's (2004) account of the interactional organization of conflict in high school classrooms treats resistance to authority in light of group cultures. Although not civic spaces as narrowly defined, classrooms reveal the intersection of power, rights, and responsibilities. Students' acts of classroom resistance are a form of ritual, in which resistance, contesting power relations, is understood through the implicit claims that develop from social relations. Resistance and its resolution depend on choices by actors and their audience. Both depend on a tight-knit community. Although a risk exists that contention will fail to produce successful redress and a return to civil relations, resistance is "a structured process that is variably enacted through the strategic framing efforts of actors" (McFarland 2004: 1250). As structured and as strategic, this contention links to the preexisting group culture.

The salience of conflict as contributing to civic order depends on recognized circuits of action, the morality of the group cultures, and the construction of intersubjectivity. These elements occur not only despite disruption but through it. A view of local cultures that ignores the value of disruption overlooks Georg Simmel's (1950: 17) injunction about the necessary linkage between unity and conflict:

> There is a misunderstanding according to which one of these two kinds of interaction tears down what the other builds up, and what is eventually left standing is the result of the subtraction of the two (while in reality it must rather be designated as the result of their addition).

Although Simmel does not suggest that moments of harmony and dispute are equally distributed in social relations, he argues that a well-functioning community depends on both. While consensus is prized, it is not the only goal.

If we value aligning lines of action, we must also appreciate how conflict contributes to alignment. Within the boundaries of a local community, the smooth alignment of actors permits rapid coordination. Yet even within the confines of an interaction order, as Erving Goffman (1967) emphasized, more than local pressures exist: actors' projects often filter through an interactional membrane as their projects are situated within a temporal landscape, affecting the understanding of pasts and expectation for futures (Tavory and Eliasoph 2013).

In practice, harmony typically signals civic comfort. But the relationship between situational smoothness and the embrace of broader projects may be problematic at times. As David Gibson (2012) demonstrates, smooth interaction may hide the unintended consequences of political projects, creating moments of groupthink, when challenge might have avoided policy traps. As I discuss in chapter 6, in examining executive branch meetings during the 1962 Cuban missile crisis, Gibson finds that many scenarios were left unexplored as leaders were overly focused on maintaining collegiality and shared understandings. They protected their group culture from challenge. Even more troubling, the 1961 Bay of Pigs decision is an archetypal case of harmony and deference overriding alternatives and minimizing the predictions of failure (Janis 1972). When participants show "courtesy agreements," deferentially accepting others' perspectives despite private doubts, a strong motivation to find a way around disagreement may prevent finding a way through it. Conflict is marginalized when it should be respected. Whereas commitment to agreement may trump longer-term concerns, in other cases commitment to those longer-term trajectories may disrupt the flow of the situational, because otherwise participants will be held accountable if their agreements fail in costly ways. The pressure to demonstrate courtesy agreements—getting along by erasing conflict—can pose an obstacle for local communities.

Emphasizing smooth interaction, face-saving, and role-taking assumes too much harmony, insufficient disruption, and an absence of recognition of the adjustment of varying interests. Consensus and disruption are found at different moments of group activity, and reflect divergent commitments to sociality. Rather than solely stressing smoothness, interaction orders inevitably present a minuet of comity and conflict as actors balance preserving situations and relationships by expressing separate values and demanding alternate futures. Further, communities hold distinct local expectations about the contours of smooth interaction, creating boundaries and contention when communities meet.[2]

Although communities can accept varying levels of conflict, actors must consider how relationships are defined by their group culture. Which disputes are permissible and which are unacceptable in light of local practices? Groups treat certain topics as usable and others as taboo (Fine 1979). While actors may disagree vehemently over ideas that do not reach the core of group identity, they should not breach unquestioned and morally central domains. As Iddo Tavory (2016) demonstrates, groups of Orthodox Jews are permitted—even encouraged—to engage in lively arguments about religious doctrine as part of participating in a civic community, but they are not to discuss their workplace friendships with non-Jews, which might challenge their communal commitment. Implicit rules reside not in the interaction itself but in interpretations of the moral standing of the interactants.

While emphasizing conflict recognizes a closer affinity between stability and disruption, incorporating otherwise improper interaction can be mobilized because norms of legitimate interaction permit a challenge to authority. For instance, homeless panhandlers may refer to the dogs walked by middle-class women to justify a conversational opening (Duneier and Molotch 1999), pulling passersby into interactions they might otherwise wish to avoid. Likewise, demonstrators in rallies address police officers, treating them as colleagues in a communal project rather than as agents of social control. Norms can subvert their ostensible intent.

Disputes and the Politics of Change

Disputes and ruptures can generate change, challenge inequality and oppression, and rearrange taken-for-granted realities. This leads to the question of when harmony becomes conflict or conflict becomes harmony. Part of the answer results from the authority of influential participants to define their collective selfhood: the group establishes a moral identity, developed through the recognition of common beliefs, acceptance of lines of action, and avoiding identities imposed from the outside. As Michael Haedicke (2012) emphasizes, analyzing external forces that shape the politics of natural food co-ops, participants use their shared culture to respond to decisions that might otherwise split the group. The group does not always succeed, given the press of other groups, but defends itself through the anchoring of values and traditions.

Treating conflict as part of interaction suggests how welcoming a group will be to new members, how demanding the process of socialization, and whether the group will permit the presence of outsiders. In observing an Australian pagan community, Angela Coco and Ian Woodward (2007: 479) found a sharp divide between those who wish for the group culture to be esoteric and those who desire more outreach, embracing popular cultural representations of paganism that might appeal to a wider public. The former group speaks of the latter as transforming pagan beliefs into an embrace of "fluffy bunnies," lacking a serious commitment. Members on each side of the conflict have their own images that they claim captures the group's central culture.

That such conflict does not inevitably lead to group dysfunction is shown in experimental research. As Steven Bernard and Pat Barclay reveal, some forms of conflict—what they term democratic competition—may increase the production of public goods and bolster group efficiency (sometimes by increasing deception to achieve these positive outcomes). These studies suggest that conflict is not distinct from order but part of it, generated through ongoing disagreements that are either existential or negotiable. Respectful competition enriches stable organizations, such as church congregations that have the resources and commitments to manage disagreements in creating a compassionate community (Becker 1999; Campbell and Putnam 2010). Lacking such resources and commitments, the group splits or dissolves.

A mesolevel analysis suggests that conflict is embedded in competing meanings that exist within group cultures. Even in the case of extended conflict, individuals depend on communal affiliations. Ultimately, the dynamics of change and the solution to the problem of order is specific to local conditions, including whether the conflict is manageable, whether it is treated as internal or external, and whether conflict fits within local decision-making (Douglas 2014). The resolution of the conflict—temporarily or permanently—consists of a moral domain negotiated through group process and consisting in the reorganization of previously established local cultures. For instance, Craig Calhoun (1982) found that nineteenth-century British radicalism and the conflicts embedded in class struggles during the Industrial Revolution were nurtured by the commitments of local craft communities undergoing external pressures and resisting these pressures while maintaining their culture. These close ties along with a recognition of threats to workers' lifeworlds provided the basis for opposition to powerful external groups, such as industrial organizations pushing a new factory system.

The connection between the existence of tight communities and their willingness to engage in civic conflict in larger and more extensive social worlds is evident in oppositional social movements, including the Levelers, the Chartists, elements of the American Civil Rights movement, and local Tea Party groups. Conflict can be mobilized internally or externally. An emotional attachment that stems not only from shared belief but also from common experiences and ongoing social relations recognizes that intergroup contention can build tight-knit group cultures. This intergroup conflict must be considered in a mesolevel understanding of the cultures of rival communities, each with a tight commitment to a local interaction order.

However, some movement structures are looser, operating as networked relations, and depending on weak ties to create powerful social pressures. This includes movements such as the 1960s antiwar movement, the Occupy Wall Street movement, or the contemporary Black Lives Matter movement. However, for these groups to last and to thrive, an organizing center is needed, even if those controlling forces are resented. Despite the appeal of freedom to act, movements are rarely effective unless local groups are coordinated under a larger umbrella. More central groups with resource power, cultural authority, and networking ability often strive to limit the actions of groups under their jurisdiction in that the actions of those locals may come to characterize the larger movement. The issue is the extent to which the movement depends on a set of small group cultures as opposed to cultural control from above (discussed in chap. 6). A tension exists between autonomy and discipline. If there is a core group, or if the core demands coordination, how is that coordination managed or enforced? This is a challenge for any broad movement that hopes to be effective on the local level as well as altering the broader patterns of society. Movements must develop a consistent perspective while maintaining the commitment that minute, diverse associations provide. The Tea Party's rapid rise and then collapse during the Obama administration reflects the importance of grassroots groups that generate strong affiliation, warm emotions, and shared activity among neighbors, but eventually their take-over by larger "Astroturf" institutions, such as FreedomWorks, diminished both their authority and the charm of the local. In developing a national movement, the imposed bureaucracy vitiated the neighborly energy, local creativity, and committed friendships on which the movement depended.

Ultimately, conflict is central to the metaphor of the Hinge, the semiautonomous intersection of individuals and institutions. Group members treat conflict as part of a recognized microculture, connecting to or distancing themselves from the institutions that surround them. Further, the conflict can be overt, as in the case of oppositional or revolutionary movements, or hidden, as with conflicts that are not addressed—but still have consequences.

Whatever its form, conflict serves multiple purposes. It can strengthen group bonds in response to external groups seen as threatening, but it can also separate. Finally, conflict can be a bridging mechanism, as when a conflict establishes new alliances among groups with similar values or goals.

Conflict does not, by itself, imply the justice of any particular claim, but is part of an interaction order in which meanings are locally constituted and relations adjusted. In Ann Swidler's (1986) terms, challenges to established systems are central to the tool kit of group

life, particularly when new ideologies are deemed necessary in unsettled times. On these occasions implicit meanings of social order are
threatened and participants must establish newly formulated rules.
Unsettled times produce unsettled groups. Some groups maintain a
firm epistemological consensus, supported by a robust local culture,
while others are in a continual process of cognitive contestation. Cultures treat argumentation in different ways (Tannen 1984), establishing rules of contention, even in ostensibly sociable groups. Unsettled
groups may actively judge their own values, beliefs, and ideologies,
and negotiate as to whether they share common purpose or legitimate
authority in the face of fractured interests.

Recognizing rough interaction and group discord, I divide conflicts
within interaction systems into three broad categories: those that are
internal to the group but can be managed, those that split the group,
and those in which group cultures are structured to justify conflicts
with other groups or with more powerful institutions. Disruption is
variable in its intensity, and the cultural forms that disputes take differ
widely. Conflict is a strategy selected by knots of social actors at particular moments, neither inherently valuable nor eternally harmful.
From this perspective, conflict is integrated into—and often integral
to—communal cultures, producing what Bruno Latour (2005) terms
the reassembly of the social.

Conflict and Cases

To examine the forms that conflict takes in the tiny publics of civil
society, I draw on three cases. The first instance involves ongoing
contention of the kind often found in political systems, even in stable
systems of mutual commitment. At times, this becomes solidified into
a factional or partisan rivalry, but it can also involve the recognition
of fundamentally differing interests. To explore continuing conflict,
I focus on the description by Andrew Deener (2016) of local politics
in Venice, California. Like many communities that balance divergent
values and diverse populations, residents of Venice debate the rules
for interaction within a political forum, who should be included, and
how legitimate decision-making should occur. How can trust be established in the face of conflicting interests and mistrust of others? In
this progressive bastion, the neighborhood council permitted civic
involvement that established a space for conflict. A discursive arena

was opened, but consensus and decorum were harder to come by. How can disagreements that result from fundamentally different interests be resolved, even if all agree, in principle, on the same overarching values? Put another way, how can an integrated community be formed when sharply different local goals exist? When are boundaries salient and when can they be bridged?

A second case inquires into how conflict can create turmoil and a breakdown of the assumptions surrounding the "normal" structure of everyday life. Sociologists have only begun to examine the structure of turmoil, challenging the ideal of a stable lifeworld (Hallett 2010). How is the mundane life of cities disrupted through the actions of homeless advocates? This is a domain of collective action studied by David Snow and his colleagues (Snow et al. 1998) in their exploration of civic breakdown. As is true with gangs and other tight-knit disruptive bands, the group, because of the commitments of participants to act in concert, can disorient a larger community through collective action.

Finally, I examine accounts of civil rights activists affiliated with Freedom Summer (Belfrage 1966; McAdam 1988; Watson 2010). How is group solidarity established in the face of committed, hostile, and sometimes violent opposition in the wider community? In this movement there were internal conflicts, such as between well-educated, liberal, Northern white volunteers and impassioned, angry, oppressed Southern black youth. The organization could manage the conflicts for a time because of the emotional energy generated by core values and by resisting external forces. However, the ongoing conflict over who should lead the movement eventually created a climate in which Freedom Summer could not be repeated. This rupture occurred despite the optimism of white students traveling south to serve as teachers and activists in ways that they considered altruistic and others defined as patronizing. After that remarkable summer, African Americans led the way. As powerful as Freedom Summer was for the participants and for the communities that were served, and as deep as its local culture at Freedom Schools and community projects, the moment was never replicated.

TROUBLE IN VENICE

How does a community—a governmental entity that hopes to create positive civic feeling—manage endogenous conflict between those with sharply distinct views of morality and of the good life? The case of Venice, California, a mixed-income, socially diverse, progressive beach community within the Los Angeles city limits provides a compelling case (Deener 2012). The city established elected neighborhood councils at which residents could discuss problems that they collectively faced. These councils are elected, city-funded, advisory boards whose members represent the local neighborhood to the Los Angeles City Council. As is often the case, the local ideas that occur through deliberation were not always discussed when they reached the city council, but the belief is that civic participation in itself has benefits (Lee 2007). The strain in this case is that even though most Venice residents defined themselves as progressive, sharp disagreements emerged, particularly over how to treat the homeless and whether to protect property values. The community council had to determine the most effective way to manage ongoing conflict—disagreements that stemmed from competing interests—while keeping community spirit intact. How is affiliation possible in the face of policy dissensus, even if, as in Venice, a fair degree of value consensus exists? This battle pitted the activist Venice Progressives, connected to the radical Peace and Freedom Party, a group that emphasized issues of affordable housing and homeless rights, against a rival group operating under the label of Team Venice. Team Venice was supported by neighborhood groups that focused on quality of life issues for current homeowners and hoped to block the expansion of social service agencies into residential neighborhoods.

The differing policy preferences provide a basis for political contestation. Deener (2016: 817–18) presents a dramatic moment of conflict:

> At a monthly Neighborhood Council meeting [with an audience of 75] ... a board member calls out Charlotte's name during the public comment portion.... A white woman in her mid-fifties wearing jeans and an oversized T-shirt, Charlotte approaches the microphone.... "For those who don't know me," Charlotte says, "I've been doing neighborhood watch in this community for almost 30 years. I go out at five in the morning. I take everything off the telephone poles. I spend my own money on graffiti, get rid of homeless people parked in and sleeping in campers and vans, and that's where you come in." Charlotte points towards a few of the newly

elected council members affiliated with a group called the Venice Progressives. She focuses most of her attention on Lindsay, a white woman in her late fifties who has been a vocal homeless advocate. With an air of disgust, Charlotte says, "You have more guts than I've ever seen in my entire life.".... A commotion develops and participants, including board members and those in the audience, are suddenly screaming at each other.... With a booming voice, [Charlotte] screams, "I don't need it, I don't need it! I just want to let you know that you board members should be ashamed of yourself. You filed a complaint with the LAPD [about her alleged harassment of the homeless], and you have taught the people living in campers to break the law, something that I have been working on! You can sit there, like you are stuck with a hanger in your mouth, but you know what, each and every one of you ..." Several other audience members who also sit on the homelessness subcommittee shout over her, "Boo, Boo! She's a racist! She's a racist! Justice for all! Justice for all! She's a racist!".... These activists remain determined to disrupt her public comment. Excessive screaming back and forth continues, on and off, for the entire four-hour meeting.

Deener's dramatic example poses a challenge for a mesolevel analysis of political involvement. Here are two groups—two tiny publics—effectively at war with each other in this civic space, a place that lacks a tradition of civility and overlapping networks outside this political space (see Baiocchi 2003). Given such strong feelings, how can Venice maintain an ongoing political process? At what point does Venice become ungovernable, at least with regard to the level of respect and trust that permits a single imagined community? When do relations among neighbors become so toxic that any sense of a shared community withers away? As Deener (2015: 5) points out, "Individuals collectively perform unity around a shared identity and in order for neighborhood conflict to persist, participants must return to the scene of the action and stabilize an ongoing drama by performing intergroup conflict." In this model, groups become visible through performing conflict, and in this case with contentious relations, each group has expectations for civic behavior: rival and intersecting circuits of actions. Charlotte, for example, reflects Team Venice's concern in her strident belief in the stable community culture that she sees threatened by homeless persons, menacing the security of homeowners.

Members of the Venice Progressives treat her concerns as typifying the "group" that they define her as representing. Further, they take her words and actions as constituting bigotry directed at vulnerable citizens that they wish to protect. This conflict is situated within a larger set of policies that extends beyond the borders of Venice, and it reflects a politics of contention that characterizes conflict in many societal domains. The interactional styles of the political spaces that a community establishes lead to this ongoing conflict that reflects disputatious practices among groups in broader communities.

Deener asserts that social conflict is a group-level performance. He suggests that the content of the argument is not all to consider. Political actors can be divided into two broad camps that do not easily map on to the ostensible debate between progressive activists and neighborhood activists. In his model, engaged citizens can be entrepreneurial activists or protective activists. These categories address whether activists are embedded in provocative groups or are aiming for solutions. These are distinct styles of engagement. Deener (2016: 830) defines entrepreneurial activists as committed to an organized political association, participating in the Venice Neighborhood Council with the aim of enacting their agenda. In contrast, protective activists seek solutions to the problems that they face as residents; they are problem-centered and align with groups only to solve those problems. In contrast to the entrepreneurial activists whose group affiliation is central to their identity, for the protective activists, membership is valuable only in light of results; group culture is secondary. Of course, in any dynamic political system intervening events potentially disrupt the flow of civic participation and identity claims. But ultimately the structure of the Venice Neighborhood Council provided a space where conflict could continue and, given the commitment to democratic process, be controlled. Commitments to groups (by entrepreneurial activists) and to issues (by protective activists) create rival civic cultures.

BREAKDOWNS AND COLLECTIVE ACTION

A standard trope in social movement theory is that social strain or breakdown leads to activism (Smelser 1962). While the empirical data on the effects of strain at the societal level are ambiguous, causing the approach to become marginalized, David Snow and his colleagues

(Snow et al. 1998) suggest that societal breakdown is observable through mesolevel analysis. This suggests that we must conceive of nodes of citizens rather than individuals or broad populations. With a support network, a commitment to resistance is amplified. Snow argues that the disruption of the quotidian, a shattering of local practices, and the questioning of everyday assumptions of order increase the likelihood of collective action. Snow postulates four conditions that disrupt the mundane dimensions of everyday life: accidents that challenge a community's routines; violations of citizens' sense of control, safety, or privacy; changes in the availability of resources; and major alterations in the forms of surveillance and social control. Each threat is revealed on the mesolevel, weakening ties to larger structures and encouraging commitments to local counterpublics. Drawing on empirical observations of the mobilization of the homeless, Snow argues that these forms of resistance generate collective action.

Each condition implies a breakdown of local culture, creating epistemic turmoil. William Gamson and his colleagues (1982) suggest that when situational definitions undercut group culture, participants feel that something fundamentally wrong or unjust is happening. With effective leaders this becomes framed as something that can and should be fixed, leading to norm-breaking collective action (Piven and Cloward 1992). When tied to a disruption of routines, everyday grievances bring people together in common cause (Johnston 1991).

In examining homeless social movements in the 1980s and early 1990s, Snow finds that initial mobilization results from a disruption of action routines. Snow and his colleagues (1998: 12) write,

> In the case of the disruption of individual routines, the typical scenario was that one or more homeless individuals found it increasingly difficult to negotiate their daily routines, and that this jolt became a kind of consciousness-raising experience that pushed some in the direction of collective action. Because of increasing numbers of homeless claimants, taken-for-granted routines, such as standing in line at soup kitchens and shelters, no longer guaranteed the expected outcome. One service provider in Philadelphia explained this when discussing a homeless individual who helped begin both the local homeless movement and the National Union of the Homeless: "To get into the shelter you had to wait in line, and if they fill up, you're just out of luck. Now these lines were not well

supervised, so the bigger boys would fight their way in. Chris is a big guy, and it really ripped him up to have to fight other men so that he could sleep indoors on a floor." It was in response ... that the founder of the Philadelphia movement decided he had enough and began to appeal to other homeless individuals and selected social service providers that the time had come to organize.

This quotation reveals how leaders and groups respond to a common problem, establishing a structure of interaction that can produce contentious politics and civic action.

In a similar vein, research by Tim Hallett (2010) on the structure of turmoil in an urban elementary school, while not connected to civic action as such, points to a similar issue of epistemic distress and the creation of an injustice frame. In Hallett's research, the school's newly appointed principal overturned the previously accepted and understood local circuits of action without the consent or support of those who worked under those new rules. As Hallett demonstrates, an attempt to recouple accountability among teachers with particular classroom practices created an ongoing state of conflict. The turmoil was constituted by a radical change in expectations, and in the process created an alternative set of meanings that provoked continuing conflict with the principal. Hallett (2010: 53) speaks of a "partisan interpretation," indicating a set of meanings that is locally constituted by distinct interest groups. Hallett links this to a mesolevel neo-institutional theory that examines the effects of loosely coupled local cultures on the structure of organizations. Early iterations of neo-institutional theory emphasized that the development of organizational meaning operates through impression management and interpersonal interaction (Meyer and Rowan 1977: 358). In Hallett's case, overstepping established work practices created collective discontent within the school, leading to disruption. One teacher gathered letters of complaint against the principal from more than two dozen teachers that she compiled into a 119-page volume, distributed to central administration. This teacher corralled colleagues into her movement, proudly explaining, "I plastered her name all over this city. Everybody I could think of I sent that book to.... It had, oh God, maybe a good 40 odd letters from various teachers" (Hallett 2010: 65). These teachers treated the organization as owned space, justifying local action. Crucial to Hallett's inhabited-institutions approach is that conflict results from how groups perceive threats to their routinized practices. Conflict in institutions results when routines and expectations are disrupted.

CIVIL RIGHTS AND CIVIL CONFLICT

The early Civil Rights movement has become so thoroughly incorporated into the grand narrative of American civic virtue that it may be hard to recall the contention in the South during the 1960s as anything other than good versus evil. Yet there was much divergence of opinions, particularly on the desirability of young (largely white) Northerners traveling to Mississippi for community organizing. Would affluent whites set the terms of the group culture of the movement? To understand the moment, we must recognize that civil rights activists depended on group affiliation as did much of the white opposition. Both played on a larger canvas. These young activists did not operate as freestanding individuals, nor were they directed by a central office in a mass organization. The Civil Rights movement, especially the 1964 Freedom Summer, depended on a reticulated group structure, a network of small projects, each with its own set of social ties. Similarly, in the black community, groups—both church groups and more explicitly political groups—organized collective action.

Those who wished to preserve the racial status quo of the segregationist South also operated through like-minded groups. The violent attacks on the young civil rights workers were rarely the acts of "lone wolves" but rather of "wolf packs." Klan klaverns or local White Citizen Councils reflected the organizational structure of the segregationist status quo. Other friendship groups acted outside of a formal group structure, and these were particularly dangerous in that they had no structure to contain extreme violence. Because of their secrecy, we know less about these groups than we do about the more open groups that constituted the Civil Rights movement, including Freedom Summer.

In our collective memory, Freedom Summer was a dramatic and even romantic moment, especially for educated, white war babies and baby boomers. While Freedom Summer was not the most consequential moment for altering racial attitudes, it captures our attention at least in part because it depended on the involvement of Northern white students to support the aspirations of Southern African Americans as best they could. Freedom Summer speaks to the possibility of racial collaboration and, perhaps, to the reality of racial hegemony. The narrative of Freedom Summer may downplay the indigenous African American organizing tradition.

The Freedom Summer project was organized explicitly and self-consciously to leverage the power of the small group. While most organizing builds off of groups, including families, neighbors, churches, and local associations, the mobilizing and educating projects of Freedom Summer made this structure particularly salient. As Charles Payne (1995) emphasizes, the students developed intimate ties with each other and often with black residents who treated them as family, or so the students believed. As one participant recounted decades later, "What have I done with my life?... I ate at the table of Fannie Lou Hamer, in her home and she called me by my name and we were friends" (Watson 2010: 123).

However, the goals and structure of the movement also led to conflict as crucial as cohesion. These students, many raised in comfortable and cocooned homes, needed to recognize the overt and sometimes deadly conflict with white Mississippians, who considered them to be agitators (as, indeed, they were) and communists (as most were not). These resentments were evident in the hostility of county sheriffs. The young students also faced—and often were dismayed by—conflicts with those black residents, ministers, and local activists whom the outsiders were determined to help with their cultural capital, but who resented assumptions of expertise. Freedom Summer faced both external and internal conflicts.

While many moving accounts are memoirs (Belfrage 1966), the most consequential scholarly analysis is that of Doug McAdam (1988: 199–219), who examines not only the group structures but also the long-term consequences, including the reality that participation embedded activists in other movement communities, shaped civic culture, and established a long-term network of engagement.

In part because of the fear of conflict with hostile publics, the group culture in Freedom Summer projects was emotionally intense. Over one thousand volunteers traveled to "schools" organized by the Student Non-Violent Coordinating Committee (SNCC). Participants were socialized during a one-week orientation session in Oxford, Ohio, sponsored by the National Council of Churches. They were then sent to forty-four local projects in towns throughout Mississippi, many living in communal Freedom Houses. Most participants were involved in voter registration projects or in teaching in so-called Freedom Schools. It was a remarkable summer, notable in part because by 1965 the ideal of interracial political action—the Beloved Community—had faded.

Groups were central to the organization of Freedom Summer. The movement was built around meetings of twenty to thirty activists who coordinated their projects. In addition, groups of five to ten people worked together. These middle-class, collegiate idealists had to recognize their dangerous politics. From the beginning, staff explained the risks involved. The black SNCC volunteers had become increasingly militant and radical over the previous years, and they shared those experiences with their white collegiate colleagues. As McAdam (2008: 67, 69) writes,

> Jess Brown, one of only three civil rights lawyers in the state, apprised the volunteers of the "unique" quality of Mississippi justice.... In a sobering and, for many, radicalizing session, [Department of Justice official] John Doar warned the volunteers not to expect federal protection while in Mississippi. "Maintaining law and order," he argued, "is a state responsibility."... In planning the sessions, one of the overriding goals had been to overwhelm the volunteers with the savagery and violence of life in Mississippi.... So in session after session, staff members recounted the litany of horror they had seen in Mississippi.

Participants engaged in role-playing episodes, such as "The Cell": "A white civil rights worker is thrown into a cell with three ardent segregationists. As the jailer opens the cell, he identifies the civil rights worker to the inmates—'Got some company for you fellas, one of those Northern nigger-loving agitators. Now you treat him nice'" (Belfrage 1966: 16). Through these performances of imagined hostility, the group bonded. The local context of civic action provided for shared emotional energy that depended on the reality of continual conflict. As one volunteer wrote, "I'd venture to say that every member of the Mississippi staff has been beaten at least once and he who has not been shot at is rare. It is impossible for you to imagine what we are going in to, as it is for me now, but I'm beginning to see" (McAdam 1988: 69). The role-playing sessions and advice about personal protection promoted a group culture that made participants conflict-aware. Participants learned to recognize the cues in the hostile world that surrounded them, a reality brought home by the murder of one young volunteer and two staff members in Philadelphia, Mississippi. The communal culture emphasized that the young volunteers were venturing into an alien climate filled with hidden danger. This cultural frame, reasonable given the "facts on the ground," made salient the division between "them" and "us" and led to hostility of the workers toward the white citizens of Mississippi as a collective category. This perspective usefully incorporates conflict into the image of a politicized society, permitting one volunteer to remark, "We know the blood is going to flow this summer and it's going to be our blood" (McAdam 1988: 71). The public recounting of fear was central, similar to the emotional bonding found among military platoons readying for battle (Kaplan 2006). At the same time, the volunteers were quick to emphasize the love that they felt, both from the African American volunteers and the sympathetic black residents of the Mississippi communities in which they were staying.

Despite this, the movement culture could not escape the social divisions and resentments of a small, intense community. Freedom Summer volunteers on each project constituted themselves as a tiny public—a small beloved community—one that could be defined, in part, by the external opposition that they faced. When, the following year, divisions emerged among those who had once been allies, the idealistic and consensual group culture was irreparably shattered.

The Conflictual Hinge

Order is not always orderly, smoothness is not necessarily smooth, and conflict can be creative: these are important recognitions for understanding the interaction order as it operates in practice. Conflict may be valuable in structuring interaction. This can be recognized if we focus not on institutions in dispute but on civic engagement and political rivalries. A contentious society can be fulfilling and progressive because the roughness of interaction can raise important issues, contesting what had been taken for granted. We may find conflict within groups and, in society, between groups.

How can systems of dispute be managed so that participants feel invested even if they are unable to achieve their goals? The history of social change suggests that groups strive for rights or resources in opposition to other groups that reject the awarding of these benefits. In some cases, a presumption exists that the demands are fully legitimate, even part of natural law. A case in point is that slavery was once considered by many as legitimate servitude, with even Biblical support, but it now stands outside every moral order. This does not mean that these current assessments will never change, but such change would surely be challenged if this moral abomination were to become treated as part of a just social order.

A mesolevel analysis of conflict recognizes that many topics might cause disruption, but what matters is the group process through which issues are challenged, defended, and debated. Moral claims, tied to local communities, shape the interaction order, as groups with interests and resources use available images to argue for what they define as justice, to gain new adherents, and to form new associations.

As the case of Venice, California, demonstrates, conflictual interaction, tied to contending groups, may be a continuing part of a local social system. Residents with different interests and divergent views of what it means to be a good citizen and varying preferences of how to argue may belong to the same civic order. The problem develops when groups rig the rules for their own interest. They would rather win dirty than lose clean. Such a stance, while temporarily successful, damages commitment to process. For a mesolevel approach to build a stable community, legitimated procedure is a guarantor of civil order.

The questioning of process provides an opportunity for various forms of breakdown in which the mundane order of life is challenged: sometimes in what has been termed "good trouble." While breakdown theories do not adequately explain how broad strains generate social movements, they reveal how local turmoil can create an interaction order based on grievances and opposition to a collective epistemology. Grievance becomes something that can be publicly discussed, a point for complaint (Weeks 2004). Attacks on the quotidian potentially lead to moral ruptures. The challenge is not a result of new commitments—although this happens as well—but from coping with a changing mesoorder and a new discursive realm. Disputes may be resolved through innovative forms of mesocommunity that in time expand from presenting a particular complaint to developing an alternative worldview.

The final aspect of conflict is evident in established social movements, such as the Civil Rights movement. An effective movement depends on the authority of the group, often constructing a culture through rituals, music, narrative, and history. An external, hostile opposition may create conditions for intense bonding, and, as a result, movement groups often emphasize the threat from their opposition. Fear of others and love for one's colleagues are intertwined. Freedom Summer was such an example. To create the cohesion to face danger, an intense mesoworld was necessary. The Beloved Community of Dr. King proved powerful, although it could not withstand racial politics and conflicts over moral authority. This strain represents an important feature of the organization of conflict. For a harmonious organization, participants need not only a commitment to action but a commitment to each other.

Civic politics often center on how conflicts are presented and managed. Engagement is about disagreements and alternatives. These begin within a close-knit community, only spreading outward when embraced by others. Conflict arises in the heart of community: a sense of "we-ness" or an imagined community that depends not only on concepts such as the state or a national language but on the routines of communal life. From this, "they-ness" follows. Citizenship is never about the individual but about individuals in contact. When contacts bridge interactional worlds, one can imagine bonds with those whom one does not know or recognize but who are believed to share values.

Ultimately, we must recognize the role of conflict in local civic orders. Although various microsociological traditions suggest that the support for smooth and easy interaction is a foundational aspect of social order and group culture, such an account misses much. Rough engagement is crucial in both smaller and wider worlds, but it finds its most powerful home in a world of tiny publics.

6

CONTROL

Patrolling Civil Society

There are only four or five who maintain the dictator, four or five who keep the country in bondage to him. Five or six have always had access to his ear, and have either gone to him of their own accord, or else have been summoned by him to be accomplices in his cruelties, companions in his pleasures, panders to his lusts, and sharers in his plunders. These six manage their chief so successfully that he comes to be held accountable not only for his own misdeeds but even for theirs. The six have six hundred who profit under them, and with the six hundred they do what they have accomplished with their tyrant. The six hundred maintain under them six thousand, whom they promote in rank, upon whom they confer the government of provinces or the direction of finances, in order that they may serve as instruments of avarice and cruelty, executing orders at the proper time and working such havoc all around that they could not last except under the shadow of the six hundred, nor be exempt from law and punishment except through their influence.

ÉTIENNE DE LA BOÉTIE, *The Discourse of Voluntary Servitude*

The sixteenth-century protolibertarian philosopher and judge Étienne de la Boétie argued that tyrants remain in power by activating a network of supporters: tyranny by group. No dictator can dictate to an empty hall. Even totalitarian states depend, in a certain sense, on consent of the governed: at least a fraction of those governed. Despots assemble a governing team whose members profit from available resources and shape policy based on their desires. Each adherent gathers a set of followers who depend on the patronage of this secondary leader. Totalitarian governments operate through a structure of oppression based on a network of groups. Like democracy, authoritarian governments are relational.

Further, oppressive control may be localized. Trauma need not be national; it can be tightly focused and spatially contained, even if it is often true that powerful groups have some awareness of the brutality that is performed under their aegis. The widely reported case of torture in 2003 at Baghdad's Abu Ghraib prison by members of the American military provides an example of how local control can be brutal, serving as a micromodel of repressive cruelty, establishing a vicious culture. The ostensible goal was to teach these prisoners not to defy the rules that the prison officers had established in their own highly controlled "civil society" (Graveline and Clemens 2010: 3–6). Control can be organized through legitimate or illegitimate means, but even in the latter case, some measure of authority is often implicit.

To maintain itself, every tiny public, democratic or not, relies on a recognized interaction order that enforces standards and demands predictability. My goal in this chapter is not to describe tyranny but to claim that social control, operating in local contexts, is part of all organized social systems. Systems of power inevitably depend on chains of relations and systems of interpretation (Reed 2017) and must be studied as such. Norms (actions that communities hold to be morally or socially proper) and routines (expectations that lead to predictable and recognized circuits of action) are essential to any theory of control. Establishing social order beyond personal desires but within the context of group cultures allows us to address Thomas Hobbes's concern. The Hobbesian metaphor is of a centralized and extended institution—the Leviathan—that enforces rules that limit the choices of individual actors. However, this erases the role of group culture on both sides of the social control boundary: the powerful and the regulated. How can individuals be free actors, while permitting the order that expectations provide and that stable institutions require? The answer is by means of the Hinge, the semiautonomous linkage of the individual and the structure through local relations.

When societies work efficiently and amiably, control is implicit, even welcomed, as it supports shared understandings of propriety. Constraints on action should not depend on the decisions of the powerful but on communal desires. Groups—or clans (Weiner 2013)— may erect barriers to participation by those defined as disruptive, disagreeable, or resistant, or may sanction them. As legal scholar Robert Ellickson (1991) underlines, local control is the ideal; through its moral weight, "order without law" emerges. In the phrase of political scientist James Scott (2012: 30), this creates a "vernacular order" in contrast to the "official order." In small-scale social systems, such as roommate dyads (Emerson 2008), committees (Haug 2013), or workplace meetings (Hallett, Harger, and Eder 2009), strategies of informal control build a desire to maintain congenial relations, encouraging accommodation and local remediation (Morrill 1995).

In other cases, external groups—often agents of the state—organize control, sometimes involving harsh punitive sanctions with the goal of disrupting disliked groups such as terrorist cells (Reedy, Gastil, and Gabbay 2013). Direct control from above is also used by authoritarian regimes, such as the People's Republic of China, when, during the Cultural Revolution, the state organized groups of five to eight members—*hsiao-tsu*—to indoctrinate and coerce citizens through political rituals as well as interpersonal surveillance (Whyte 1974). State actors can access resources that permit explicit control. However, the control of group members works best when authorities discreetly glove power. Given that surveillance is never complete, if groups internalize the rules of powerful actors, they support the preferences of those authorities.

When the need for more powerful and extended social control is perceived, groups are structured to preserve social order. We see this when our legal system addresses threats to community. Courts (and juries) are constituted as small groups (Burnett 2001; Diamond and Rose 2005; Manzo 1993). Justice requires mesolevel decision-making. The legal system relies on group consensus to maintain what the community—and those knots of citizens that comprise it—considers desired morality and institutional legitimacy.

Civic-Minded Control

To understand the dynamics of control, we must consider how civic-minded organizations operate. Institutions cannot enforce surveillance without group process. Controlling organizations, whatever their civic purpose, can be thought of as polities: ministates (Weber and Wäger 2017). In this, organizations justify an interaction order while distributing resources to those under their aegis.

Civic organizations respond to a networked institutional ecology, depending on micronetworks of group life. Although scholars have recently emphasized the agentic role of individuals in institutional life (Battalina 2006; Hardy and Maguire 2008), extending models of interaction to account for the importance of meaning-makers (Fligstein 2001; Barley 2008), these meaning-makers belong to local communities. We must not assume that these projects link the individual with the institution, ignoring the hinge that connects them. In connecting the macro and micro basis of control, groups comprise a mesorealm through which social control is formulated by colleagues. These local communities, relying on a robust interaction order, may be characterized by authority from the top or resistance from below. Both constitute institutional control, made manifest through collaboration. It is not just that groups link the micro and the macro; rather, the mesolevel has properties that in its local power permit control.

The reality that groups operate in a behavioral space situated between individuals and structures is crucial to enacting control. It is easier to surveil those with social relations when they gather together. From the standpoint of those to be controlled, voluntary allegiance operates through conformity, identification, and internalization (Kelman 1973). Conformity demands mimetic action. This is the traditional image of constraint with penalties for not conforming. The other two mechanisms suggest the powerful affiliations of actors to the groups to which they belong, either seeing social relations as worth preserving (identification) or treating local standards as an interpretive model to embrace (internalization). The cultures of civic organizations, coupled with their resources, bolster coordination between institutional demands and the responses of actors.

As prominent as culture has become in the social sciences, this was not always so. Before the cultural turn of the early 1980s (Friedland and Mohr 2004), culture was marginal in explaining the actions of organizations (Morrill 2008: 15). However, the turn allowed scholars to treat culture as integral to social control. In its macroconceptualization, scholars refer to characteristics of national or even Western culture (e.g., Munch and Smelser 1993; Meyer and Jepperson 2000). These analyses treat culture as characteristic of societies, assuming homogeneity of values and similarity of demography. However, because most communities are characterized by cognitive, affective, and behavioral diversity, these analyses are inevitably imprecise, ignoring the local, negotiated, and grounded features of culture. As a result, culture is difficult to operationalize, a swirling mist (Ghaziani 2010) rather than an observable object. Examples of the macro use of culture, often with vague referents, are found in discussions of "rationalized myths" (Meyer and Rowan 1977) or "institutional logics" (Friedland and Alford 1991). In these traditions, culture shapes actors by virtue of their position in an institutional field, rather than through an interactional order. This tradition ignores the recognition that culture is something through which people make claims, deploy for negotiation, and use to create affiliation. In contrast, a mesolevel approach argues that culture is a social practice in daily life. People, embedded in communities, acting in concert and in conflict, and building on shared experience, collectively interpret cultural meanings and then act accordingly (Hallett 2010; Hallett and Ventresca 2006). The actor as well as the institution shapes civic life.

Institutions as Control Systems

To understand how mesolevel scholars conceptualize systems of control in local politics, we must recognize that most institutions—with their associated organizations—have a hierarchical component. Because of their depth, reach, and resources, they often serve as the face of control. An array of organizations contributes to a robust civil society.

If organizational theory has not always taken the mesolevel into account, emphasizing the bare-bones structural skeleton of organizations or their role in an organizational ecology, over the last two decades control theories have increasingly emphasized the microfoundations of institutional life (Powell and Colyvas 2008; Barley 2008; Fine and Hallett 2014). This approach has generated attention to several rich theoretical veins: individual agency within institutions (Battilana 2006), the interests of institutional entrepreneurs (Dimaggio 1988; Hardy and Maguire 2008; Battilana, Leca, and Boxenbaum 2009), and the skills of those who hope to refashion institutions (Fligstein 2001; Fligstein and McAdam 2012). In addition, there is institutional work, constituting the "purposive action of individuals and organizations aimed at creating, maintaining, and disrupting institutions" (Lawrence and Suddaby 2006: 216; Lawrence, Suddaby, and Leca 2009). Together these projects emphasize that actors collaborate to achieve local interests. Power need not be antidemocratic or even inherently coercive (Lukes 2005), but it inevitably is part of an interpretive process operating within a set of social relations (Reed 2017).

Recognizing the role of local communities is an alternative to the danger of portraying institutions as "disembodied structures acting on their own volition while depicting actors as powerless and inert in

the face of inexorable social forces" (Colomy 1998: 267). At the same
time, emphasizing the importance of the group prevents "microchauvinism" (Turner and Boyns 2002), in which "a sharply defined
purposive 'actor'" becomes the engine of change (Jepperson and
Meyer 2011: 57). Microchauvinism elevates individuals as creators of
institutional action but may downplay the reality that social systems
require people to collaborate. We must be skeptical of any atomistic
account that explains social life only through individuals maximizing
their interests through forms of control (DiMaggio and Powell 1991:
3, 9). Interests are never as certain or as unambiguous as such choice
theories typically assume.

In contrast to these approaches, I argue that the control that organizations exert arises because interacting groups promote an organizational agenda, an effort that uses available organizational resources
to alter society. They treat power as fundamentally civic, whether others concur or resist.

Of the current approaches that examine organizational control, inhabited institutionalism has the greatest affinity with a group culture
model of civic action (Scully and Creed 1997; Hallett and Ventresca
2006). I do not dismiss other approaches, such as those emphasizing institutional logics (Thornton, Ocasio, and Lounsbury 2012) or
institutional work (Lawrence and Suddaby 2006: 216), but these are
less attuned to how groups create a robust and self-referential culture. For an inhabited-institutional approach, the driving force is negotiation among invested groups, producing new routines (McGinty
2014; Maines 1977). By incorporating meaning, action, and hierarchy,
the inhabited-institutionalist framework balances individual desires
against the normative power of joint action. Institutional practices
merge with interactional orders in setting forms of constraint (Binder
2007; Aurini 2012; Everitt 2012, Haedicke 2012; Nunn 2014). Too often, however, the focus on how groups and their cultures shape these
choices ignores that these effects reverberate outside the organization (Dorado 2013). Such negotiations are crucial within a network
of groups that transforms and organizes local interests in ways that
shape social order. As described in chapter 3, civic culture is often
structured through associations. In this way, private interests coalesce
to create a local consensus. While agency is essential, the agency of
individuals is integrated into the agency of the organization and the
institutional field. We see this when recognizing that much social con-

trol is backed by state power or by social movements that contest that power. These institutions are inhabited by active agents, but in their civil role they are assumed to produce a collective pressure. Civic cultures have consequences because of collective agreement, even if the means by which those agreements are established is through negotiation.

Culture as Control

Culture does not exist merely as a set of rules, images, or objects, but is used in local communities, channeling and limiting civic life (Fine and Harrington 2004). Through culture, people make claims about shared pasts and about the desirability of prospective futures. This view is consistent with a tool-kit approach, but it rejects the idea that culture is a thing (a tool) in order to embrace the idea that culture is a practice (a tactic) to control and order interaction through the routines of circuits of action. Shared projects, reflecting common interests, provide the hinge through which local communities control intersubjective experience for common ends. This perspective asserts that, in open and democratic systems, the control of culture depends on the use made of it in tiny publics. Here the rights of communities within a larger politics are apparent, and, as a result, control is not imposed from the outside but involves collaboration.

Of course, in modern extended societies knots of citizens cannot develop their own rules. However, if they believe that power emanates from vertical and horizontal bands of consent, citizens often accept these rules and sanctions. Control, when embraced, is embedded in a network of groups, each respecting the voice of the others.

Erving Goffman's (1983) discussion of the interaction order justifies the mesolevel analysis of social control, asserting that interaction is not an unpredictable agentic response to events and situations, but that it is ordered, a result of understood control mechanisms. Goffman (1983: 4) writes that "at the very center of interaction life is the cognitive relation we have with those present before us, without which relationship, our activity, behavioral and verbal, could not be meaningfully organized." In privileging the organization of interaction, Goffman asks how cultures create control and predictability. By recognizing, participating in, and showing deference to normative and patterned expectations, group members treat their associations as stable, ongoing, and consequential. This stability is not generated within the immediate encounter but depends on a recalled past. As successful interaction from previous encounters serves as a template for ongoing relations, the past becomes a resource to create orderliness. In this, Anne Rawls (1987) suggests that "imperatives that are not structurally defined" are organizing principles that build local commitments, a claim central to mesoanalysis. Culture is both cause and effect of interaction and affiliation.

In extending analysis of the interaction order to social control, I integrate Goffman's insights of how interaction creates routines with the recognition that groups frequently rely on meanings embedded in those groups to which they are most committed. This includes groups found in offices, shop floors, and neighborhoods. However, given differing interests and backgrounds, negotiation is essential for building ongoing, flexible, but durable relations (Strauss 1978). Negotiations are more than "merely" immediate because they shape the future within a context of joint pasts.

Ultimately, both anxiety and confidence about the necessity of control are evident within an interaction order. In this, group response depends on resources and social relations. Groups need not accept the legitimacy of external control, but they must recognize the consequences of challenging that control. In the simplest model, an authoritative group decides and then through the reach of its resources and sanctions, individuals follow or reject those demands. However, this view excises the way local communities make choices in practice. In this, social relations organize authority, relying on the interpretations and the support of communal nodes. Presidents have cabinets and dictators have juntas and workplaces have teams. From these groups, decisions are transmitted to other groups that create policies to put the decision into effect. Those "on the ground" must implement the policies. In turn, those on whom the policy is imposed must respond, even if the response is to ignore the policy if feasible. Although some individuals act independently, families, cliques, neighborhoods, or movements often energize a collective response. Social control, accepted or resisted, involves a push-and-pull among groups. Civil societies inevitably require some forms of control, but their effectiveness results from the beliefs, resources, and relations of those who choose and those who are chosen.

Three Control Systems

To analyze control systems in light of their group cultures, I present three cases. I begin by examining government decision-making on the small-group level, exploring the problem of groupthink and ways around it as evidenced in the failed Bay of Pigs invasion (Janis 1972) and the successful conclusion of the Cuban missile crisis (Gibson 2012). Drawing on accounts of these events, I examine the dynamics of how group culture facilitates or limits decision-making. Groupthink has been a durable concept in social psychology and political science (Sunstein and Hastie 2015). Decision-making invariably depends on the existence of a group culture. Some groups have resources—material or cognitive—to shape events, creating a skein of significant consequences. It is not merely the existence of rules and practices that matters, but how those rules and practices affect social relations and local cultures.

I then describe how a larger organization attempts to control and constrain the smaller groups under its rubric. This is a general problem for social movements that hope to balance the benefits of central decision-making and resource control with the vibrancy and commitment of local action. When does the center speak for the periphery and, if it does, does this diminish local autonomy? Conversely, do the actions of local groups define the organization as a whole? In the face of critical outsiders, the choices of a local group may be treated by opponents as characterizing the organization as a whole. Although this tension between the center and the periphery also reflects the struggles of the Tea Party or the Occupy movement, I return eighty years to the heyday of the America First Movement (Fine 2006). This movement, expanding rapidly in the early 1940s, proved hard to control by the organizers at headquarters. The anti-interventionist passion in some groups edged toward a robust isolationism or even pro-German sentiment. The problem was how the central organization could constrain chapters, particularly given oppositional groups that used the presence of local excesses to characterize the movement as a whole.

Finally, delving into the heart of social control, I examine a set of ethnographies of police. A police force is an archetypal vector of control, being the primary guardian of social order with which citizens interact. I focus on dual forms of control: the control that the police organization has on local station houses and patrol squads, and how police units control the citizenry. Police on the street find themselves in a control bind. Officers are controlled by forces above that demand professionalism and political subtlety without permitting much discretion. These officers must then control those outside their occupational community who may resist their demands. The blue line is often blurred, and street-level bureaucracy can be attacked for going too far or not far enough. Together these cases remind us that, while control is essential for social order, the choices that are made are a result of the intersection of local conditions and external limits set by others.

EMBRACING AND ESCAPING GROUPTHINK

Elites in a political hierarchy represent the pinnacle of control, but the process through which these groups operate is not so different from any decision-making group. Group choices depend on a set of internal dynamics among the participants in which reputation, interpersonal skill, alliances, and personality all play a role. As Christoph Haug (2013) points out, meetings often have the goal of determining future action. They depend on those present, who speaks, who is listened to, who is persuasive, and the established connections among attendees.

One salient difference between elite meetings and other gatherings is that, because of their resources and because of the deference shown by groups that are expected to enforce their decisions, choices in such settings have extensive and lasting reverberations. Privilege matters and authority cascades. This reflects what Isaac Reed (2017) terms "chains of power," emphasizing the ties among groups in enforcing authority.

Accounts of major foreign policy decisions (and the disasters that sometimes result) typically involve "a tiny group of individuals talking with one another in a small number of meetings" (Jasper and Volpi 2018: 30). Once a resolution is established, others are charged with implementation. While all decisions are local, some force others to respond. This is particularly evident when decision-makers are treated as legitimate authorities or when they have established consequences for those who resist.

Authoritative committees make choices that are widely publicized and that, over time, are judged valid or harmful. However, whether right or wrong, the strong presumption is that these decisions should be obeyed and enforced. How do decisions emerge as a matter of group practice? Much has been written on leadership, and surely the voices of influential individuals count greatly, but often the process is collective, illustrating the internal dynamics of group culture. Groups with a common goal and strong affiliation are likely to be satisfied with their outcomes (Thompson 2014). Still, in some situations—what Irving Janis (1972) labeled groupthink—cohesion prevents incorporating alternative perspectives or external insights.

Theories of group dynamics provide a model that addresses the mesolevel pressures that policy-makers confront. This is a crucial instance in which group culture has potentially long-lasting effects. In the case of Paul 't Hart's (1994) careful analysis of the group basis of policy failure, cohesion, conformity, and deindividuation are crucial. However, the group must also be seen as a cultural unit built on ongoing social relations, despite the reverberations involved. These groups operate within political worlds with their own rituals, traditions, rules of discourse, and performances. Culture provides standards by which the group evaluates potential actions and judges the claims of members.

Even in analyzing elite decision-makers, an emphasis on group culture combines recognition of generic processes with the content of the specific relations. These actors participate in a "game of esteem," building on common experiences, ongoing friendships, and long-standing rivalries. As Irving Janis (1972: 8) points out,

> The group dynamics approach is based on the working assumption that the members of policy-making groups, no matter how mindful they may be of their exalted national status and of their heavy responsibilities, are subjected to the pressures widely observed in groups of ordinary citizens.... Members tend to evolve informal objectives to preserve friendly intragroup relations and this becomes part of the hidden agenda at their meetings.... The more amiability and esprit de corps among the members of a policy-making ingroup, the greater is the danger that independent critical thinking will be replaced by groupthink, which is likely to result in irrational and dehumanizing actions directed against out-groups.

A cost exists in a strong group culture in that the desire to preserve bonds among members shapes internal culture dynamics. In tightly networked settings, being a naysayer has reputational consequences. Because of their vast documentation, along with the salience of the decisions, foreign policy decisions in the Kennedy administration with regard to Cuba serve as models for understanding decisions gone wrong as well as decisions made right.

Compare the decision-making process behind the successful resolution of the 1962 Cuban missile crisis with that behind the failed Bay of Pigs invasion the previous year. Granted these reflected two distinct geopolitical contexts, even though both involved the strained relations between the United States and the Castro regime in Havana and the Soviets in Moscow. Scholars treat the Bay of Pigs decision as reflecting the limits of groups, while the former reveals how elite groups can achieve successful outcomes. American foreign policy leaders planning the Bay of Pigs attack lacked adequate input, did not consider all available options, and ignored the malign effects of cohesiveness when they rejected nonconforming ideas (Janis 1972: 5). Groups often—although not inevitably—choose more dangerous options, labeled the risky shift, that can produce heightened victories or devastating defeats (Stoner 1968). Polarization is evident in experimental studies of laboratory groups, although some studies find that with a different framing, groups may become more cautious. This failure of decision-making may have contributed to the more successful decision the following year in the response to the Cuban missile crisis. The recognition of the previous outcome provided a barrier to risky action. The framing that President Kennedy set for the group discussion, as he avoided provocative confrontation in the October 1962 crisis, seems, in retrospect, to have been shaped by the earlier experience (Allison and Zelikow 1999).

By examining these two diplomatic cases, we "read history backwards." We know the outcomes, but had the Bay of Pigs invasion overthrown Castro or the Cuban missile crisis led to nuclear devastation, diplomatic historians—those that survived!—would have searched for other explanations, labeling the two sets of meetings in vastly different ways.

My goal is not to trace policy concerns that affected these outcomes but to examine the dynamics of group culture that channeled the decision-making. The substantive and policy choices behind the decisions have been presented elsewhere (Allison and Zelikow 1999; Fursenko and Naftali 1997), although without emphasizing the interpersonal relations within the meetings. In each instance, a hierarchy existed with President Kennedy as the final arbiter (Neustadt 1990: 182). As commander in chief, Kennedy had authority to set policy on these issues of global consequence.

In the Cuban missile crisis, Kennedy depended on an elite group, the Executive Committee of the National Security Council (ExComm), consisting of Vice-President Lyndon Johnson, Secretary of State Dean Rusk, Secretary of Defense Robert McNamara, the chairman of the Joint Chiefs of Staff, the director of the Central Intelligence Agency, and departmental undersecretaries, former ambassadors, and other presidential advisors. These men had a shared history and tangled, intense social relations, having served with—and sometimes against—each other in government and in other policy spheres. Many had connections with the Georgetown set, described in chapter 2. Friendship, respect, and rivalries were crucial as their relations shaped their conversations and their policy preferences. While we cannot determine to what extent personal relations shaped policy advice, long-term relations and short-term emotions provided a context for talk. In his account of the ExComm meetings, based on available tapes, Sheldon Stern (2003: 416–17) reports,

> Kennedy's management of the ExComm discussions was subtle and understated but remarkably effective. JFK virtually never lost his temper, at least, Dean Rusk might add, not during the high point of the crisis, and remained all but imperturbable in the face of sometimes severe criticism from the Joint Chiefs, the ExComm or the leaders of Congress.... The views of ExComm members, of course, shifted, evolved and even reversed direction in response to the changing diplomatic, political and military situation, their own beliefs and the arguments of their colleagues.... Some participants ... were nearly always diffident and reflective; some were tough and assertive; some were eager to lead, despite the enormous stakes involved; others were content to follow and say very little.... Only the tapes or a narrative can adequately convey the undercurrent of friction that developed between President Kennedy and McGeorge Bundy at the ExComm meetings. "Mac," as his colleagues called him, had a well-deserved reputation for brilliance—and abrasive-

ness.... He spoke his mind freely and seemed to genuinely enjoy the intellectual challenge of these high-stakes discussions.

President Kennedy watched closely, aware of group dynamics, sending some participants out of the room and calling for a dinner break when disagreements became too sharp. While these accounts do not trace personal relations and the long-term group culture, they capture how the group developed understandings that responded to ongoing events as well as to the flow of talk and argument.

David Gibson (2011: 1–2) emphasizes that this case reveals the salience of microcontingencies, recognizing that the course of history depends on localized events and face-to-face copresence. The group context and interactional structure of the administration's executive committee proved crucial in incorporating diverse perspectives, perhaps responding to memories of the failed Bay of Pigs attack. The outcome depended on discourse. Gibson (2012: 160) writes,

> The decision is actually reached through talk, rather than through the working of a solitary mind.... [Kennedy] saw the virtues of the National Security Council meeting format, and opted to assemble his advisers in one place rather than have them approach him individually ... and to encourage free and open exchanges rather than impose an artificial structure that might have inhibited participation or otherwise sent the wrong message about formality and protocol. Kennedy thus bound himself to make decisions, to the extent possible, that were sensible and justifiable against the backdrop of what I have referred to as the "discursive state," meaning what has been said up to the moment of decision.

This is a powerful instance of the Hinge: the linkage between individual and structure as mediated through the local context of group dynamics. Politics depends on social relations and images of the proper functioning of the interaction order. By establishing an executive committee and granting it authority (and potentially blame), Kennedy recognizes the value of debate in political culture and its limits. Because these actors are considering the future in what Mische (2009) terms foretalk and I label futurework (Fine 2007), they extrapolate from a set of potentially relevant pasts, searching for a shared interpretation of how pasts link to futures, a set of temporal trajectories (Tavory and Eliasoph 2013).

By constituting the committee as open to a wide array of voices, participants hoped to avoid the weaknesses of the closed mindset that led to the Bay of Pigs fiasco or, on another occasion, the bureaucratic mistakes that led to the *Challenger* launch disaster (Vaughan 1996). Group decisions are no assurance of a desirable outcome, but they provide for collective investment and ongoing social relations. Conflicting interpretations are brought into dialogue, preventing an impasse in which the most extreme decisions hold sway (Wagner-Pacifici 2000).

The fact that in a political context individuals have ongoing relations permits them to draw on detailed personal knowledge to choose an effective rejoinder and to create the granular conditions of group-work. Awareness of the backgrounds and histories of participants allows colleagues to judge the context of their claims beyond the content of the claim itself. Further, given that individuals are engaging in a status contest, certain types of responses may be treated as desirable. Secretary of Defense Robert McNamara's reputation as a policy dove caused him to shape his remarks in order to escape that interpretation. These forms of talk are meaningful not simply for their overt content but in their relationship to the speaker. A thread exists between the speech act and the interactional domain in which it is enacted. Further, talk within groups often consists of stories (Martin 1992), either events in the past (afttalk) or hypothetical ones (foretalk). To gain power the stories must appeal to consensus.

This leads Gibson (2012: 159) to argue,

> Insofar as a decision arises out of talk, and there is no "right" answer simply waiting to be discovered or agreed, that decision emerges from the intersection of individuals' perspectives and interests; conversational rules, procedures, and vicissitudes; and external events that may impinge on the decision-making process before it has run its course.

Put differently, groupthink is an outcome of grouptalk.

In political decision-making, powerful groups have a duty to decide. Of course, the decision to threaten a blockade and to demand the removal of missiles from Cuba had huge implications for groups in other places with different agendas and amounts of control. We cannot assess with certainty what was happening in the Soviet upper circles, but we know the major players in their decision-making apparatus were engaging in parallel discussions and attempting to interpret the implications of the American decisions (Allison and Zelikow 1999: 328–29). Nor do we know precisely how Kennedy's orders were put into effect through the choices of naval officers or interpreted in discussions in Congress, in newsrooms, and in living rooms. Decisions, demanding action, reverberate throughout a social system. These debates underline the salience of local cultures, worlds of actors working together within a structure. In this case, their challenge might have led to the nuclear annihilation of those with no voice in the decisions but, thankfully, did not. This fateful possibility was known only after the fact. However, the reality of relationship histories and group practices was recognized at the time. This dramatic instance of elite control reminds us that decisions at the top flow to other groups charged with fulfilling them and affect the life chances of those who only learn of them later.

CONTROLLING CHAPTERS

Groups routinely demand limits on the actions of participants. This control often operates through consensus, a shared sense of propriety. Of course, many groups struggle to establish a joint vision, and some are unable to achieve it, requiring sanctions or exclusion of those who do not accept what others treat as the local moral order.

This can be a challenge within a face-to-face group, but what happens when an association is constituted as a network of groups? This is a particular challenge for groups that depend on the presence of chapters, even if the chapters have only thin links to a central authority. Movements desire large membership both for financial support and for what supporters can achieve when acting together. The challenge is that independent groups can be treated as speaking for the broader organization. This can become a dilemma when these local groups express beliefs of which the central headquarters disapproves or wishes to hide from the use of opponents. This constitutes what James Jasper (2004) describes as an "extension dilemma." How can an association that operates within a contentious political space control its members and patrol its borders?

To address this extension dilemma, I examine the America First Committee, founded in June 1940, the influential political group that prior to Pearl Harbor pushed to keep America out of the European conflict. Before the Japanese attack, most Americans opposed involvement in the war in Europe. The America First Committee (AFC) hoped to pressure Congress and the Roosevelt administration not to intervene, creating a local chapter-based movement that opponents derided as isolationist. The memory of the killing fields of the Great War was still raw in the minds of many Americans, and the desire of the Roosevelt administration to aid Britain made it apparent to many that the United States was sliding into the European conflict. The attack on Pearl Harbor marginalized isolationists, and this rapid justification for war made conspiracy theories plausible for many on the margins of political discourse.

As a mass movement, the AFC was organized through local chapters. This had advantages in generating emotional energy, organizing local rallies, and building on network recruitment (Snow et al. 1986). Yet such a system depended on chapters accepting the strategies of the national headquarters, even though this removed autonomy from local activists. In reality, chapters had diverse politics: a few seemed sympathetic to the Nazi regime, others despised Roosevelt, and some displayed a measure of anti-Semitism. The culture of each group depended on the beliefs of their volunteers and leaders. Perhaps some groups were infiltrated by those who wished to discredit the organization by extreme pronouncements. Even if these groups did not reflect the policy of the national organization, the actions of a chapter could be used to typify the organization as a whole. Controlling these local cultures was difficult at best and often impossible.

As a result, the headquarters attempted to create a system that might be described as border control. The main office hoped to exclude those that they considered undesirable. Being anti-interventionist was not sufficient, since other beliefs might stigmatize the movement. Those sympathetic to Nazi or Fascist aims, those with anti-Jewish attitudes, and those who supported the Soviet-Nazi pact might find the America First Committee an appealing home if not excluded.

In a letter to chapter organizers, Robert Bliss, the Director of

Organization, emphasized: "There is no room in our program for Nazis, Fascists, Communists, Bundists, or any persons with leanings that place the interests of a foreign country ahead of those of the United States. We do not countenance anti-Semitism nor antiadministrative activity. We are non-partisan" (Fine 2006: 416). The organization even asked prominent citizens to provide references for potential leaders of local chapters, writing, "Pertaining to our connection, actual or prospective, with the person named above, we desire information concerning his (or her) standing and integrity." Contributors of over $100 were investigated and some checks returned, including a check to an Oregon chapter for $20 from the German War Veterans, even though there was no evidence that the group was connected with the German-American Bund. Those associated with the Bund or with Father Coughlin's Social Justice Movement were informed that they were not wanted. Even Henry Ford was dropped from the board of directors because of earlier anti-Semitic statements.

Particularly at the local level, these activists might define the culture. This was seen as such a significant problem that R. Douglas Stuart Jr., the AFC national director, wrote chapter chairs, "It is not unlikely that certain elements which seek to promote racial and religious intolerance may mistakenly conclude that they will now be welcomed in the ranks of America First. Careful as we have been, we must now scrutinize each membership application with redoubled care." This cost the organization considerable time and expense (Fine 2006: 416).

Beyond the intensive review of potential members, hoping to preserve the purity of the organization, the behavior of local chapters had to be policed. Chapters were told not to cosponsor events with other organizations without prior approval from national headquarters. Visits to politicians by local groups could be counterproductive, and chapters were ordered to exert control: "There are instances wherein a people's lobby in Washington becomes more destructive than constructive.... During the extension of the service bill unpleasant incidents arose and we must ask all chapters to exert a more rigid control upon whom they ask to represent them on a trip to Washington" (Fine 2006: 417). While less connected to local group cultures, the control of those who distributed literature or even attended public rallies proved problematic. Chapters were informed that they should request police protection. In time, the organization was tarred with the comments of the celebrated aviator Charles Lindbergh at an address in Des Moines, Iowa, in which he suggested that Jews were behind the push for military involvement, a claim that many considered explicitly anti-Semitic. Lindbergh was so identified with the organization and so closely linked to the group at headquarters, serving on the board of directors, that he was retained, although his presence caused some liberals and Jews to keep their distance. In contrast to those on the local level, his central position could not be eliminated. The words of Lindbergh were used by opponents to typify the character of members and the goals of the organization.

Through action and talk, the America First Committee tried to police the chapters and the cultures that characterized the organization. But given the porosity of movement boundaries, such attempts were imperfect. In a world of interlaced groups, control from above is a challenge, especially without surveillance and with a belief in the value of local control. Control is far easier to enforce with strong boundaries, but when multiple groups participate within the same network, local cultures inevitably produce divergent beliefs and actions.

BLUE PATROLS

The most palpable agent of state control is the police force, an institution that is organized by groups on multiple levels. Researchers have conducted insightful ethnographies of police activity, riding in police cars and observing in station houses. As a result, the cultures of police have been well documented. While we often speak of "the police," this misrepresents life on the street: the creation of a street-level bureaucracy (Lipsky 2010). This local bureaucracy is the nexus in which state actors come into contact with citizens, helping or constraining them according to policy and discretion. It is understandable that scholars suggest that their site of observation represents the police force in general, rather than a squad in particular, but, as a result, the robust local cultures of police may be ignored. Accounts of police practices reveal that cultures differ. In the words of sociologist Peter Moskos (2008: 1–2), who spent over a year policing in Baltimore's impoverished Eastern District, "The so-called Blue Brotherhood is not a monolithic entity as much as a tent under which a diverse clan of cousins constantly feuds and squabbles." Or as Jennifer Hunt (2010: 7–8) explained, no monolithic police culture exists, even within a single urban department, but, in contrast, there is a matrix of subcultures whose members share different orientations to the job and in which different normative orders are dominant at different times.... Even within occupational subcultures there is considerable variation in how individuals and groups of officers view traditional values, including notions of secrecy and loyalty, perceptions of the external environment as dangerous and hostile, conservatism, alienation from the community, and tension between cops and management.

These multiple police cultures are established by local units based on the traditions of the police force. In her analysis of specialized units in the New York police department, Hunt (2010: 8) depicts a dramatic difference in the culture of SWAT teams from that of emergency services.

On the most basic level, police often patrol in pairs that are characterized by high levels of cohesion. The internal space of the "cop car" creates an intense culture, as the pair must rely on each other in situations that call for fast cognition and wide discretion with potentially life-altering consequences (Van Maanen 1988: 109–12). The possibility for errors of judgment leads to each officer "having their partner's back."

Informal relations set the conditions of work and provide an alternative framework in contrast to formal rank (Hunt 2010: 14). Anthropologist Didier Fassin (2013: 208), observing the police in a Parisian suburb (an ethnic banlieue), found that patrol teams held varying attitudes toward residents and, as a result, had different perspectives on confrontation. Fassin writes,

> The hierarchical relations within their small teams of three were not such that a sergeant could impose his way of behaving or thinking on a patrol officer: hence, practices still varied, and some racist violent officers allowed their habits free rein even when they were under the command of these two [less hostile] sergeants; nevertheless, the climate seemed less hostile than in other crews.

The teams with their styles of action, moderated through authority and seniority, affected how citizens were treated. Although Fassin assumes that individual attitudes are central, the dynamics among partners with their mutual commitments, shared histories, and desire for harmony create group culture. The face-to-face relations of a patrol team create a potent cultural dynamic. As Jonathan Rubinstein (1973: 438–39) emphasizes in *City Police*, partners are social units:

> Partnerships are founded on equality of responsibility and rewards. The men share everything and must have confidence in each other.... The men do not necessarily become close personal friends, but they must be compatible since they spend a great deal of time together.... These forced coalitions rarely develop into friendships that extend outside of working hours, but the men manage, they discuss their family lives and their personal problems. It is understood that partners will not discuss with third parties any work in which they are mutually engaged.

This encourages secrecy in resisting civilian control. If the officers are engaged in illicit or corrupt activity or operate contrary to official guidelines, they act, in effect, like a street gang with the structure of a secret society. Hunt (2010: 75) presents a powerful example of how an intense partnership creates a group culture that shapes the practice of policing:

> There were jobs that pushed Ryan to the limits, like instances of domestic violence, which made him feel angry enough to kill the guy who beat up his wife or abused their child. In times like that, Dolan's eyes might get hard and beady but he would keep cool, soothing his partner and keeping his temper in check. Ryan, in turn, often took a leadership role, calming Dolan down when he got nervous or a little impatient. Sometimes, when Dolan got up on the wrong side of the bed, he would respond angrily to an irritation that others would let roll off their backs. Ryan's mere presence would serve to keep down the heat that bubbled inside and Dolan would restrain himself. When Ryan felt depressed or burdened by too much thought, he could count on Dolan to crack a joke or otherwise lighten his load.

Accounts of the dyadic culture of partners emphasize that the culture is not only satisfying but also affects how they patrol, shaping their performance as controllers of the public order.

Beyond the culture of partners, there are shifts, stations, divisions, and other organizational forms in which police officers develop close connections, common knowledge, and microcultures. New recruits are accepted provisionally once they demonstrate that they deserve trust. As Jonathan Rubinstein (1973: 438) asserts, "The only way the need for secrecy and privacy can be met without compromising the squad's ability to fulfill its collective responsibilities is by the continuous formation and dissolution of cliques and coalitions." Authority depends on social relations. This use of culture in enforcing normative order is evident in the nicknames awarded to professionally problematic individuals, such as "Off-at-Seven George," or "The-Eternal-Flame Edward Who-Never-Goes-Out" (Van Maanen 1988: 58). Peter Moskos (2008: 35–36) emphasizes this same practice of localization in the case of Baltimore policing:

> As a Baltimore police officer, I couldn't pass as a New York City cop because I can't speak the local lingo. While policing is fundamentally the same in different cities, there are many linguistic differences between locales.... In New York City to "jack somebody up" means to beat them up; in Baltimore it means an aggressive frisk. Baltimore and New York City police have different terms for many similar items such as ambulance ("ambo" in Baltimore versus "bus" in New York), searching a suspect on the street ("jack-up" versus "toss"), beating a person ("thump" versus "jack-up"), an out-of-the-way place to rest ("hole" versus "coop"), and a good police officer ("real PO-lice" versus "cop's cop").... In general, any professional courtesy you receive as a police officer (not receiving a traffic ticket, free coffee, getting into a night club) decreases as distance increases, in part because of the inability to know with certainty that the person really is a police officer.

Localism is powerful in state control as in other activities that shape civil society. This is not to deny that a transsituational or even national police culture is meaningful and recognized. However, officers learn this culture through their organizational environments, evident in police training, working together, transferring, and developing rapport with officers outside of their work units. It is not only the culture of the police within an organization that is consequential, but also the culture of police communities as inhabited institutions.

Controlling Groups

Groups are both controlled and agents of control. They depend on being embedded in associations and networks that provide resources and mandates of authority. Organizations often determine relations among groups, and this matters in how control operates in practice. We have a clearer sense of how control operates when we bracket the larger system as a site of legitimation and focus on smaller units. In this, we see how decisions flow from group to group.

Recognizing that action units constrain and channel the choices of other units allows us to see how individuals and structure enforce control through group life. Organizations, institutions, and structures are inhabited, not by isolated individuals, but by individuals whose ongoing contact creates traditions, rituals, and histories that can be used in a self-reflexive way as an idioculture.

Models of control emphasize hierarchy: the layering of groups. How does one local community direct the actions of another? This is a mesolevel analysis of chains of power (Reed 2017): interpretations of legitimate action among groups with different amounts of power or resources. The chain depends on a ladder of groups with each dependent on another, constituting a cascade of authority.

This process occurs within the context of political decision-making, where the influence of elites is supported by institutional legitimacy. Groupthink, a form of cultural dysfunction, reveals how knowledge and normative boundaries infect systems of control.

The ties between periphery and center are evident in extended associations that operate through chapters or local outposts. Can an organizational center control those within their purview? Patrolling boundaries can be challenging, dependent on the moral authority or resource control of a central organizational unit. Rather than treating an extended organization as a single domain, in reality it often consists of loosely coupled structures.

Finally, some organizations, such as the police, have the authority to enforce control among a diffuse network of individuals and groups. These institutional actors—and the military is a prime example—are structured as a linked network of small units from top to bottom. This permitted the torture at Abu Ghraib to be treated as legitimate, even absent formal approval from above. The performance of trauma was, in this circumstance, a mark of authority.

The police force, like the military, is a multisited organization in which power is embedded in social relations. However, these organizations, explicitly tied to social control, are structured like many organizations that lack control as a specific mandate. In all cases, how this control is managed depends on a close-knit camaraderie that group cultures provide in the face of challenge. The presence of dependable others with whom bonds have been established creates the trust necessary to perform the dangerous and dirty work of control.

While the first chapters examine civic organizations that assume harmony in their local action circuits, this is not always true as communities face those with rival interests or disruptive intent. In such a situation, conflict and control are evident. Resource-rich groups, especially those that receive the ability to direct behavior from the support of state systems, use their resources to enforce a vision of the right and proper. Control is as much a part of civic culture as are coordination and civility.

7

EXTENSIONS

Tiny Publics and Distant Worlds

There is no limit to the liberal expansion and confirmation of limited personal intellectual endowment which may proceed from the flow of social intelligence when that circulates by word of mouth from one to another in the communications of the local community. That and that alone gives reality to public opinion. We lie, as Emerson said, in the lap of an immense intelligence. But that intelligence is dormant and its communications are broken, inarticulate and faint until it possesses the local community as its medium.

JOHN DEWEY, *The Public and Its Problems*

I have focused single-mindedly on how face-to-face groups create cultures and how individuals develop relations that link them into civil society. However, anyone less fixated on knots of local action will recognize that concentrating on bounded groups and the strong ties within them misses much. The decisions of individuals ("players" in the terms of Jasper and Volpi [2018]) both shape and are shaped by those with whom they associate. People become politically active through voting, voluntary contributions, participating in online discussions, or attending demonstrations with friends. Further, those groups with which we engage often depend on intersecting and larger communities, and in this way they constitute fragmented fields, distinct from face-to-face groups that are often more unified. In this chapter, I explore group extensions, examining implicit groups, dispersed cultures, widespread networks, and not-so-tiny publics. We might speak of this as constituting "extension work": how a local community comes to fit into a more extended social domain and how it may shape that domain. A local analysis must not ignore the influence of—and on—large-scale organizations, subcultures, media worlds, and online communities.

I do not dismiss extended networks or ignore mass-membership organizations but argue that such extended social systems depend

on the influence of a grid of tiny publics and the identities that derive from belonging to local communities. Larger structures involve
a fragmented mesh of small groups but not an undifferentiated mass
or a nation of isolates. The question is how media, acquaintances,
and technologies of socialization and surveillance link local domains.
How do groups fit into "society"? How is civic structure scalable from
local sites of action into complex institutional webs?

While small communities have been dominant for much of human
history, the existence of empires—ancient and modern—and extended metropolises suggest that a broad structure of political power
has the potential to overwhelm local control, even when powerful
decision-makers are a group themselves. Still, these expansive systems depend on coordination and collaboration.

The stability of empires depends on small groups in the court, military, church, and countryside. But we cannot simply reduce empires
to such groups. As I described in considering social control, influential groups have mechanisms for diffusing power. Human history is
an account by which some groups expand their influence to shape
responses of others, establishing a civic hierarchy. While not the first
empire, the Roman Empire and its Pax Romana reveal the development of extensive systems of control. Empires may limit local systems
of governance, reinforcing centralized power.

Even more impressive, given its reach and longevity, is the Catholic
Church with its headquarters in Rome and its outposts throughout
the world. The establishment of house churches throughout Pales-
tine, Anatolia, Greece, and the rest of the Roman Empire by Saint
Paul and fellow evangelists reveals how centralization and localization can coexist. Other religions, some more and others less centralized than the Church of Rome, reveal how communities fit into an
expansive organization. The more locally diffuse Protestant Reforma-
tion demonstrated that centralization has costs and is not inevitable.

By the nineteenth century, large-scale voluntary associations began to develop outside the auspices of church and state. As Richard
Brown (1974: 43) pointed out in his examination of voluntary associations in Massachusetts in the 1830s,

> Localism and insularity were being challenged, if not actually de-
> stroyed. People remained bound to the old organizations of family,
> church, and town, but now they possessed additional ties.... Some-

times the contact was direct.... More often, the contact was psychological, coming from memberships in countywide or statewide organizations and the publications such activities produced.

Many associations developed a three-tier system: local, regional, and translocal. Members maintained personal contacts while also committing themselves to groups that were more extensive. As Theda Skocpol (1999: 66) pointed out,

> Membership in local units of translocal federations offered connections to and organizational routes into broader social and political movements. People loved being part of larger "brotherhoods" and "sisterhoods" and often were inspired to join endeavors to which they knew thousands of others across their state and nation were also committed.... During recurrent group conventions Americans from different parts of states and parts of the country met one another, learned about other people's homes, and exchanged ideas about group and civic affairs.

Skocpol (2003: 78) argues persuasively that local and translocal structures were mutually supportive. In this, larger organizations had advantages in creating a sense of national significance, even while members enjoyed each other's company. Leaders visited local chapters and the organizations sponsored funds for travel to far-flung chapters (Skocpol 2003: 86). Rules and rituals shared across national organizations enabled travelers to connect with other members when far from home. This is true for organizations as diverse as the Masons, Rotary, Alcoholics Anonymous, and even the Ku Klux Klan. While the Klan of the 1920s has not been considered in this light given its political agenda, its clubby, fraternal (and sororal) sensibility places the local klaverns in much the same category as the Masons or Odd Fellows (Gordon 2017). Further, as Skocpol (2003: 92) emphasizes, an association begins with a core group, and then members fan out establishing chapters to spread the word and the fellowship. Fraternal and civic groups rushed to create local chapters that not only provided for emotional affiliation but also supported the larger organization. The model for voluntary associations is that of new religions, whether Christianity, Mormonism, or Scientology (Meeks 2003; Bushman 2005; Wright 2012). Establishing local chapters did not merely result from spontaneous enthusiasm by a group of friends but was due to organizers traveling from central headquarters. By this mechanism, intense and cohesive clubs emerged, providing a shared culture for individuals who often were unfamiliar with each other but desired a tight-knit allegiance.

In time, each group transformed the traditions of the founding association, incorporating its own variations. Local practices came to support a national purpose. As Skocpol (2003: 97) writes,

> Classic American voluntary associations were *not*, therefore, expressions of small-is-beautiful localism. On the contrary, multiple tiered national federations were the key institutional supports of American voluntarism because they simultaneously sustained intimate solidarities and facilitated connections to wider worlds.

This structure characterized many American civic groups as well as groups in other nations.

Organizations are strengthened through local relations as well from a belief that participants are contributing to a salient civic purpose. While the local group provides personal satisfactions, contributing to the organization generates a belief in national involvement or even global connections. By the twentieth century, voluntary organizations, such as Rotary, were proudly international in scope.

If this is not an example of small-is-beautiful localism that dismisses the larger society, it does represent large-is-comforting localism in which belonging to a network of intimate solidarities permits a powerful form of identity. Rituals are performed with beloved brothers and sisters, but they are performed with the possibility of contributing to shared projects that those at headquarters determine serve organizational interests. In this way, groups are crucial to the American associational structure but are also connected to larger groups-of-groups, constituting a national fellowship. The challenge is that if chapters are weakened, the association might become an empty shell, reduced to infrequent ritual gatherings. Under these circumstances, what had been a vibrant form of community becomes a bureaucratic entity with headquarters distributing newsletters and appealing for individual donations but lacking vibrant local chapters. Only the rare organization, like Alcoholics Anonymous or Rotary, can keep its local structures strong while maintaining an extended organization.

A second element must be considered to appreciate the extension of mesolevel structures and the creation of translocal connections: the role of the mass media. The idea of the "mass" in "media" must be unpacked to understand how media support the local. The mass media extend social relations beyond the local, allowing groups to experience what other groups have produced. For an extended community, perhaps the greatest value of the media is the potential to create a focused public that extends beyond the local. Even when trading in matters that are small and seemingly mundane, media educate. They disseminate information that permits local conversations. A common culture connects those who might otherwise be isolated or separated into narrow social realms: David Hume's conversible world. The publicity given to sports in modern society is an example. To the extent that much of the citizenry tracks sports events, connections with strangers, whether temporary or extended, are possible. Of course, not every event falls under a universal knowledge canopy (sports knowledge is often highly gendered, for example, and knowledge silos in politics are clear), but we assume widespread awareness. While we might hesitate in defining this as public intelligence, civic awareness allows for commitment, opportunities for interaction, and historical memory.

Minute communities interpret and evaluate these cultural topics whether they are sports, politics, or entertainment. Other groups have the responsibility to produce and publicize these events. A football team is a group as is the cast of a television show as is a political campaign. Once again, groups exist all the way up and all the way down chains of power and hierarchies of knowledge. Many groups hope that a network of groups will spread their productions. Some productions receive wide exposure and can be referred to with the assumption that others will be aware of the reference. Mass media can reach a wide audience, although this outcome has become more challenging with more media outlets and with an increasingly fragmented media landscape.

Shared memories are central to how media shape the relationship of citizens to civil society. Communications scholar Michael Schudson (1989) presents five processes that serve as mechanisms through which cultural objects fit into public recall. Following Ann Swidler's (1986) phrasing, Schudson refers to culture as a tool kit. In a self-reflexive way, groups rely on the interaction order—the structured and recognized form of cohesive engagement—to create routines in their communal bubble that tie media portrayals to moments of participation. In this analysis, Schudson explores cultural forms that are widely known within a population but that originate and gain meaning in local spaces. His model emphasizes big media and large audiences, downplaying domains of interaction. However, knowledge and memory have effects because they are found within communities. Despite the reality that media outlets depend on those that produce and distribute their products, the media stream is distinct from the groupiness of its consumers. Communities of consumers take these messages and alter them as needed. Specifically Schudson addresses mechanisms that characterize the potency of a cultural object: retrievability (the availability of the memory of the object), rhetorical force (its power to engage its audience), resonance (whether the audience can use the object to interpret their surroundings), institutional retention (whether local institutions support memory), and resolution (whether the object can be used to solve group problems). Memory does not simply float in mind or in structures but develops through a relational order. When groups have similar dynamics, local choices become part of extended cultures.

Collective Histories

Collective memory theorist Jeffrey Olick describes two cultures of memory, distinguishing between collected memories—the similar memories of many individuals—and collective memories—memories that are embedded in civic structures. He separates parallel micromemories and macromemories that operate as social facts, typically with institutional support. Olick (1999: 333) writes, "Two different concepts of collective memory compete—one refers to the aggregation of socially framed individual memories and one refers to collective phenomena sui generis." In connecting the two, he downplays the mesolevel spaces of memory. Olick is not alone in distinguishing the micro and the macro in the creation of national histories (Spillman 1997; Brubaker and Cooper 2000). However, power does not reside in an unpeopled state; rather, self-interested actors make this happen if they can persuade others to judge their actions and rhetorical claims favorably. In the case of diasporic support for home nations (Israel and Ireland), Dan Lainer-Vos (2013: 154) emphasizes the key role of activist groups in creating a national cause through networking and recruitment to ethnic associations. Groups provide the glue through which national affiliation (or, perhaps, disaffiliation) is generated.

Recall is supported through group discussions. While individuals are the keepers of personal memory and while institutional systems provide for material storage and the ritual consecration of memory, a usable past is central to communal identity. Groups form at political events, such as the 1848 Seneca Falls Convention, attended by Elizabeth Cady Stanton, Lucretia Mott, and Frederick Douglass, and, as a result, participants share experience and build affective ties. This gathering gave rise to the organization of the "Ultras" in which Stanton and Mott were central, providing a structure for the subsequent involvement of Susan B. Anthony. However, more than this, the meeting provided an origin story, a moment that was consecrated in justifying the movement.

National holidays and the constructed memories that support them become real because families or friends attend fireworks celebrations and other festivities (Santino 1994). Effective holidays gather people together to embrace family (Thanksgiving), faith (Easter, Passover, Ramadan), age (Halloween), or nation (Independence Day, Bastille Day). These are not occasions that individuals celebrate nor are they occasions where the celebration is entirely collective, despite occasional large gatherings, services, or broadcasts. Instead, their power derives from an in-gathering of acquaintances. This is demonstrated powerfully in folklorist Simon Bronner's (2011) analysis of how building Sukkot huts provides an opportunity for local Jewish communities to bond and to express their commitment to religious practices and to each other. These huts represent shelters in the wilderness. As Bronner emphasizes, their construction and their sharing for the weeklong holiday, including eating and sleeping in the huts, bolster microcommunities in a way that connects to a local Jewish present as well as to the larger Jewish past. Constructing these huts requires social relations as it historicizes these relations and the religious beliefs that support them. Holidays lacking an interpersonal element (such as Columbus Day or President's Day) are less effective in supporting commitment. The continuing challenge of Martin Luther King's Birthday is to find strategies, perhaps through volunteering, that transform a vacation day into a day that creates a shared public.

Mutual presence and the emotional energy that this brings contribute to moral socialization. Copresence at an event and the recognition of common narratives make history collective (Tilly 2006: 209). States can enact social control and individuals can award personal recognition, but groups permit communal memories to become integrated into the self.

Tiny Publics in the Air

In describing the role of tiny publics in civil society, I have emphasized groups that operate through face-to-face interaction. This is the classic approach to communal life. However, mediated social relations deserve explicit attention. The idea of a "republic of letters" (Goodman 1994) recognizes that written communication creates lines of collaboration that both incorporates and transcends group cultures. Technologies of aural communication, such as the telephone, serve the same purpose (Fischer 1992). Email can be conceived as a rapid postal system and texting has some of the immediacy of conversation without a visual component. Social media is a form of communication that will surely evolve until technologies and desires stabilize. These communication channels provide both freedom and constraint. They permit opportunities for revolt and additional layers of surveillance. Like all systems that promise freedom, social media also produce inequality and build power structures. While these sites encourage interaction, establish membership criteria, and depend on rules of conduct, these are often looser and less enforced than those found in face-to-face domains. Further, they have the potential to create groupings that might be unlikely if spatial copresence were all that was considered.

What are the consequences of social media on tiny publics? How does cyberspace create the possibility of group cultures, even in the absence of face-to-face interaction? Can online and offline community be integrated, creating an extended mesoculture? It might appear that the creation of an online network of intimate strangers is distant from group dynamics. These are thin social systems, constructing a world with weak local cultures. However, as Lance Bennett (2012: 20) argues, new media create opportunities for the personalization of politics and, consequently, permit the gathering of those who embrace similar identities. What appears to be institutional fragmentation leads to vibrant communities and to the development of new interaction orders with their own norms, morals, and expectations (Chayko 2008).

We are witnessing change in the use of social capital. Robert Putnam (2000) bemoans the decline of face-to-face groups and clubs, such as bowling teams and Parent-Teacher Associations. The Facebook generation might seem to have no need for such assemblies, satisfied with an occasional meet-up. Indeed, Eric Klinenberg (2012) has pointed to the reality that increasing numbers of young people are choosing to reside alone, rejecting even the possibility of a roommate dyad. Although this is true, it does not predict an atomized society. "Isolates" in their living quarters are not necessarily isolates in their social lives, either in person or online. Coordination is essential for any social system.

Face-to-face interaction that was visual and auditory (and occasionally tactile and olfactory)—a sensory symphony—has been replaced by fewer channels. Letters privilege vision, recognizing that the feel of the stationery and the smell of a perfumed billet-doux had some effects. Telephonic communications privilege the auditory in a setting that, like face-to-face communication, encourages dialogue. Instant messaging and texting blend the visual and the dialogic, while social media expand the potential audience beyond the dyad or microgroup.

However, what about other forms of electronic communication that spread to a wider audience? Perhaps we overemphasize the prominence of electronic communication. Despite the attention to popular memes, few messages go viral. According to the *Atlantic Monthly* (Meyer 2013), Facebook communities are smaller than we might imagine. The individual Facebook user has approximately a hundred "friends"—a tiny public—and these friends tend to be linked. Twitter users have a smaller network: each active user (someone who has tweeted in the past month) has sixty-one followers, despite the attempts by the company to expand the size of networks. In contrast to Facebook, these Tweeters are less likely to follow each other, but they have traits in common. If a user tweets, a small group may respond or retweet. Although some blog-based protests begin with temporary communities with thin interpersonal connections but common values, through the online network dispersion of information, shared identification often emerges (Courpasson and Dany 2013). Activation through social media does not develop immediately, but because small nodes link with other small nodes, a larger network is possible. When many nodes are activated simultaneously, a collection of tiny publics can appear to be a mass movement when viewed from above, even if the network involves separate groupings of friends, only coalescing for an engaging occasion. Given the diffuse structure, the challenge is to create identification from those whose commitment is local.

Extended Worlds

What kinds of networked social communities exist beyond the boundary of the small group, while still supported by interaction orders? To what extent do people know each other, to what extent do they respond to each other, and to what extent do they identify with a bounded public? Can we plausibly speak of these extended worlds of identity as tiny publics? I believe that these structures matter, although these are to be differentiated from face-to-face communities.

Most extended domains—and, in particular, online communities—are organized so that centralized control is difficult. The normative order, often facilitated through social relations, depends on the salience of identification. As a result, crucial forces that keep disruption in check and that keep relations smooth are absent, leading to the possibility of ruptures. Participants can more readily distance themselves from embracing proposed values when they perceive others as strangers. This is particularly applicable in online communication in which participants in a digital culture may be anonymous, hidden by a handle or an avatar. Everyone is wearing masks.

To describe group cultures and their extensions, I examine three cases. I begin with activist and terrorist cells and their integration into political networks. While violent attacks and democratic engagement are distinct, and terrorism is treated as an attack on civil society, both activists and terrorists rely on tight-knit groups, extended networks, and provocation. I compare John Brown's group that attacked Harpers Ferry (Fine 1999) and radical Islamist terrorist groups (Sageman 2008; Horgan 2014) with civic political activist groups in postauthoritarian Brazil (Mische 2008).

Perhaps the social movement that best captures the spirit of the age of social extensions is that which motivated the Arab Spring, particularly as centered in Cairo in 2011. This second case involves the mass movement that was driven by a combination of local groups as extended through social media. As Hatem Hassan (2015) points out, informal small groups—Popular Committees—protected local communities, streets, or even housing blocks during the crisis, particularly as residents feared that outsiders might attack or cause disruption. Even though the totality of these groups was fragmented, individual groups built social relationships and rules of informal action. They created standards for local performances and, as they linked with other groups, they engaged in extension work. The committees were established as friends arrived to play cards, chess, soccer, video games, or smoke hookah, drink tea, joke, or gossip, but they often overlapped with neighboring or nearby groups.

For actors to be considered a movement, rather than a network of thinly linked local groups, coordination is required. Their performances needed to share a cultural logic in which participants could simultaneously feel that they were part of a small group and a larger community. These popular committees must connect to other forms of social activism to extend beyond the locality. They do so to the extent that their performances of allegiance are similar, recognizable, and sharable. Access to cell phones and computers contributed to producing large-scale activism. As Asaf Bayat emphasizes, the activism depended on local relations, but relations that were understood as characteristic of those in a large community. Crowds and gatherings were not composed of anonymous strangers but of friendship groups, neighborhood acquaintances, and informal contacts whose behaviors—performances of shared identity—were readily identifiable. This allowed for the creation of extended networks (Leenders 2012). What appears to be an undifferentiated mass is actually a granulated gathering of knots of acquaintances. Arab Spring, as detailed by Bayat (2013) and Castells (2012), demonstrates the intersection of the local and the digital in the creation of mass movements.

This leads to the third case: online activism or what has been termed the "Netroots movement" (Kerbel 2009). While the goal is rarely to organize a demonstration, online political discourse provides a means by which citizen activists participate in political discourse. This occurs within a social world, not in isolation. Communities can be portable (Chayko 2008). Groups even arrange conclaves in which personal friendships enhance online connections. This is a crucial feature of many extended social worlds. The realm of online relations may be thin, but thicker meet-ups exist. This permits these gatherings to have some features of wispy communities in which intense face-to-face interaction is occasional, while less intimate communication continues over time (Fine and Van den Scott 2011).

NETWORKS OF ACTION AND TERROR

If any political group underlines the potency of small groups in politics, it surely is the terrorist cell. Because they are so intensely private, perhaps we should not consider these cells as tiny *publics*. The intimacy and secrecy necessary to plan violent actions depend on a tight group culture. These groups remind us that, as described in chapter 3, the civic virtue of local action may also be civic vice. Groups bond, create a shared identity, plan, and train, but they also band against others. Even cells that belong to the same insurgent movement, such as those of the Front de libération du Québec, may develop substantially different cultures and hold to distinct models of "legitimate" revolutionary action (Reedy, Gastil, and Gabbay 2013: 600). Consequently, those tasked with counterterrorism must consider the contours of local cultures as they attempt to degrade group capacity, produce disruption, or moderate the commitment to violent action.

But a small group in isolation is rarely sufficient. For societal consequences, the group must belong to a network. Those who desire substantial change cannot simply rely on a few committed members; they must grow the movement, expanding their influence through the bodies that they gather. This is equally true for believers in the strategy of terror and participants in democratic contentious politics. The two approaches differ in many ways, including in the respect given to those who disagree. However, parallels exist. Terrorists, like activists, wish to shape the polity. They attempt to persuade, act strategically, and perform dramatically in ways that they hope will lead to a better society. While these claimants are often intolerant of other views and limit public debate, the commitment to local action, to discourse, and to "social betterment" is characteristic of all who participate in civic culture. In order to extend their reach and to encourage broad changes, the terrorist group typically bridges to or develops from a larger network of those with similar perspectives.

In like fashion, activist movements build on a network, and often the discussions of strategies are closed to those outside the inner circle, although such groups are more open than terrorist cells. These movements must determine how best to communicate with local activists as well as reaching a broader public. In democratic polities, activist networks recognize the political legitimacy of opponents (if not always their moral legitimacy) and attempt to engage opponents through talk or action.

In attempts to extend influence, the similarities between activists and terrorists are notable; both depend on local commitment and extended publicity. Of course, as targets of surveillance and by targeting opponents, terrorist groups have a different structure than activist groups, even if both aim to disrupt the status quo. A terrorist group operates as a secret society, whereas activists openly welcome an influx of members.

Activism, with its willingness to engage in contentious or disruptive politics, is discomforting to its opponents but is treated as democratic engagement, a commitment to voices of popular dissent. However, for both terrorists and activists, political action is simultaneously local and tied to wider networks.

Terrorist cells typically demand that participants hide their allegiance. This structure makes the group boundary salient. Much discussion of terrorism focuses on its secretiveness: a serpent with hidden fangs and a long tail. Whether the metaphor is accurate, this image is frightening. Yet even terrorists—whether found in cells of a larger organization or lone-wolf knots of friends—depend on a group context. John Horgan (2014) presents a model of radical Islamicist terrorism that suggests that violence arises not from a deep ideological commitment but from local social relations that are extended into a broader network. This does not suggest that beliefs, ideology, or personality are irrelevant but rather that their effects occur within the context of a cadre: a web of connected cells. However, maintaining a disciplined organization under conditions of surveillance, disruption, and battle is challenging, as the decline of the ISIS caliphate makes clear. As long threads exist, examining terrorism networks only through a mesolevel analysis in which local relations generate the conditions that are truly global is misleading. However, ignoring these local relations is inadequate as well. In global terror, making the interaction order central may seem odd, yet deciding to put one's life on the line is a rare choice that must be highly motivated. As Randall Collins (2008) argues, a commitment to violence depends on a commitment to sociality. Friends and social relations produce terrorist engagements and then provide the support through which such connections continue, ignoring values that are more pacific.

I draw on the literature on contemporary terrorism that emphasizes the salience of group dynamics, especially the approach of security expert John Horgan and psychiatrist Marc Sageman. Both propose what Sageman (2008: 23) describes as a "middle-range analysis" that examines processes of interaction. As Horgan (2014: 11) writes, "Most terrorist movements are relatively small, (semi-) clandestine collectives." Like the fraternal associations described in chapter 3, intense political groups are "brotherhoods." Horgan advocates a group dynamics approach, emphasizing a sequence of involvement, engagement, and disengagement.

While the group dynamics model as postulated by Horgan characterizes contemporary terrorism, it also applies to terrorism prior to the internet, as it describes the intersection of a group and a more expansive community. Recruitment by friends in a relational network is crucial to group growth. This is particularly effective in recruiting those whose networks are not extensive. Considering young Moroccan men, Andrea Elliott (2007) finds that jihadis "are more likely to radicalize together with others who share the same passions and affiliations and daily routines." Listening to movement songs or videos in a group context can be a powerful inducement (Bartlett and Miller 2012). Sageman (2008: 66) notes,

> About two-thirds of the people in the sample [of known terrorists] were friends with other people who joined together or already had some connection to terrorism. [One pathway is] a "bunch of guys" who collectively decided to join a terrorist organization. This was a collective decision, not an individual one. A second common pathway was that of joining childhood friends.

As Horgan (2012: 91) suggests, immersion has an allure. Radical Islam is a social club from the start.

In some instances, no preexisting connections exist. The group is the site of socialization. Sageman (2008: 8–11) describes Ahmed Omar Saeed Sheikh, convicted of beheading Daniel Pearl, a *Wall Street Journal* reporter. Sheikh's life, as described by Sageman, reveals that other individuals and the groups to which he belonged led him to jihad. Rather than coming to these social encounters with clear beliefs, the local culture shaped them. Sageman (2008: 7–9) writes,

> While recuperating in Split [Croatia], Omar met Abdur Rauf, a Pakistani veteran of the war in Afghanistan.... Rauf belonged to the Harakut-ul Mujahedin, one of the many small Islamic guerilla groups that proliferated in Pakistan and Afghanistan.... Omar arrived in Lahore "with zeal and intention to undergo arms training and joining the mujahedin," according to his diary. He shopped around for the best group for his need. The diary continued, "Decide HUM best option. Leave for Afghanistan via Islamabad." In August 1993, he arrived at the Khalid bin Waleed training camp, which was associated with al Qaeda but used by many of the myriad Islamist guerrilla groups.... Back in London, Omar started martial arts classes for a group of Muslims and tried to interest his old friends and classmates in joining the jihad.

While many details are specific to Sheikh's story, the power of communal influence transforms him from a student at the London School of Economics to a terrorist stalwart. Sheikh did not join with friends, but his commitment to community made commitment to radical ideas possible. Groups are not inevitably effective, as most participants drop out, sometimes affiliating with less militant associations. However, without group participation, Sheikh would have had a different life. While not dismissing ideology and shared images of oppression, the group dynamics approach treats ideology as an effect of social relations, rather than as its cause (Horgan 2014; Munson 2008).

Although emphasizing group culture is valuable, this approach can separate terrorists from the larger environment. Here media are influential. Terrorists act in a world of hot images and cool narratives, accessed through magazines, television, chatrooms, and word-of-mouth. An injustice frame solidifies collective passion, providing a basis by which groups connect. Even "isolated" groups require a mediated environment, a space of shared stories and beliefs.

While the internet is a ready means of connection, bolstering and occasionally replacing face-to-face affiliation, radical networks existed prior to online communication and modern techniques of surveillance. These included anarchist and anticolonialist groups. Consider the case of John Brown and his band (Oates 1984; Finkelstein 1995). Brown, a militant abolitionist, was the first American executed for treason.[1] In 1859 Brown gathered two dozen men to attack the federal arsenal at Harpers Ferry, Virginia (now West Virginia). This militancy mirrored his battles against Southern sympathizers in "Bleeding Kansas" in 1856. In the Harpers Ferry attack and its aftermath, ten of Brown's supporters and five federal troops were killed. Whether Brown wished to provoke insurrection among Southern slaves is unclear, but he recognized that public attention required relying on his abolitionist network. After the attack, abolitionists, including Brown himself, described the action as heroic, hoping to inspire further militancy. He swayed female supporters with "romantic abolitionism" and inspired male supporters with the "heroism of violence." Accounts of Brown's militant action spread rapidly, based on powerful narratives that built commitment. The original shock of the assault on federal troops was justified, aided by accounts by New England intellectuals, friends of Henry David Thoreau, and abolitionists allied with William Lloyd Garrison (Fine 1999: 232). The magazines and newspapers of the period, coupled with meetings, religious services, and lectures, would now parallel an internet chatroom.

A local culture requires moral legitimation by which groups justify themselves as they recruit. While each historical moment is unique, similarities exist between John Brown's band and today's terrorist cells, whether Islamicist, Irish Republican, or White Nationalist. A belief in the justice—and the heroism—of violent action builds a network. However, narratives are not sufficient; a supportive social climate must activate the audience, whether in school, prison, mosque, or online. Each challenges individuals to commit, recognizing the existence of similar others. Because of their immediacy and global scope, internet chatrooms provide opportunities for this allegiance. While Sageman (2008: 123) suggests that because of the internet, Islamicist terrorism will not die, the reason is that narrative accounts generate benefits equivalent to an intense sociality. If those vanish, terrorism might lapse, no longer being "where the action is." Back to hookah parlors or online gaming.

With some exceptions, the same is true of activist movements. Here participants accept the boundaries of legitimate political protest and the possibility of defeat. The challenge, as Ann Mische depicts it in her examination of Brazilian youth politics in the 1990s, is that multiple groups (in her case, those on the left) compete for the same potential followers. Each group must create a culture and a style of action and each must find a movement niche. To create a "partisan public" (Mische 2008: 20), a movement recruits from a broad population to gain sufficient adherents. Groups network and negotiate with others within their intersecting political worlds, differentiating themselves through style and the recognition of political boundaries. These idiocultures "entail distinguishable cultural practices that identify members, help them build relationships, establish boundaries with outsiders, and give meaning and orientation to actions" (Mische 2008: 38). While internal cultures generate commitment, so do connections among groups with their cultures and extensions. Mische (2008: 48) emphasizes that actions at group intersections are particularly crucial as "actors located at the intersection of multiple groups have unique opportunities for building publics, which often require them to mediate between diverse identities and interests." These are boundary-spanners, engaged as brokers among competing communities. Those able to inspire cooperation among tiny publics are crucial to the mesolevel construction of political action. For any activist group to have broad effect, it must create a culture in which relations create intense commitment, rely on preexisting images, and build a broader network.

TAHRIR IN THE AIR

Increasingly we reside in a bubble of social media; many spend hours perusing a variety of sites that constitute our networks, even if we are not personally aware of the others who share our cyberspace. This poses a challenge for those who emphasize the power of face-to-face communication. What, if anything, does social media reveal about the significance of groups in society? Both much and little. Online communication reduces the cost of reaching others, permitting one to be embedded in widely spread networks. Sometimes the allegiance to a community is thin, and norms of civility are at risk. I can participate in a chatroom without long-term commitment. When we speak of a message or video "going viral," we refer to this form of thin communication. Online discursive spaces lack the stickiness of embodied places and we may dart in and out of these sites.

In contrast, some online domains, whether formally open or limited, have the feel of a small group. Over time, participants know each other by their words, emojis, and avatars. The chatroom, discussion board, and email Listserv have characteristics of the small group, and individuals may choose to meet in physical space.

In examining social media as an extension of local civic action, we integrate the intimacy of groups with that of anonymous public spaces. The question is how does social media or online communication organize social gatherings? In a fundamental way, this is not a new problem. Mobs, crowds, and demonstrations have long used those media that were available, whether gossip networks, pamphlets, town criers, church bulletins, radio announcements, graffiti, telephone calls, or mobile loudspeakers. Social media is a recent form of those types of communication that have been available to the politically active. Yet the speed and ease of communication transform engagement in that widespread information diffusion now occurs in real time.

Some particularly dramatic examples of how social media encourages protest within civil society were the demonstrations during the Arab Spring, focusing on Cairo's Tahrir Square. These events captured the world's attention, although several years later their impact was smaller than imagined at the time. Perhaps these gatherings were not so different from demonstrations in Beijing's Tiananmen Square twenty-two years previously, where college students were networked (although then without the aid of Facebook). Activists must energize followers, and the available technology can be central for this goal.

Asaf Bayat (2013: 15) begins his analysis with a paradox; he speaks of "social nonmovements," referring to "the collective action of non-collective actors who embody shared practices of large numbers of ordinary people whose fragmented but similar activities trigger social change, even if not guided by ideology or recognizable leadership and organization." This account of nonmovements in a world of social media refers to how groups gather without a consensual hierarchy of leaders. If microgroups are present at the start, the commitment of participants gives them power in the absence of an established structure. However, for a movement to grow, tiny publics are insufficient. How does coordination occur when large numbers must be organized?

The remarkable achievement of the protests in Tahrir Square—the April 6th Youth Movement—was to bind disparate groups together in common cause, despite all of their differences. According to Bayat (2013: 24), the movement linked some seventy thousand young people, largely through internet communication. In turn, these demonstrations leveraged other groups and networks. Many groups formed in private spaces, subsequently reaching out through online communication. The movement was sparked by a vlog by a young activist, Asmaa Mafhouz, who called for a mass gathering on Tahrir Square on January 25, 2011, to protest rising food prices and government oppression. Activists labeled it "the vlog that helped spark the revolution." As Manuel Castells (2012: 55–56, 59) writes,

> From Internet networks, the call to action spread through the social networks of friends, family and associations of all kinds. The networks connected not only to individuals but also to each individual's networks. Particularly important were the fan networks of soccer teams, mainly al-Ahly as well as its rival Zamolek Sporting, who had a long history of battling the police…. Thus, Internet networks, mobile networks, pre-existing social networks, street demonstrations, occupations of public squares and Friday gatherings around the mosques all contributed to the spontaneous, largely leaderless, multimodal networks that enacted the Egyptian revolution. The role of pre-existing offline social networks was also important, as they helped facilitate the canvassing of pamphlets in the digitally excluded slum, and the traditional forms of social and political gatherings in the mosques after the Friday prayers. This multimodality of autonomous communication broke the barriers of isolation and made it possible to overcome fear by the act of joining and sharing.

Networks built on networks, creating a communications meganetwork that depended on widespread, and sometimes anonymous, communication, as well as face-to-face commitments. Here was a movement that was composed of the Muslim Brotherhood and other Islamicists, of the impoverished and dispossessed, of young secularists with ties to the West, and of Coptic Christian communities. Each had grievances with the Mubarak regime; their vast differences were shelved during the protest (but reemerged later). What is crucial is that these groups stood outside the control of formal organizations and political parties (Castells 2012: 4). This does not mean that formal organizations did not strive to control the movement; after the immediacy of the events, they succeeded in doing so. This was the case with the Muslim Brotherhood, which attempted to capture the movement, using the protests as a basis of their original electoral triumph. In the United States, Tea Party activism presents a similar case. The movement had great authority while it was locally based and informally networked, but when it was captured by large-scale organizations such as FreedomWorks, with their considerable resources and organizing expertise, energy dissipated. Both cases suggest that networks of friends and associates take priority during moments of activism. When local groups lose control, the movement is at risk. This is the dilemma of folding tiny publics into mass organizations.

In Cairo, the vast Tahrir Square quickly filled with individuals, friendship groups, and small assemblies mobilized through their networks, now taking on new roles and trading apathy for activism. To watch the huge gatherings of millions over those few days was stirring, appearing to be a spontaneous mass outpouring, even if it was a conclave of groups. While social media were once limited to the young, tech-savvy, and well educated, eventually diverse citizens have joined cybernetworks. As of 2010, 80 percent of Egyptians had cell phones and 25 percent were connected to the internet. By 2011, five million users were on the Arabic edition of Facebook. Twitter and texting were common. The number of users of all kinds of social media has exploded. Mobile phones, with their immediacy and their ability to send text messages and other forms of online access, allow for speed to replace accuracy. Given that much information has not been validated, rumor is central (Shibutani 1966; Fine and Turner 2001).

Rapid communication makes national or even global activism possible in real time, linking local connections to mass engagement. This was exemplified in the Occupy movement, where personal connections undergirded anonymous relations. Intense moments of historical change reveal how social movements build on close relationships and on anonymous connections through what Castells (1996) labels the "network society."

NETROOTS AS NEW POLITICS

American political discourse has shifted over the past quarter-century, reflecting the flowering of platforms for political writers and the increased diversity of civic perspectives. Podcasts permit everyone to be a star, or at least potentially so. However, the question is whether these new venues of communication are populated by isolated individuals hunched over their computers in bedrooms or basements, or whether their connections to interactional orders allow for new possibilities of engagement. When one examines evolving changes in technological systems before the changes have stabilized into a recognized system of norms, rights, and responsibilities, one must write with a large eraser or rapid delete key.

A widely used buzzword is "Netroots," mirroring the idea of grassroots progressivism, that first came to public attention with the 2004 insurgent, but ultimately unsuccessful, presidential campaign of Vermont governor Howard Dean. Dean attracted a coterie of young supporters who had familiarity with internet communication. Early on, many net activists were progressive Democrats, and their most impressive electoral triumph was the 2008 presidential campaign of Barack Obama. The political scientist Matthew Kerbel (2009), in describing the Netroots movement, writes about politics at this exhilarating moment, suggesting that liberal activists have an advantage over conservatives but also that the progressive politics of the activists were hostile to the traditional Democratic establishment. The results of the 2010, 2014, and 2016 elections, and the incorporation of progressives into the Democratic Party, might provide pause. Today a vibrant and influential conservative blogosphere exists, whatever label it is given. In addition, considerable concern is directed at foreign trolls, especially Russians, who attempt to affect American politics.

My concern is less about the content of Netroots activism but about the establishment of communities that privilege the local scribe. How does the mesolevel of analysis fit into online politics? Does an online community exist? For Mary Chayko (2008: 6–8), these can be conceptualized as portable communities. Kerbel emphasizes the networking of networks, as friendship ties of one participant may extend the friendship ties of others. Likewise boyd (2014) stresses the role of "networked publics" in the creation of adolescent subcultures through the readership of blogs and other online texts, sharing ideas without sharing physical space, combining a writer's desires with a broadcast audience. Mass diffusion (an anonymous audience) merges with a sense of community (an engaged audience). The establishment of community is bidirectional. First, networks are linked through personal relationships, and this contributes to a sense of belonging, comfort, and companionship (Chayko 2008: 114). However, people also search out those communities whose ideas mirror their own identity and ideology. As a result, Facebook and other media platforms permit—even encourage—users to define who should be in their online community, while using this networking to attract advertisers. These connections, however they might be utilized by corporations, have the potential to lead to direct political action but may also include a variety of less intense civic engagements, such as volunteering, social movement support, or community service.

Communities of commitment can on occasion be passionate. Markos Moulitsas emphasizes, for example, that the Daily Kos website constituted a deeply engaged social world:

> We are a community. We celebrate our successes. Like the two marriages that have emerged from the Daily Kos community.... And you've shared your happy moments as well as with your pictures. Of your babies. And your cats. We also grieve together.... Without my planning or prodding, you started organizing. You started talking to each other and deciding, on your own, to take charge of your politics.... But it wasn't just talking. (Kos 2007)

The death of a prominent blogger, even one whose personal qualities are unknown, promotes an outpouring of grief (Kerbel 2009: 114). While Netroots sites begin as virtual communities, they do not end there. As Kerbel (2009: 10) writes:

> Those who choose to stay [in a blogging community] feel a sense of belonging that suggests the virtual community pays emotional benefits similar to real-world interpersonal engagement.... And at times when online associates have had the opportunity to meet in person, by their own report they were supportive and respectful in a way more suggestive of friends reacquainting than strangers meeting for the first time. This points to the progressive blogosphere as a source of social capital for those who invest in online activism, despite the fact that much of the time they are alone in front of a computer screen.

The assumption is that their purpose transcends physical isolation, but also that at ritual moments, such as at Netroots Nation gatherings, their virtual commitment can evolve into physical connections.

Meet-up groups allow us to recognize that online community can create an offline beachhead, perhaps becoming more solidified. A dramatic example of how a ritual gathering becomes a romantic origin story of the founding of community is evident in this account of an early Netroots meeting by a participant at the Yearly Kos meeting. "Gina" emphasizes the cooperation and fellowship of a group that once was composed of strangers but became intimates. In the details that she presents, Gina captures the power of face-to-face group culture as transformed from online culture:

> I said in my closing remarks Saturday evening that this convention was built on a foundation of trust. Markos set it out when he first created the structure of our community where we riff raff are trusted to create our own content and manage our own community. In return, the community trusted us by investing and showing up. And speaking of trust ... now that Hyperbolic Pants Explosion's camera has been returned, nothing at this convention was stolen.... But once again an example of who we are and what we can expect even on the smallest of levels. (Gina 2006)

In Gina's view, the gathering of over a thousand participants generated a culture and set of stories that could then reflexively shape the community online, although with the assumption that those who met face-to-face had a deeper connection from additional visual and auditory knowledge. (As is said, "on the internet nobody knows that you are a dog.") Gina's account shows how the broader community can have a virtual quality, while maintaining an inner circle.

Whether one relies on physical or virtual knowledge, community creates intimacy. While self-selection and recommendations from associates determine who will visit which website, a tight-knit world can emerge as bloggers define themselves as a community (Kerbel 2009: 117). Pungent debates occur with the sense that community matters. If a person, typically an outsider, is deliberatively provocative, desiring to undercut the community (a "troll"), exclusion—literally excommunication—may be required. Further, hierarchies among virtual participants mirror hierarchies in nonvirtual communities. As one casual member points out, "Virtual community is pretty good among the top bloggers, but less so for those further down the pecking order" (Kerbel 2009: 117). In other words, dynamics of inclusion and exclusion by means of social capital, hierarchy, and common belief occur both online and offline.

Ultimately, this reflects similarities and tensions between a community of the air and one on the ground. Both are forms of mesocommunity, but the ability to extend community is greater if one is not limited by the demands and constraints of spatial proximity.

The Extended World

Focusing on small groups to the exclusion of larger communities is misleading. Small groups, while always present, are often tied to large networks and institutions that can access more resources. Although expansive institutions depend on groups to mobilize actors, these organizations have power because people and their tiny publics agree that these larger entities matter. The availability of resources makes these beliefs plausible. While authoritarian governments require committees, departments, and boards, for local communities, elites are rarely seen and government is typically present in the form of police, bureaucratic offices, and other street-level agents. This is true even in societies in which the state hopes to be protective, not oppressive.

Given that the world can be a divided and contentious place, those who engage in extension work, moving local concerns into a broader civic sphere, are challenged. Alliances and networks must be developed and shaped; boundaries with contending groups must be considered. The content and logics of cultural images must be presented to appeal to a wider network, and this can occur as members of one group perform in displays to which other groups are audiences. New forms of online communication aid this process of extension, as open and expansive discursive places can allow participants to transcend local spaces.

Media could not exist without groups to produce and distribute content, but, in contrast to face-to-face community, their distribution often reaches large numbers of viewers and listeners simultaneously. Not all of these audiences are groups, as individuals may consume media in isolation, but media reports are often notable narratives that are legitimate topics of local discussion. Whether the audience is composed of individuals or groups, media create collective memory. However wide the network, it establishes shared awareness for tiny publics.

In examining change in civil society, I emphasize the potency of political actors, but I also emphasize the limits of attempts to provoke change. In many ways, terrorist organizations mirror other activist groups. In each case, the local group confronts a broader collectivity that itself is ultimately comprised of and dependent on local groups. Mass action is not possible without the commitments of participants to shared goals over which they do not have full control. This is how a mesolevel analysis contributes to the sweep of history. The arc of social order operates through the intersection of groups. Local scenes when viewed together and at a distance are society writ large.

Conclusion

CIRCUITS OF ACTION

A nation can be maintained only if, between the state and the individual, there is intercalated a whole series of secondary groups near enough to the individuals to attract them strongly in their spheres of action and drag them in this way into the general torrent of social life.

ÉMILE DURKHEIM, *The Division of Labor in Society*

Throughout this volume, I have argued that local action serves as the hinge that connects persons and institutions. As a hinge, the mesolevel is a semiautonomous realm that links these other levels of analysis. Of course, this perspective must not deny the significance of either the micro or the macro, but it suggests that the two are inextricably related in that both persons and societal structures depend on group action. To this end, I weave threads of scholarship from sociology and beyond to claim that civic action depends on local engagements. I am not the first to argue that groups and interactions matter in public engagement, but I hope that this detailed treatment builds a compelling case that tiny publics are as significant as are persons and structures. A robust, comprehensive sociology depends on the joining of the personal, the institutional, and the local.

Focusing on the mesolevel edges us closer to recognizing how individuals align with political systems through participation in communal sites. Mass publics are inevitably built on the amalgamation of tiny ones. While media representations, institutional constraints, and state power are real, each depends on group organization and, in turn, groups respond to these macrosystems.

The public sphere is a realm of local action. Lacking this recognition, the linkage of individual and state is underspecified. While researchers properly analyze the creation of affiliative communities from a macroperspective, ignoring the granular conditions of communal participation leaves such analysis insufficient. Civic attachment is felt through families, classrooms, workplaces, clubs, social movements, union locals, and political campaigns. The presence of like-minded others creates collective representations and shared engagements on which institutions depend. Affiliating with a political system is not merely an idea but involves identity and action. A theory of political commitment is tethered to social psychology.

I have organized this project by means of two intersecting structures. Each of the seven substantive chapters examines a concept that is central to civil society and that depends on local action: coordination, relations, associations, places, conflict, control, and extensions. In this conclusion, I briefly recap the importance of each.

However, beyond these concepts—or perhaps above them—I rely on four themes that when integrated constitute my argument that the mesolevel is the hinge between the micro and the macro. These themes appear in each of the chapters, linking my approach to civil society and political engagement with cultural sociology, interactionism, and an action-based sociology. As explained in the introduction, I use the interaction order, group culture (idioculture), circuits of action, and tiny publics as the basis of a mesolevel analysis of the civic. I hope to develop a local sociology through the lenses of joint action, culture, routines, and politics.

Themes of the Hinge

INTERACTION ORDER

I start with interaction: people doing things together in light of surrounding structural conditions. Interaction must be orderly. Of the many concepts developed by Erving Goffman (1983), the interaction order may be the most fruitful in permitting an integrated sociology. In his final statement—his coda—Goffman argued that interaction provides the basis for structures, just as it is shaped by those structures. Perhaps there was something Bourdieusian in his attempt to emphasize the ongoing significance of understood practices. This should not be surprising as Goffman was heavily influenced by Émile Durkheim's emphasis on the shared cultural representations of secondary groups. Within Goffman's analysis is the claim that interactional practices constitute a field of meaning and of actors, tied to identification and social relations. The concept of the interaction order recognizes that interaction is not freely constructed at each moment, but that it depends on the expectations and constraints that characterize social systems.

I take this claim to heart. The interaction order demonstrates that public engagement depends on tacit proprieties. Behavior is not free-floating and newly minted but is channeled. This does not suggest that impression management is tangential but rather that some choices have costs, tied to the likely response of others. On occasion, the costs may be onerous.

While the interaction order presents opportunities for coordination, it also provides limits. Any sociology of the mesolevel and any analysis of civic participation must begin and must end with people acting in concert in light of perceived encouragements and barriers.

GROUP CULTURE

Together with interaction, shared meaning is a defining feature of mesolevel analysis. As a social psychologist who has examined culture from the start of my career (Fine 1979), I have emphasized what I have termed "idioculture" or group culture. Shared culture cements people by revealing a common past and an ongoing, referential process. Interaction is never sufficient but is found in webs of interpretation and is perceived as stable. These meanings are not personally held but instead emerge through social relations and internal group dynamics. As relations continue, the group culture expands as experiences grow by accretion. To gain power, group cultures must be understood and referenced by those in the local community. Borrowing from Marx, we might imagine the interaction order as providing the base microstructure of material life and the idioculture as constituting the cultural superstructure. Both are necessary for a social psychology of culture.

If one argues, as I do, that groups constitute the fundamental foundation of social order, this happens because participants treat those groups as having meaning that leads to identity formation and provides a model of how society should be organized. When groups differ, participants need to integrate multiple sets of rules, acting in light of the context. For collective identity—essential to long-term commitment—participants must share ideas, beliefs, customs, and rituals and recognize this sharing. How could an association be resilient without a common core?

CIRCUITS OF ACTION

By linking interaction and culture, I address how the recognition of common practices contributes to group belonging. Awareness supports stability. These connections between expected routines and group engagement constitute what I term circuits of action. By their presence, their recognition, and their acceptance, understood practices build group cohesion. I reject the idea that behaviors are scripted or tightly organized, but shared expectations support patterns of civic engagement. These practices are embedded within group culture. Each routine makes the performance of subsequent routines more likely. In other words, traditional behaviors define the group through routine, custom, and a normative order. Without circuits of action, interaction orders must be continually built anew.

TINY PUBLICS

The fourth theme is that of tiny publics, perhaps the most significant in light of civil society. Here I focus on civic engagement as defined broadly, eschewing a narrow politics while emphasizing broader communal participation. There are many interaction orders, many group cultures, and many circuits of action. These provide the basis of tiny publics. However, tiny publics are not mere conclaves of individuals. In contrast, they are communities that respond to the broad political sphere. Tiny publics *constitute a public*: a committed node of participants who see themselves as belonging together and believe that they are working in common cause toward social betterment. This is true even if, as often occurs, people belong to several tiny publics simultaneously. Tiny publics are not merely groups but communities. Put another way, these groups have a face that looks outward and are situated so that other groups are aware of their presence. Publics are distinct from what we might label as privates. Whether they desire to promote or to retard change and whether they are democratic or authoritarian, tiny publics are integral to any political order.

AN INTEGRATION

While each of these themes is valuable in itself, my argument depends on integrating all four. The mesosociological approach depends on treating interactional regularities as central to understanding how people collaborate in a variety of projects. Unlike scholars who see society as arising from structures in which individual agency is marginalized, my approach makes central the choices of how to act with others. Only in this way is coordination possible; only in this way can social relations be fostered.

However, as I have argued, interaction orders must be grounded in a set of appreciated meanings. These shared understandings—this culture—are based in the group. In other words, meaning is locally constructed. These insights are not merely individual preferences but develop from the groups in which actors participate. That a person often belongs to many groups simultaneously (and sequentially) makes embracing local traditions a question of negotiation. Every approach that is grounded in a social psychology must engage with both interaction and culture.

The third major theme—that of circuits of action—provides the stability that every social system requires. Groups share experiences, and these experiences, when recalled as identity markers, constitute the collective memory of the group. This permits the knitting together of a community's past, present, and ultimately its future. As related to interaction, this constitutes those circuits of action that are meaningful routines or understood practices. Choices of interaction are not created anew at each moment, but expectations provide guide rails and traditions create confidence in the responses of others.

To make this model relevant to civic engagement, I focus on groups that I term tiny publics. Interaction orders, group cultures, and circuits of action exist even in groups that are not outward-looking or concerned about the welfare of the community. A public has the feature of being civic in orientation, and a tiny public provides the recognition that there are features of small-scale communities—local domains—that permit shared commitment and common identity.

The model that I propose must be expanded and refined. No theory can rely on a single perspective. However, if we hope to take a meso-sociological analysis of civil society seriously, this a place to begin.

Building Blocks of the Hinge

COORDINATION

If the world were comprised of hermits, we would not adjust our actions in light of the desires of others. Civic action would consist of not interfering: a libertarian romance. Coordination would be unnecessary. We would act without interacting. However, this image of a world filled with hermits has little value in a civil society where shared identities are crucial. In contrast, were we to be sheep, our bleats would be identical. If our task were dutifully to follow demands over which we have no control, we would not rely on collaborations or negotiations. In contrast to a politics focused on the individual, on the mass, or on the state, the mesolevel emphasizes communal choices. Civic worlds are inhabited. Coordination is the basis through which attachment produces a joint political project.

Consider the challenge of "neighborliness." When do people feel obliged to aid each other? When do expectations of support exist without an overarching and sanctioned system of coordination, such as what an organization or state might provide? This is Robert Ellickson's (1991) focus in *Order Without Law*. A formal system of law produces some forms of coordination, but the most effective social systems are self-organizing. Farmers are a prime example because their spatial distance from centers of bureaucratic surveillance encourages informal systems of aid. These help networks may emerge temporarily without many defined structures, as when someone helps another who drops a package or slides on a patch of ice, but I focus on cases in which the system of mutual aid is recognized and is integrated into local culture.

We also find coordination in solving common problems. Here the parties have what Muzafer Sherif and his colleagues (1961) term superordinate goals. To achieve a desired end, people work together even if they must transcend previous conflicts. A case in point is what Danielle Allen (2014) describes as "democratic writing." We need not refer to such a dramatic historic case as the creation of the Declaration of Independence to recognize that collaboration to achieve civic goals is a virtue. Even without a formal association, citizens jointly determine how best to use their skills to contribute to the commonweal. A model of a good society rarely emerges from the mind of an individual. Even revered figures, such as Martin Luther King Jr., Mahatma Gandhi, or Nelson Mandela, required a collaborative team, as in the case of Abraham Lincoln's "team of rivals." These may be central figures, but they are also front men.

Perhaps the most dramatic example of the art—and the limit—of collaboration is self-governance of the commons. Can a community limit shared resources? The fact that, over time, governance proved difficult has been called the tragedy of the commons. It emphasizes the challenge of self-governance without external control. However, the reality was that for centuries, villages maintained order so that meadows were not overgrazed by cows and sheep, preventing community members from maximizing their own personal benefits. Whether a tragedy or a romance, the commons, long-studied by historians, economists, political scientists, and sociologists, demonstrates that coordination is a political project, constrained by both external and internal forces that might disrupt it. Whatever the form of civil society, willing collaboration within a local culture is crucial for ongoing relations and for laying the groundwork for a democratic and respectful polity.

RELATIONS

Whether described as social capital, favor banks, or simple friendship, relations within a community are profoundly consequential for civic culture. Personal affiliations may matter as much as blood ties in stabilizing social order. Although a tradition exists of distinguishing primary relations from secondary ones, dividing intimates from acquaintances, and strong from weak ties, the divisions may obscure as much as they illuminate.

Relations are crucial to establishing influence. The assumption is that the wider and deeper a friendship net, the more advantaged one will be, although such advantages depend on whether we focus on those with many ties or those with the most committed ties. The person with horizontal connections, whose relations permit a wide reach, has advantages in connecting with those who have extensive resources. In contrast, an individual with deep, vertical ties creates a group of associates who serve as guides and protectors.

In democratic theory from Aristotle on, many suggest that friendships are the basis of democratic participation. Perhaps it is not what exchange with friends can provide but rather that the presence of friends allows one to affiliate confidently within a wide social system. Friendship is a backdrop for a public sphere. Put another way, firm friendships limit suspicion and cynicism.

My examples describe different sociable publics: an impoverished community, a middle-class friendship culture, and an elite group of political influencers. Notable are the similarities among these social worlds and how they each provide mutual support. Whether what is traded is childcare in the impoverished community, sociability for discussing national politics among middle-class retirees, or access to power by those with extensive networks and influence, relationships are the basis for empowerment and for belonging to a caring community. Friendship and its markers of loyalty, reciprocity, and affect create a hinge between persons and institutions that sustains civil society.

ASSOCIATION

Associations solidify social relations. These are groups that political theorists treat as characteristic of modern democracies in general and of American society in particular, although, of course, they are also found outside of democracies (Riley 2010). In the public sphere, such groups establish a space separate from the power of the state and assert that some forms of political activity stand outside state control. While we might conceive of democracy as the ability of the individual to claim rights, I argue that an association of citizens claims those rights. Individual citizens have constrained authority and limited ability to speak. A civil society results from tiny publics presenting visions of the proper goals and legitimate reach of government.

In addressing how citizens confront the state, we often consider social movements. As Kathleen Blee (2012) notes, in any sizable community many such groups exist, each with an agenda, each with a meaningful group culture, each with action preferences, and each with a public persona. Effecting social change is difficult; each organization must determine how to retain members as well as which claims will extend their influence with their audience. As Blee emphasizes, many movement organizations collapse and others fail to achieve their objectives. Still, they may produce a welcoming discursive space.

Not all associations connect citizens with direct political activity. Volunteering does not necessarily imply a commitment to act in support of change. In the case of volunteer groups concerned with drug use, members drew a bright line between a desire to improve their community and the desire to engage in policy debates. While some might label this apathy, a commitment to apathy serves civic purposes as it supports the standing forms of political process. To contribute to a community does not mean that every association must participate in contentious politics.

Further, the existence of associations does not presume that associations serve all equally. Not all associations have open membership; exclusive associations contribute to a mesolevel structure of political activity as well. These groups justify commitment for those allowed to join.

The presence of associations, whether political or civic, open or selective, reveals the power of local publics to address issues about which citizens care and on which they are motivated to act. Associations, claiming the right to speak for the governed, create a civic backing from which routinized interaction is possible.

PLACE

Collective action requires space to unfold. To the extent that politics involves public performance, it demands a stage (Edelman 1985). Recognizing the salience of locations in which mesopolitics is enacted underlines the importance of *acts* of citizenship. Politics is more than structural demands or private cognitions. No government, however totalitarian in its intent, can prevent private prayer, gossip, or whispers among intimates. There are many hidden arbors.

Tiny publics demand a locational, ecological politics. This expands the Bourdieusian argument, extending the concept of habitus by asserting that the construction of identity depends on the geography of fields of action. Bourdieu and other field theorists argue that it is through common sites that participants create collective action. Habitus generates a feedback loop of "meaningful practice and meaning-giving perceptions" (Bourdieu 1984: 166), but fields are places of action. One simultaneously judges oneself and others in light of one's surroundings and acts on this judgment.

Some spaces are open to all, while others are limited as associations establish access rules. In this way, the distinction between the coffeehouse and the salon is analytically important. Both institutions, founded during the emergence of the idea of civil society in the eighteenth century, helped birth a public sphere, a world of discussion apart from direct state control. However, they differed markedly in their politics of access. In a market economy, "third places" exist that are open to all with sufficient resources. Coffeehouses, the archetypal form of eighteenth-century English sociability, are such spaces. They encourage, but do not demand, commitment. At first, the political coffeehouse was a novelty, a place "where the action is," but, over time, the openness of the coffeehouse proved problematic. Presence was not inherently status-enhancing. In France the salon, a closed social space of discussion and debate, generated a spatial politics that lasted until the overthrow of elite culture.

While these examples reflect specific organizational characteristics, they also suggest a more general problem. How are spaces allocated to citizens? In the case of elite sites, salons or retreats like the Bohemian Grove, Davos, or Renaissance Weekends, the boundaries are well patrolled. Yet in other cases, such as the coffeehouse or the town meeting, the decision to attend depends on choices made by potential participants and their imagination of whom and what they might find. Spaces are, after all, not only sites where individuals might gather, but where individuals might meet others in ways that prove meaningful.

CONFLICT

A danger exists in conceiving social relations as inevitably harmonious and in asserting that desired interaction is placid: the more social relations, the more coordination, the more association, the better. To be sure, there is some truth to this claim. However, smooth interaction is not inevitable nor always desirable. A robust theory of civic life must incorporate the presence and the value of conflict. Contention is a hallmark of democratic governance.

Just as group culture can build interpersonal connections and social capital by assuming moral accord and social deference, it can also illuminate divisions within and between groups. Movements, while being associations, must stand for something. New values or policy changes typically follow from group demands. Although visionary or charismatic leaders may prove powerful advocates of change—encapsulating the group's self-image in the form of a charismatic persona—these heroes require a team to support their efforts in unsettling the status quo. As a result, conflict is built into mesolevel analysis. Over time, groups can expand and reach corners of the population that were not a part of the original circle of commitment. Groups may develop alliances, but they may also engage in rivalrous confrontation. As I have described, the Civil Rights movement provides a complex case. Even within an activist community, such as Freedom Summer, divisions existed, and each group was confronted by opposing groups, less open but no less committed.

While movements provide a model for dynamic change, conflict is not always embedded within discrete organizational forms. In political spaces and in institutional contexts, groups can find themselves in rivalrous contention. While particular groups may gain dominance, a possibility of reversal always exists.

Within organizations, the process of contestation is more complex, and some organizations teeter on the cusp of turmoil. These organizations often rely on external support, and conflict reflects the hope that organizational leaders can be persuaded to alter policies in the face of continuing pressure or in response to departures from the organization. Just as conflict does not always destroy the overall idea of democracy itself, so it can be a valuable feature of a group-based democracy. Local cultures may involve ongoing conflict and still maintain a commitment to community.

CONTROL

Conflict and control are intertwined: the yin and the yang of political systems. Challenges to the system may be met with challenges to the challenges. Forces of control are neither mysterious nor omniscient, but, like groups that desire change, they depend on an interaction order. No matter which group decides what will be treated as outside the boundary of propriety and legitimate contention, the process through which this is determined involves group choice in light of the social space. In the ideal, agents of control protect and preserve civil society rather than limit and constrain it. Controlling change can be as much a part of democracy as encouraging that change: in both cases, practices of power are central.

Exploring what we might label "command capital" is essential for determining how the ordering of civil society is possible. As a result, ethnographies of police activity provide a rich body of data. The police must maintain order, but what does order mean on the mesolevel? Who is included within an orderly or a protesting public? Who is excluded? When do police officers disrupt groups in public and when do they protect them or let them be? Who draws the line between order and chaos? Members of complex societies desire order, calling on the police as the bulwark of peace, but the police are neither an anonymous nor an autonomous institution. Rather, a police department is an organization that depends on its own group cultures, which stretch from political overseers to the command structure to station houses, detective squads, and police partners. Each layer has its own idioculture that overlaps, controls, and contends with others while responding to immediate circumstances.

In a world in which control is expected, how do citizens confront the challenges of change agents? If we think of political participation as a game between opponents, each has interests, strategies, and resources. Additional control derives from information access. Here groups face the danger of groupthink, ignoring diverse sources of knowledge. How do governmental agencies, businesses, or social movements gain the broad set of knowledges from which to make effective decisions? The history of policy deliberations reveals abject failures as well as happy outcomes. However, whatever the contour of information, decisions result from the knowledge that actors access, not the information that is theoretically available.

EXTENSIONS

Despite the salience of interaction regimes and group cultures, focusing on the local at the expense of broader domains blinds us to the complexity of an extended world. Groups build on groups, and, as I have suggested, there are groups all the way up and all the way down. To imagine the world as an archipelago of tiny publics lacking bridges—or, using another metaphor, without ladders to reach groups above or below—is misleading.

Extensions happen because knowledge domains are larger than the small group. Collective memories can be widely shared. Hopes and fears of how a social system might change depend on an imagined future and a shared past, and the sites of imagination and sharing can be well populated. Together we think forward as well as backward, both with friends and among strangers.

The linkages among groups create structures that we recognize as diffuse units such as governments or translocal associations. Despite the reality that we engage with local offices and with their employees, we treat them as part of a coordinated bureaucracy. This macrostructural imaginary makes sense in that participants seem to have a common goal and set of procedures that may erase the variability of interaction (Fine 1991).

Face-to-face interaction—the world of tiny publics—is reshaped, in part, through the consequences of online communication. Social media channel interaction orders to downplay embodied and embedded connections in favor of connections that are based on an assumption of common interests and the presence of shared discourse. The question becomes how to integrate the power of the local, which provides stability and commitment, with online communication, which spreads beyond those who "know" each other as multidimensional copresent beings.

Contemporary terrorist groups reveal the complexities of the intersection of the local and global. Terrorist cells may develop from friendship groups or informal neighborhood ties, later joining with others. Even training camps connect a group into a larger system. Networks of groups are as important as networks of individuals.

Still more dramatic is the role of cybermedia as the basis of community. The world of blogs—people writing on the air—is a striking example. People become acquainted through their mediated personas, rarely gathering in physical space. As a result, they can establish a political movement that does not depend on routine face-to-face connections but mobilizes through online communication.

This type of group reveals its power when we consider how large-scale activist engagement occurs. Movements such as the Arab Spring, the Green Revolution in Iran, Occupy Wall Street, and even the Tea Party utilized social media to coordinate. As with other forms of activism, people often arrive at events as part of groups, but, in addition, online messages have the potential to be disseminated through a network beyond the local. These extensions can be activated without the deep group culture that was essential in preinternet movements.

Recognizing the existence and the importance of extensions prevents embracing the misleading belief that tiny publics operating in a shared space are all that matter. While these publics are influential, emphasizing interaction above all transforms civil society into a mere appendage of the local, ignoring its wide and lasting effects.

Citizens Together?

Although not political in a narrow sense, my interpretation of civic engagement recognizes the rhetorical imagining of equality and the operation of inequality. Groups may define all members as equals—perhaps as citizens with identical rights—but does this definition hold? Likewise, the treatment of those outside the boundary of the group may include them as part of the larger polity or may exclude them as aliens or as illegals. In reality, neither individuals nor groups have equal access to resources, and this advantages some groups and persons in enhancing their life chances while penalizing others.

A challenge for any mesolevel analysis is to determine how tiny publics, as locally constituted, gain authority to promote the interests of members of the group or of a larger community. I do not address how civil societies *might* operate but how they *do* operate as interactional regimes that depend on social relations.

Democratic society depends on groups mobilizing in a shared civic project, supporting a commitment to the political process. While the characteristics, motivations, and goals of tiny publics vary, each is shaped by institutions and publics that surround it. In practice, some bridging publics strive to incorporate pluralistic perspectives while, for others, the boundaries are more tightly fixed and the group is a homogeneous band, skeptical of those surrounding.

Citizenship implies a reading of the idea of civility that builds on the existence of local communities, sites through which civility is modeled and through which membership is assigned. However, civility is distinct from politeness or passivity. Contentious politics, division, and disruption, when operating within bounds, can be valid. Even in the case of political aggression, while the acts that characterize the violent group may stand outside democratic, participatory norms, the discourse may contribute to moral debates, as in the case of the radical abolitionist movement.

The justification for the idea of the citizen, whether supportive of the status quo or in revolt, depends on the belief that one is not alone. Patriotism is not a sentiment of isolated individuals but assumes the standing of others who are similarly situated and who share attachment in sites of collective activity or institutional control. Further, patriotism is a group sentiment linked to times and places of collective commemoration. These can be private gatherings, such as Thanksgiving dinners, or public celebrations in which many families or friends share a space, such as at Independence Day fireworks. With a belief in our linked fate, we are not alone.

However, simply believing that one citizen is similar to another is insufficient. The creation of sets of relations recognizes a community with which we have common cause and with which we can work, building what we cannot construct alone. We need places where selves can meet and recognize their joint stakes and shared activities.

We find much variation in group cultures. Some societies operate with robust and solid groups, whereas elsewhere, perhaps because of distinct styles of interaction, technologies of surveillance, or forms of social control, local participation may be truncated. Examining how inequality arises and what its effects are is essential for understanding the availability of citizenship and diverse commitments to equality. As the properties of tiny publics vary, we can compare local worlds in nations and regions, creating a comparative mesopolitics. This potentially provides a sophisticated understanding of how the cultures, resources, and demographics of groups shape the organization of societies and their commitment to full participation. This permits a "politics of politics," as understood through the chain of tiny publics with their access to resources and the persuasiveness of their authority claims.

Opening the Hinge

I have presented an array of empirical studies that, taken together, justify the utility of a local analysis of civil society. However, for the approach to be useful it must be applicable to a wide range of projects.

Let us consider a project in which I am currently engaged. Having written extensively on political and literary reputations (Fine 2001), I became interested in the current debates over the history of the Civil War and how the war (and, in particular, the Confederacy) should be commemorated. As an ethnographer, I began to observe gatherings of "history buffs" in Illinois, Missouri, Mississippi, and South Carolina. Drawing on the themes discussed here has been helpful. Examining distinct communities with different views of Civil War history (some more supportive of Unionist sentiment; others of Southern greatness; some interested in the mud and blood of military engagements; others in the social and political aspects of the conflict) reveals distinctive local cultures. Interests vary from network to network.

More than this, these groups' patterns of legitimate action—the interaction order—differ as well. I learned that the rules of interaction varied on issues as to how detailed the historical arguments should be, how identification should be shown to prominent actors, to what extent disagreements are legitimate, and how "politically correct" my informants had to be. Issues of slavery, segregation, and racial bias require considerable sensitivity in all groups. But as the groups developed and coalesced, participants understood what constituted legitimate practices, and it is here that I was able to observe the circuits of action. The choices of participants provided the opportunities for others to respond or to ignore.

Finally, given the now fraught politics of Civil War commemorations, these participants find themselves as members of tiny publics. Perhaps when Civil War history was more esoteric, more consensual, and less fraught, this would have been less evident, but today what one is willing to claim about the "War Between the States" (or the "War for Southern Independence" or the "War of Northern Aggression") has civic implications that can discredit or ennoble. Gray and blue lives matter. The debates are now heated in ways that would not have been so true at the war's centennial. History is a lever through which the public sphere rolls on.

In this, I am not presenting a developed set of findings but rather suggesting that the mesosociological model can provide directions for research and analysis. These ways of approaching the world of history buffs and national collective memory can also be utilized for the variety of domains about which sociologists care.

A Note before Closing

I do not aspire to provide either caustic or anodyne assessments of contemporary politics. Partisans exist for this task. I have long admired Erving Goffman's (1974: 14) plaint: "I can only suggest that he who would combat false consciousness and awaken people to their true interests has much to do because the sleep is very deep. And I do not intend here to provide a lullaby but merely to sneak in and watch the way people snore." Goffman treats his colleagues in the academy with the same bracing skepticism with which he had previously viewed those in the psychiatric profession. Those who wish to work for the "common good" have a challenge in determining what this good includes and what it excludes, and, most particularly, who should define what is common and how resources should be transferred to make the good, better.

We live in an age in which many fear that their foes are edging toward totalitarianism. Others see their opponents as dangerously racist or otherwise blighted or as slightly—or deeply—deranged. The existence of these deep chasms does not invalidate my approach but supports it. I do not suggest that all silos have the same architecture. Nor do I deny that media reach large swaths of the population. Rather I point out that institutions of diffusion (Fox News, the *New York Times*, MSNBC, the *Wall Street Journal*) produce the "news" through a set of work groups. Audiences are not composed of isolated consumers, but those that talk with each other, processing this news and treating it as notable, worthy of being shared and discussed. To be spread, culture must first be created by group action and, to be influential, it must be interpreted in groups that care. Minute communities in Maine may hear the same information as those in Missouri or Montana, but groups with distinct perspectives will process it differently. Whether the Trumps are a crime family or tribunes of the unheard, these communities are primed to share their beliefs. The same is true of the wunderkinds of the Resistance or the Amazons of the Squad. What we require is to treasure the widely spread archipelagoes of publics, and to hope that we have sturdy spans above the crashing waves of ideology.

Beyond this, we embrace political systems not because we love the system as such but because we admire and trust those who surround us with recognizably similar comforts and anxieties. Fortunately, there are numerous shoals in the social sea. A Leviathan is unnecessary when there are many schools of fish. The diversity of mesostructures—spaces of community—reduces the need for a single power center.

Those who believe in the power of tiny publics to create civic culture must make this case persuasively. Too often, the mesolevel is treated as secondary to individual preferences or structural demands. But joint action matters. Affiliations among persons create affiliation with society. Allegiance emerges in local worlds in which citizens act together and then extends to a wider world that is more expansive but perceived as similar in kind. Circuits of action are forms of practice that connect individuals and institutions through the traditions of a powerful community that is more than a person and less than a structure. Adherence to the local depends on awareness of an extended world. This recognition is the Hinge on which civil society depends.

Afterword

THE COVID HINGE

Two decades ago, we commonly spoke of the world as divided into pre-9/11 and post-9/11: September 10th and September 12th. The structure of life at that dark time seemed to have been dramatically and permanently altered by the attacks on the World Trade Center. We had to search for a new normal in the smoke and dust. Over time, the changes brought about by that attack seem less monumental, though not entirely insignificant.

This work of theory takes as its fundamental assumption that local communities matter. We engage with each other in groups and develop cultural practices and behavioral routines through sharing a space, linking self and society. Our co-presence is crucial in creating group cultures, circuits of action, and interaction orders. We reside in a world of tiny publics.

But as I write these lines in the late spring of 2020, we might be inclined to wonder about this conceit. Will we speak of the pre-COVID world and the post-COVID world? Will our new normal be recognizable in light of our old normal? Will we return to life as it has been lived and as I have depicted it?

There is a widely quoted Sufi proverb: This too shall pass. In addition, consider the well-known French saying, "Plus ça change, plus c'est la même chose." The more things change, the more they stay the same. These are homages to the sticky staying power of the status quo. Yet, we know that things sometimes do change in ways that are dramatic and consequential.

Perhaps COVID-19 will fade with the summer heat, largely forgotten, much like SARS or the Spanish Flu. In time, our anxieties will likely lift, along with our spirits. Soon we may party again. Salut! Or perhaps the novel coronavirus will be a constant companion, kept under control through treatments or vaccines, bedeviling us and menacing the medically exposed like the seasonal flu. In either of these cases, the interaction orders of which I write will only be slightly shaken. Epidemics such as polio and typhoid over decades have left few behavioral changes as they have been managed and forgotten. Perhaps AIDS will be the model where changes that promote safer sexual practices have occurred. However, given prevention and treatment (although without a vaccine), the fears of the 1980s have largely retreated. Several years from now, perhaps we will be left with elbow bumps and air kisses. These do not a changed society make.

But what if the effects are lasting? Suppose COVID-19 continues to infect and mutate with immunity evaporating. Might we live in a virtual society with two classes of workers: those who can work online from home and those in place in a risky world? This division largely mirrors our current division between highly trained elites and those who serve them. In such a divide, medical personnel are the rare hands-on professionals.

Alternatively, imagine two classes of citizens: Those with long-term immunity and those still at risk. Will those protected go freely, while the vulnerable remain hidden? Will we force the frail and elderly out of the public sphere, ostensibly for their own benefit? In each of these cases, we may find ourselves with two sharply bifurcated interaction orders. If the COVID-19 monster remains, we can imagine social relations segmented by exposure to the virus. No doubt this will affect the claims made in chapter 4 about the importance of place. We may categorize spaces by risk. Perhaps associations, as described in chapter 3, will no longer operate as meeting sites. One can make a plausible argument that the effects of COVID-19 might make a me-solevel analysis of less relevance or of greater importance. The current disruption reveals how much we have taken our interpersonal activity for granted. In the long-term, COVID-19 will reveal a group-based analysis to be more or less relevant, or possibly both.

A Vanished Hinge

Given the vexation of "social distancing," the importance of the groups on which we depend is revealed, but also perhaps has seemed to diminish. Relationships became fraught and unstable, filled with the mistrust of infection. In much of the United States, and, indeed, in much of the world, we no longer meet in face-to-face groups, a demand based on the claim of emergency powers by those who govern us.

We depend on platforms. While technology allows for the transfer of knowledge, these digital meetings often lack the healthy informal back-and-forth that is characteristic of local interaction. With the control of discussions by the host, debate becomes more formal and there is less opportunity to create reflexive group cultures. Nowhere is this clearer than on now empty college campuses. Professors can lecture online, but much education depends on sororities, choirs, intramural basketball, political clubs, yoga classes, and drinking buddies. In their absence, is a university collegiate?

At this moment, we realize how much of group life occurs on the margins, flitting around the main topic. With the enforced closure of "third places," the spaces of convivial gathering are limited. Will those spaces be used in the same way as before? Lacking the expectation of meeting others, will the group cultures that have been so treasured wither away? Or are the desires for interpersonal connection so powerful that groups will find a way to assemble? Currently, as we huddle at home, group life seems attenuated and it is possible that much of our social life occurring in those online spaces will not allow for expressive cultures, focusing on instrumental task work as we cope with the fatigue of mediated interaction. Online Happy Hours, although a curiosity, are curiously unsatisfying.

These changes may create a demand for a new interaction order, both online and in person as long as restrictions last. What will a world in which physical distancing is the norm be like? The crucial features of everyday interaction—the micro-negotiations, the nonverbal communication (the winks and nods), the tactile messages, and the backchannel contacts—may evaporate. When everything is on the surface in online spaces, the nuances on which local cultures depend can be lost.

A Varnished Hinge

If we accept the changes by which group action and live co-presence are limited, we might reasonably wonder about the value of an approach that argues—repeatedly—that the group is where the action is. New routines because of COVID-19 might seem to marginalize the relevance of a mesolevel analysis. If we do not congregate, does our desire for attachment matter?

I suggest, in contrast, that we might argue the opposite. We do not know when (or if) we might ever again rally in large crowds, shop in congested malls, or pray with strangers in the sanctuary of mega-churches. Perhaps we will accept a world in which gatherings are limited to fifty people or to ten. This is a world of granulated publics. The assembly of mass publics has been placed on hold, leaving open the question of whether they will return.

In chapter 7, I examined the role of group extensions, emphasizing online connections. To be online does not mean that one lacks a set of friends. Sometimes one's communications reach a large audience, but message boards, Facebook groups, and hangouts often have a modest audience. These constitute minute communities and develop norms for interaction and local collective memories. Given our need for community and given the size of an effective Zoom call, tiny publics might be the rule. Already we are creating suggestions for proper online meeting etiquette, recognizing the value of explicit routines that constitute newly formulated circuits of action. The pandemic may encourage considerations of group interaction in the absence of large meetings and conventions.

We are still learning how civil society might operate in the absence of gatherings. Is voting in person necessary? Do legislative sessions require officials to be in spatial proximity? And what do demonstrations look like online? If we believe in privately owned websites as a forum of democracy, should they be required to permit the same degree of freedom of speech as in the public square, even if these expressions are offensive? Are Facebook, YouTube, Instagram, and Twitter public utilities? While this does not speak to their scalability as such, it raises issues of which group sets the boundaries of civic culture. Whatever the platform of communication, we will find an organizing group, more than a person and less than a crowd. Conflict and control will always depend on local coordination. While the location of discourse may change and while forms of intimate interaction may alter, groups provide for a division of labor and a sense of community. No virus is likely to alter this reality.

Even if we are locked down, quarantined, distanced, and masked, the group form is still important. The rapid growth and acceptance of virtual communities are a tribute to this. If the skepticism of face-to-face communication lasts (and, as noted, it might not), people will figure out how to adjust together.

≈

I am left to speculate. Guesswork constitutes sociological analysis. And you, my reader, years hence will know far better than I how this virus has shaped our interaction practices. Readers even farther into the future can look back and wonder how wrong we were. Or perhaps they will admire us as seers. We stand at an inflection point, but some inflections have small effects, barely bending life's direction.

I hope that in this volume I have made a persuasive case that groups and local communities matter deeply in ordering society. Platforms will change and places of contact will shift, but the need for minute communities does not disappear. President Trump emphasizes that we are in a war against this novel virus. While we might be skeptical of using this metaphor to energize a frightened public, let us remember the insight of Edmund Burke: every war requires little platoons.

May 2020
At home, Glenview, Illinois

NOTES

Introduction

1. Although the saying reached a wide public as the title of First Lady Hillary Clinton's (1996) book, it has African roots. These nonpartisan sentiments are as closely aligned with conservative political theory (such as that of Edmund Burke) as with progressive beliefs.

2. Waverly Duck (2015: 17) suggests that this commitment to interactional practices is common in impoverished neighborhoods where rules about proper drug transactions protect those who are not in that scene.

3. Goffman's concern in his essay, as in much of his writing, is to examine occasioned encounters in which the parties are not in extended, meaningful contact. He emphasizes fleeting exchanges, such as those between clerks and customers, while still pointing to the centrality of "deeper" relations that depend on biographic awareness and local cultures.

4. I thank Michael DeLand (pers. comm., 2018) for this formulation.

5. In other domains, notably open access to technology, the idea of the commons remains viable.

Chapter One

1. This stands in sharp contrast to eighteenth-century liberal economists, such Adam Smith (1776) and, especially, Bernard Mandeville (1714), who held that by individuals acting according to their own self-interests all would eventually benefit.

2. Not all land—perhaps not most land—required a parliamentary-backed system of enclosure in England, as much depended on private agreements. However, ultimately even such systems depended on the force of law (McCloskey 1975: 125).

3. Arthur Stinchcombe (2001: 5), speaking of the value of formality, recognizes the dark side of informality in which oppression can occur in the name of tradition and shared understandings.

4. This harmonious response to strain is not inevitably the case, for example when social structures are washed away in the aftermath of disasters, as Kai Erikson (1977) powerfully describes in the case of the Buffalo Creek Flood in West Vir-

ginia. In this case of community destruction, residents were disoriented and lost interpersonal connection. Recent instances of natural disasters, such as flooding in New Orleans after Hurricane Katrina, reveal a threat to local identity but also an effort to aid others. The fragmenting of community and the attempt to preserve it are both evident.

5. Groups may establish specific occasions to welcome new members. When tradition allows for *punctuated recruitment*, it creates a system of cohorts. These are sets of entrants into collective life. Because of their backgrounds or because of the civic issues that confront them, generational groups may develop distinctly different politics (Mannheim 1952). Social movements, given the intensity of their relationships, are often structured through the socialization of generations (DeMartini 1985), and within groups the transfer of power between generations must be negotiated (Braungart 1975; DeMartini 1992). In her examination of cohort structures in feminist organizations in Columbus, Ohio, Nancy Whittier (1997) finds that cohorts develop characteristic interaction patterns, rely on different identities, and address different concerns. Patterns of microrelations, once established, are revised over time because of altered social relations and distinct cultural practices. In more political terms, microcohorts embrace particular master action frames, a phenomenon that may lead to political change as in the nations of Eastern Europe in the late Soviet era (Johnston and Aarelaid-Tart 2000).

6. Perhaps the creation of Wikipedia entries contains some of the same features of "democratic writing," as the texts are amended and revised by a collection of "authors." Of course, in the case of Wikipedia, the face-to-face contact that has traditionally been tied to collaborative writing is absent as many contributors may be anonymous aside from their words.

7. In these sites, despite a communal agreement as to their value, debates over competing interests and the free-rider problem can create strain, demanding incentives and penalties to create an organized "commons."

8. As emphasized in the introduction, my use of "association" excludes large organizations that are not based on deliberation and personal awareness, except when I discuss the role of small decision-making groups within these larger organizations. I focus on interaction scenes, face-to-face or the digital equivalent.

Chapter Two

1. I focus on social affiliations ("Platonic friendships," we might label them) in contrast to romantic relations or colleagueship (friendly acquaintanceships in the workplace). Both of these realms contribute to civil society, although they stand outside of my analysis here. Civil society is also based on who has the rights to couple based on demographic or citizenship status, as well as how coworkers provide support for each other in and out of surveillance of employers.

2. While in practice not every friendship will lead to political capacity, friendships, when confronted with challenges that require thinking outside the bond, have that possibility.

3. It is imprecise to speak of "gay culture" or "gay community." In contrast, there are numerous sexual cultures and communities, which take distinct forms and operate in distinct places with no single common fate. I thank Japonica Brown-Saracino for this point (pers. comm., 2018).

4. The slogan, now widely used, was originally the title of an essay by Carol Hanisch, published in a 1970 feminist volume, *Notes from the Second Year: Women's Liberation*, which addresses the tiny publics of consciousness-raising groups. See "The Personal is Political" by Carol Hanisch, January 2006. http:// http://www .carolhanisch.org/CHwritings/PIP.html (accessed December 14, 2019).

5. Vargas (2015) notes that to implement the Affordable Care Act the Obama administration hired "health navigators," whose role was to provide a socially supportive entry to signing up for healthcare, otherwise a worrisome experience. To engage the uninsured poor, navigators created "cultures of camaraderie" that hoped to persuade clients that these navigators were honest brokers in the choice of health care and that they had a shared fate. Even though these were not preexisting friendships, navigators, like successful salespersons (and con artists), must persuade others that they share a perspective, and, thus, their advice can be treated as an act of friendship.

6. With the harsh debates over immigration, the term "citizen" has become emotionally and politically loaded. How do groups that are socially inside and legally outside deserve attention, especially as many of their neighbors and coworkers (not to mention their offspring) are inside the boundaries of the state. This is an important issue, but not one that I address here. In this manuscript, a citizen is a recognized and legitimated member of a civil society.

7. I am grateful to Paul Lichterman for this formulation (pers. comm., 2018).

8. Sinclair (2012: xiv) finds that political contributions to Congressional candidates are linked to relations among family and friends. Citizens, involved in campaigns, often ask those in their groups to make donations.

9. Mario Small (2017) finds that for certain topics, talking to acquaintances—not strangers, not intimates—can be particularly helpful. Weaker ties may permit a more candid discussion than talk with those close relations who may care too much about the issues involved.

10. Some propose the value of establishing intergroup dialogue programs that can and occasionally do produce an expansion of discourse (Eliasoph 2012; Walsh 2004: 191). The challenge is that discussion groups often begin with friendship ties rather than end with them.

Chapter Three

1. I acknowledge Baptiste Brossard for this reference (pers. comm., 2018).

2. Seymour Martin Lipset (1985: 141) asserted that, compared to other nationalities, "Americans are more likely to take part in voluntary efforts to achieve goals." Contrasting small-town America with southern Italy, Edward Banfield (1958: 17) portrayed American communities as constituted by a dense web of communal

organizations, finding that "Americans are used to a buzz of activity having as its purpose, at least in part, the advancement of community welfare." Tocqueville (2001: 243), from his perspective, commented about prerevolutionary France, "When the Revolution broke out, one would have searched in vain in the greatest part of France for ten men who had the habit of acting in concert in a regular manner." In a series of lectures in the early twentieth century, Max Weber worried about the lack of civic focus and democratic orientation of voluntary associations in Germany in contrast with the United States (Koshar 1986: 4–5). Even in the United States, during the mid-nineteenth century, Masons and other fraternal groups faced hostility. Opponents saw them as exclusionary and antidemocratic. As Ralph Waldo Emerson (1883–87, III, 252, cited in Schlesinger 1944, p. 20) put it, "At the name of a society all my repulsions play, all my quills rise and sharpen." He observed that men participate in clubs based on the belief that "I have failed, and you have failed, but perhaps together we shall not fail." But even if not members of a repulsive club, Emerson and his transcendental friends benefited from a close-knit community. Joining with others is considered the "American way." Elinor Ostrom's (1990) description of cross-national civic action reveals that the capacity for group activity to solve public problems is not a constant. The United States remains near the top globally in voluntary association membership (Curtis, Grabb, and Baer 1992; Curtis, Baer, and Grabb 2001; Putnam 2000: 449).

3. I thank Michael DeLand for this formulation (pers. comm., 2018).

4. Many clubs and voluntary associations, at least until recently, were exclusively open to one gender.

Chapter Four

1. Examples are recent incidents in which white residents call the police to deal with African Americans who are assumed not to belong or who violate minor rules. The police patrol propriety and do not only deal with threats to life and property.

2. Examples are the shops in which workers meet to discuss their shared complaints, as in the case of the glassworkers of Carmaux finding their craft transformed (Scott 1980).

3. This is evident in ethnographies of beauty salons for older women (Furman 1997), baseball bleachers for working-class fans (Swyers 2010), branch libraries for inner-city residents (Klinenberg 2018), and opera loges for those with musical capital (Benzecry 2011).

4. Some public spaces, such as manicured parks in suburbs, are often empty, aside from manufactured events.

5. Coffeehouse culture was also common in the Middle East, where these spaces were seen as hidden from government surveillance and present for the development of a public sphere. The repression of these free sites arose from the belief that discussions among friends and acquaintances within the coffeehouse might lead to resistance to authorities. On occasion coffeehouses were banned on grounds of morality or politics, as well as because of the intoxicating beverage itself (Hattox 1985).

6. Consider Georg Simmel's (1950) comment about those Parisian men—the *quatorzième*—who could earn a living by always being ready to attend a gathering (in proper attire) in the case of thirteen diners. For Simmel this "fourteenth man" is an extreme example of the division of labor, but it also speaks to the institution of the salon. I thank John Parker (pers. comm., 2018) for this reference.

7. The physical features of these cases matter as well. The town meeting with its images of hard benches and plank floors conjures the image of egalitarian relations. This stands in contrast to the camp-like atmosphere of the Bohemian Grove, a luxurious temple of ease. The coffeehouse with individual tables contrasts with the town meeting in which all parties are oriented to the front of the hall. I thank Paul Lichterman for this analysis of how layout contributes to imaginaries of community (pers. comm., 2018).

8. Discussant comments, Tanner Lecture on Human Values, Princeton University, March 2015.

9. The culture of social class matters here. The same forms of conversation and politeness were not found among manual laborers or farm workers, and these workers did not have access to the same spaces as the bourgeoisie.

10. German communities organized table societies and literary clubs during the seventeenth century (Habermas 1989), finding a means by which small groups could participate in public dialogue.

11. This mirrors the claim of Elijah Anderson (2011) that the "cosmopolitan canopy" constitutes an island of civility in a sea of segregation. In a classed society, the coffeehouse is a cosmopolitan canopy.

Chapter Five

1. In this section and throughout this chapter I acknowledge my discussions and collaborations with Iddo Tavory.

2. This is a dilemma for the integration of communities of color with Euro-American communities. I thank Jonathan Wynn for this insight (pers. comm., 2018).

Chapter Seven

1. Brown was executed because he was convicted of treason to the Commonwealth of Virginia, not treason to the United States.

BIBLIOGRAPHY

Adut, Ari. 2012. "A Theory of the Public Sphere." *Sociological Theory* 30: 238–62.
———. 2018. *Reign of Appearances: The Misery and Splendor of the Public Sphere.* New York: Cambridge University Press.
Agulhon, Maurice. 1982. *The Republic in the Village: The People of the Var from the French Revolution to the Second Republic.* Cambridge: Cambridge University Press.
Alberoni, Francesco. 2016. *Friendship.* Leiden: Brill.
Alexander, Jeffrey. 2006. *The Civil Sphere.* New York: Oxford University Press.
———. 2017. *The Drama of Social Life.* Cambridge: Polity.
Allen, Danielle. 2004. *Talking to Strangers: Anxieties of Citizenship Since Brown v. Board of Education.* Chicago: University of Chicago Press.
———. 2014a. *Our Declaration: A Reading of the Declaration of Independence in Defense of Equality.* New York: Liveright.
———. 2014b. "Social Capital vs. Democratic Knowledge: A Manifesto." Unpublished manuscript. Institute for Advanced Study, Princeton, New Jersey.
———. 2015. "Reconceiving Public Spheres: The Flow Dynamics Model." Pp. 178–207 in *From Voice to Influence: Understanding Influence in a Digital Age,* edited by Danielle Allen and Jennifer Light. Chicago: University of Chicago Press.
Allen, Robert. 1992. *Enclosure and the Yeoman.* Oxford: Clarendon Press.
Allport, Gordon W. 1954. *The Nature of Prejudice.* Cambridge: Addison-Wesley.
Amann, Peter. 1975. *Revolution and Mass Democracy: The Paris Club Movement in 1848.* Princeton, NJ: Princeton University Press.
Amir, Yehuda. 1969. "Contact Hypothesis in Ethnic Relations." *Psychological Bulletin* 71: 319–42.
Anderson, Benedict O'G. 1991. *Imagined Communities.* Rev. ed. London: Verso.
Anderson, Elijah. 1979. *A Place on the Corner.* Chicago: University of Chicago Press.
———. 1992. *Streetwise: Race, Class, and Change in an Urban Community.* Chicago: University of Chicago Press.

——. 2011. *The Cosmopolitan Canopy: Race and Civility in Everyday Life*. New York: W. W. Norton.

Anderson, Elizabeth. 2014. "Social Movements, Experiments in Living, and Moral Progress: Case Studies from Britain's Abolition of Slavery." Lindley Lecture, University of Kansas. http://kuscholarworks.ku.edu/handle/1808/14787. Accessed March 4, 2015.

Andrews, Kenneth, Marshall Ganz, Matt Baggetta, Hahrie Han, and Chaeyoon Lim. 2010. "Leadership, Membership, and Voice: Civic Associations That Work." *American Journal of Sociology* 115: 1191–1242.

Arditi, Jorge. 1998. *A Genealogy of Manners: Transformations of Social Relations in France and England from the Fourteenth to the Eighteenth Century*. Chicago: University of Chicago Press.

Arendt, Hannah. 1958. *The Human Condition*. Chicago: University of Chicago Press.

——. 1963. *On Revolution*. New York: Viking.

Aveni, Adrian. 1977. "The Not-So-Lonely Crowd: Friendship Groups in Collective Behavior." *Sociometry* 40: 96–99.

Back, Kurt, and Donna Polisar. 1983. "Salons und Kaffeehauser." *Kölner Zeitschrift für Soziologie und Sozialpsychologie* 25: 276–86.

Baiocchi, Gianpaolo. 2003. "Emergent Public Spheres: Talking Politics in Participatory Governance." *American Sociological Review* 68: 52–74.

Baiocchi, Gianpaolo, Elizabeth Bennett, Alissa Cordner, Peter Klein, and Stephanie Savell. 2014. *The Civic Imagination: Making a Difference in American Political Life*. Boulder, CO: Paradigm.

Bales, Robert Freed. 1954. "In Conference." *Harvard Business Review* 32: 44–50.

Banfield, Edward. 1958. *The Moral Basis of a Backward Society*. Glencoe, IL: Free Press.

Barley, Stephen. 2008. "Coalface Institutionalism." Pp. 490–516 in *SAGE Handbook of Organizational Institutionalism*, edited by R. Greenwood, C. Oliver, R. Suddaby, and K. Sahlin-Andersson. Newbury Park, CA: Sage.

Barley, Stephen, and Gideon Kunda. 1992. "Design and Devotion: Surges of Rational and Normative Ideologies of Control in Managerial Discourse." *Administrative Science Quarterly* 37: 363–99.

Bartkowski, John. 2000. "Breaking Walls, Raising Fences: Masculinity, Intimacy, and Accountability among the Promise Keepers." *Sociology of Religion* 61: 33–53.

Bartlett, Jamie, and Carl Miller. 2012. "The Edge of Violence: Towards Telling the Difference Between Violent and Non-violent Radicalization." *Terrorism and Political Violence* 24: 1–21.

Basseches, Josh. 2015. "The Micro-Foundations of Legislative Policymaking." Unpublished manuscript, Northwestern University, Evanston, IL.

Battilana, Julie. 2006. "Agency and Institutions: The Enabling Role of Individuals' Social Position." *Organization* 13: 653–76.

Battilana, Julie, Bernard Leca, and Eva Boxenbaum. 2009. "How Actors Change

Institutions: Towards a Theory of Institutional Entrepreneurship." *Academy of Management Annals* 3: 65–107.

Bayat, Asef. 2013. *Life as Politics: How Ordinary People Change the Middle East.* 2nd ed. Stanford, CA: Stanford University Press.

Bechky, Beth. 2011. "Making Organizational Theory Work: Institutions, Occupations, and Negotiated Orders." *Organization Science* 22: 1157–67.

Becker, Howard S. 1982. *Art Worlds.* Berkeley: University of California Press.

———. 1986. *Doing Things Together.* Evanston, IL: Northwestern University Press.

Becker, Penny Edgell. 1999. *Congregations in Conflict: Cultural Models of Local Religious Life.* New York: Cambridge University Press.

Belfrage, Sally. 1966. *Freedom Summer.* London: Andrew Deutsch.

Bell, Michael J. 1983. *The World from Brown's Lounge: An Ethnography of Black Middle-Class Play.* Urbana: University of Illinois Press.

Bell, Michael M. 1995. *Childerley: Nature and Morality in a Country Village.* Chicago: University of Chicago Press.

Bellah, Robert, Richard Madsen, William M. Sullivan, Ann Swidler, and Steven M. Tipton. 1991. *The Good Society.* New York: Knopf.

Bennett, W. Lance. 2012. "The Personalization of Politics: Political Identity, Social Media, and Changing Patterns of Participation." *Annals, American Academy of Political and Social Science* 644: 20–39.

Benzecry, Claudio. 2011. *The Opera Fanatic: Ethnography of an Obsession.* Chicago: University of Chicago Press.

Berezin, Mabel. 1997. *Making the Fascist Self: The Political Culture of Interwar Italy.* Ithaca, NY: Cornell University Press.

Berger, Peter, and Thomas Luckmann. 1966. *The Social Construction of Reality: A Treatise in the Sociology of Knowledge.* Garden City, NY: Anchor.

Bernard, Steven, and Pat Barclay. 2014. "Democratic Competition for Rank Increases Both Cooperation and Deception in Small Groups." American Sociological Association, San Francisco.

Billig, Michael. 1995. *Banal Nationalism.* London: Sage.

Binder, Amy. 2007. "For Love and Money: Organizations' Creative Responses to Multiple Environmental Logics." *Theory and Society* 36: 547–71.

Black, Barbara. 2012. *A Room of His Own: A Literary-Cultural Study of Victorian Clubland.* Athens: Ohio University Press.

Blee, Kathleen. 1992. *Women of the Klan: Racism and Gender in the 1920s.* Berkeley: University of California Press.

———. 2012. *Democracy in the Making: How Activist Groups Form.* New York: Oxford University Press.

Blee, Kathleen, and Amy McDowell. 2012. "Social Movement Audiences." *Sociological Forum* 27: 1–20.

Blenko, Marcia, Michael Mankins, and Paul Rogers. 2010. *Decide and Deliver: Five Steps to Breakthrough Performance in Your Organization.* Cambridge, MA: Harvard Business School Review Press.

Blumer, Herbert. 1969. *Symbolic Interactionism.* Englewood Cliffs, NJ: Prentice-Hall.

Bonilla-Silva, Eduardo. 2018. *Racism without Racists: Color-Blind Racism and the Persistence of Racial Inequality in America.* 5th ed. Lanham, Maryland: Rowman and Littlefield.

Bourdieu, Pierre. 1984. *Distinction: A Social Critique of the Judgment of Taste.* Cambridge, MA: Harvard University Press.

boyd, danah. 2014. *It's Complicated: The Social Life of Networked Teens.* New Haven, CT: Yale University Press.

Bratman, Michael. 1992. "Shared Cooperative Activity." *Philosophical Review* 101 (2): 327–41.

———. 1993. "Shared Intention." *Ethics* 104 (1): 97–113.

Braungart, Richard G. 1974. "The Sociology of Generations and Student Politics." *Journal of Social Issues* 30 (2): 31–54.

Brissett, Dennis, and Charles Edgley, eds. 2005. *Life as Theater: A Dramaturgical Sourcebook.* 2nd ed. New York: Routledge.

Britton, Marcus. 2008. "'My Regular Spot': Race and Territory in Urban Public Space." *Journal of Contemporary Ethnography* 17: 442–68.

Bronner, Simon. 2011. *Explaining Traditions: Folk Behavior in Modern Culture.* Lexington: University Press of Kentucky.

Brooks, David. 2014. "Startling Adult Friendships." *New York Times* (September 19): A29.

Brown, Richard. 1974. "The Emergence of Urban Society in Rural Massachusetts, 1760–1820." *Journal of American History* 61: 29–51.

Brown-Saracino, Japonica. 2009. *A Neighborhood That Never Changes: Gentrification, Social Preservation, and the Search for Authenticity.* Chicago: University of Chicago Press.

———. 2017. *How Places Make Us: Novel LBQ Identities in Four Small Cities.* Chicago: University of Chicago Press.

Browning, Christopher, Catherine Calder, Brian Soller, Aubrey Jackson, and Jonathan Dirlam. 2017. "Ecological Networks and Neighborhood Social Organization." *American Journal of Sociology* 122: 1939–88.

Brubaker, Rogers, and Frederick Cooper. 2000. "Beyond 'Identity.'" *Theory and Society* 29: 1–47.

Brunkhorst, Hauke. 2005. *Solidarity: From Civic Friendship to a Global Legal Community.* Trans. Jeffrey Flynn. Cambridge, MA: MIT Press.

Bryan, Frank M. 2004. *Real Democracy: The New England Town Meeting and How It Works.* Chicago: University of Chicago Press.

Burghardt, Steve. 1982. *The Other Side of Organizing: Resolving Personal Dilemmas and Political Demands of Daily Practice.* Cambridge, MA: Schenkman.

Burke, Edmund. 1790. *Reflections on the Revolution in France.* London: J. Dodsley.

Burnett, D. Graham. 2001. *A Trial by Jury.* New York: Alfred A. Knopf.

Bushman, Richard Lyman. 2005. *Joseph Smith: Rough Stone Rolling.* New York: Knopf.

Butler, Judith. 2006. *Gender Trouble: Feminism and the Subversion of Identity*. New York: Routledge.

Button, Mark, and Kevin Mattson. "Deliberative Democracy in Practice: Challenges and Prospects for Civic Deliberation." *Polity* 31: 609–37.

Calhoun, Craig. 1982. *The Question of Class Struggle: Social Foundations of Popular Radicalism during the Industrial Revolution*. Chicago: University of Chicago Press.

———. 2001. "Public Sphere: 19th and 20th Century History." Pp. 12595–99 in *International Encyclopedia of the Social and Behavioral Sciences*. Amsterdam: Elsevier.

Campbell, Andrea Louise. 2003. *How Policies Make Citizens: Senior Political Activism and the American Welfare State*. Princeton, NJ: Princeton University Press.

Campos-Castillo, Celeste, and Steven Hitlin. 2013. "Copresence: Revisiting a Building Block for Social Interaction Theories." *Sociological Theory* 31: 168–92.

Capdeville, Valerie. 2016. "'Clubbability': A Revolution in London Sociability?" *Lumen: Selected Proceedings from the Canadian Society for Eighteenth Century Studies* 35: 63–80.

Carlsson, Chris, and Francesca Manning. 2010. "Nowtopia: Strategic Exodus?" *Antipode* 42 (4): 924–53.

Cassell, Joan. 1977. *A Group Called Women: Sisterhood and Symbolism in the Feminist Movement*. New York: David McKay.

Castells, Manuel. 2012. *Networks of Outrage and Hope: Social Movements in the Internet Age*. Cambridge: Polity.

Chakravarty, Anuradha, and Soma Chaudhuri. 2012. "Strategic Framing Work(s): How Microcredit Loans Facilitate Anti-Witch-Hunt Movements." *Mobilization* 17: 175–94.

Chayko, Mary. 2008. *Portable Communities: The Social Dynamics of Online and Mobile Connectedness*. Albany: SUNY Press.

Chen, Katherine. 2009. *Enabling Creative Chaos: The Organization behind the Burning Man Event*. Chicago: University of Chicago Press.

Chua, Amy. 2018. *Political Tribes: Group Instinct and the Fate of Nations*. New York: Penguin.

Chua, Lynette. 2012. "Pragmatic Resistance, Law, and Social Movements in Authoritarian States: The Case of Gay Collective Action in Singapore." *Law & Society Review* 46: 713–48.

Clark, Burton. 1972. "The Organizational Saga in Higher Education." *Administrative Science Quarterly* 17: 178–84.

Clark, Susan, and Woden Teachout. 2012. *Slow Democracy: Rediscovering Community, Bringing Decision Making Back Home*. White River Junction, VT: Chelsea Green.

Clinton, Hillary. 1996. *It Takes a Village and Other Lessons Children Teach Us*. New York: Simon and Schuster.

Coco, Angela, and Ian Woodward. 2007. "Discourses of Authenticity with a Pagan Community." *Journal of Contemporary Ethnography* 36: 479–504.

Cohen, Jean, and Andrew Arato. 1992. *Civil Society and Political Theory*. Cambridge, MA: MIT Press.

Coleman, James. 1990. *Foundations of Social Theory*. Cambridge, MA: Harvard University Press.

Collins, Patricia Hill. 2000. *Black Feminist Thought: Knowledge, Consciousness, and the Politics of Empowerment*. New York: Routledge.

Collins, Randall. 1981. "On the Microfoundations of Macrosociology." *American Journal of Sociology* 86: 984–1014.

———. 2004. *Interaction Ritual Chains*. Princeton, NJ: Princeton University Press.

Cooley, Charles Horton. 1902. *Human Nature and the Social Order*. New York: Scribner's.

Corte, Ugo. 2013. "A Refinement of Collaborative Circles Theory: Resource Mobilization and Innovation in an Emerging Sport." *Social Psychology Quarterly* 76: 25–51.

Coser, Lewis. 1956. *The Functions of Social Conflict*. New York: Macmillan.

———. 1974. *Greedy Institutions: Patterns of Undivided Commitment*. New York: Free Press.

Courpasson, David, and Françoise Dany. 2013. "Friends behind the Screen: Enacted Solidarity in the Radicalization of a Blog Protest." Paper presented at the Academy of Management meetings. Orlando, Florida.

Cousin, Bruno, and Sébastien Chauvin. 2014. "Globalizing Forms of Elite Sociability, Varieties of Cosmopolitanism in Paris Social Clubs." *Ethnic and Racial Studies* 37: 2209–25.

Cramer, Katherine. 2016. *The Politics of Resentment: Rural Consciousness in Wisconsin and the Rise of Scott Walker*. Chicago: University of Chicago Press.

Crossley, Nick. 2011. *Towards Relational Sociology*. New York: Routledge.

Curry, James. 2015. *Legislating in the Dark: Information and Power in the House of Representatives*. Chicago: University of Chicago Press.

Curtis, James, Douglas Baer, and Edward Grabb. 2001. "Nations of Joiners: Explaining Voluntary Association Membership in Democratic Societies." *American Sociological Review* 66: 783–805.

Curtis, James, Edward Grabb, and Douglas Baer. 1992. "Voluntary Association Membership in Fifteen Countries: A Comparative Analysis." *American Sociological Review* 57: 139–52.

Dahl, Robert. 1961. *Who Governs?: Democracy and Power in an American City*. New Haven, CT: Yale University Press.

———. 1989. *Democracy and Its Critics*. New Haven, CT: Yale University Press.

Davetian, Benet. 2009. *Civility: A Cultural History*. Toronto: University of Toronto Press.

Davis, Jenny, and Tony Love. 2017. "Self-in-Self, Mind-in-Mind, Heart-in-Heart: The Future of Role-Taking, Perspective Taking and Empathy." *Advances in Group Processes* 34: 151–74.

Dawson, Michael. 1995. *Behind the Mule: Race and Class in African-American Politics*. Princeton, NJ: Princeton University Press.

bibliography

De la Boétie, Étienne, and Paul Bonnefon. 2007. *The Politics of Obedience: The Discourse of Voluntary Servitude*. Montreal: Black Rose Books.

De Tocqueville, Alexis. 2001 [1856]. *The Old Regime and the Revolution*. Chicago: University of Chicago Press.

———. 2003 [1835]. *Democracy in America and Two Essays on America*. London: Penguin.

Deegan, Mary Jo. 1990. *Jane Addams and the Men of the Chicago School, 1892–1918*. New York: Routledge.

Deener, Andrew. 2012. *Venice: A Contested Bohemia in Los Angeles*. Chicago: University of Chicago Press.

———. 2015. "Pathways and Contingencies in Neighborhood Participation: Reassembling Intergroup Conflict." Unpublished manuscript.

———. 2016. "The Ecology of Neighborhood Participation and the Reproduction of Political Conflict." *International Journal of Urban and Regional Research* 40: 817–32.

DeLand, Michael. 2018. "The Ocean Run: Stage, Cast, and Performance in a Public Park Basketball Scene." *Journal of Contemporary Ethnography* 47: 28–59.

Della Porta, Donatella. 1988. "Recruitment Processes in Clandestine Political Organizations: Italian Left-wing Terrorism." Pp. 155–69 in *From Structure to Action: Comparing Social Movements across Cultures*, ed. Sidney Tarrow, Bert Klandermans, and Hanspeter Kriesi. New York: JAI Press.

DeMartini, Joseph. 1985. "Change Agents and Generational Relationships." *Social Forces* 64:1–16.

———. 1992. "Generational Relationships and Social Movement Participation." *Sociological Inquiry* 62:450–63.

Derrida, Jacques. 1997. *The Politics of Friendship*. New York: Verso.

Devere, Heather. 2013. "Amity Update: The Academic Debate on Friendship and Politics." *Amity* 1: 5–33.

Dewey, John. 1954. *The Public and Its Problems*. Chicago: Swallow Press.

Diamond, Shari, and Mary Rose. 2005. "Real Juries." *Annual Review of Law and Social Science* 1: 255–84.

DiMaggio, Paul. 1988. "Interest and Agency in Institutional Theory." In *Institutional Patterns and Organizations: Culture and Environment*, edited by Lynne Zucker. Cambridge, MA: Ballinger.

DiMaggio, Paul, and Walter Powell. 1983. "The Iron Cage Revisited: Institutional Isomorphism and Collective Rationality in Organizational Fields." *American Sociological Review* 48: 147–60.

Djupe, Paul, and Christopher Gilbert. 2009. *The Political Influences of Churches*. New York: Cambridge University Press.

Domhoff, G. William. 1974. *The Bohemian Grove and Other Retreats*. New York: Harper & Row.

Donati, Pierpaolo. 2011. *Relational Sociology: A New Paradigm for the Social Sciences*. New York: Routledge.

Donati, Pierpaolo, and Margaret Archer. 2015. *The Relational Subject*. Cambridge: Cambridge University Press.

Douglas, Gordon. 2014. "Do-It-Yourself Urban Design: The Social Practice of Informal 'Improvement' Through Unauthorized Alteration." *City & Community* 13: 5–25.

Dubofsky, Melvyn. 1969. *We Shall Be All: A History of the Industrial Workers of the World*. New York: Quadrangle.

Duck, Waverly. 2015. *No Way Out: Precarious Living in the Shadow of Poverty and Drug Dealing*. Chicago: University of Chicago Press.

Duneier, Mitchell. 1992. *Slim's Table: Race, Respectability, and Masculinity*. Chicago: University of Chicago Press.

———. 1999. *Sidewalk*. New York: Farrar Straus Giroux.

Duneier, Mitchell, and Harvey Molotch. 1999. "Talking City Trouble: Interactional Vandalism, Social Inequality, and the 'Urban Interaction Problem.'" *American Journal of Sociology* 104: 1263–95.

Durkheim, Émile. 1964 [1893]. *The Division of Labor in Society*. New York: Free Press.

———. 1965 [1912]. *The Elementary Forms of the Religious Life*. New York: Free Press.

Edelman, Murray. 1985. *The Symbolic Uses of Politics*. 2nd ed. Urbana: University of Illinois Press.

Eder, Donna, Suzanne Staggenborg, and Lori Sudderth. 1995. "The National Women's Music Festival: Collective Identity and Diversity in a Lesbian-Feminist Community." *Journal of Contemporary Ethnography* 23: 485–515.

Ehrenberg, John. 1999. *Civil Society: The Critical History of an Idea*. New York: New York University Press.

Eliasoph, Nina. 1998. *Avoiding Politics: How Americans Produce Apathy in Everyday Life*. New York: Cambridge University Press.

———. 2012. *Making Volunteers: Civic Life after Welfare's End*. Princeton, NJ: Princeton University Press.

Eliasoph, Nina, and Paul Lichterman. 2003. "Culture in Interaction." *American Journal of Sociology* 108: 735–94.

Ellickson, Robert. 1991. *Order Without Law: How Neighbors Settle Disputes*. Cambridge, MA: Harvard University Press.

Elliott, Andrea. 2007. "Where Boys Grow Up to Be Jihadis." *New York Times Magazine* (November 25, 2007): 70–81, 96.

Emirbayer, Mustafa. 1997. "Manifesto for a Relational Sociology." *American Journal of Sociology* 103: 281–317.

Emirbayer, Mustafa, and Mimi Sheller. 1999. "Publics in History." *Theory and Society* 28: 145–97.

Erickson, Karla. 2009. *The Hungry Cowboy: Service and Community in a Neighborhood Restaurant*. Jackson: University of Mississippi Press.

Erikson, Kai. 1963. *Wayward Puritans*. New York: Wiley.

———. 1977. *Everything in Its Path: Destruction of Community in the Buffalo Creek Flood*. New York: Simon and Schuster.

Evreinoff, Nicolas. 1927. *The Theatre in Life.* New York: Brentano's.

Farrell, Michael. 2001. *Collaborative Circles: Friendship Dynamics and Creative Work.* Chicago: University of Chicago Press.

Fassin, Didier. 2013. *Enforcing Order: An Ethnography of Urban Policing.* Cambridge, UK: Polity.

Faulkner, Robert. 2014. "Shedding Culture." Unpublished manuscript, University of Massachusetts.

Feigenbaum, Kenneth. 1959. "Sociable Groups as Pre-political Behavior." *American Behavioral Scientist* 2: 29–31.

Fenno, Richard, Jr. 1978. *Home Style: House Members in Their Districts.* New York: HarperCollins.

Fine, Gary Alan. 1979a. "Small Groups and Cultural Creation: The Idioculture of Little League Baseball Teams." *American Sociological Review* 44: 733–45.

———. 1979b. "The Pinkston Settlement: An Historical and Social Psychological Investigation of the Contact Hypothesis." *Phylon* 40: 229–42.

———. 1987. *With the Boys: Little League Baseball and Preadolescent Culture.* Chicago: University of Chicago Press.

———. 1991. "On the Macrofoundations of Microsociology: Constraint and the Exterior Reality of Structure." *Sociological Quarterly* 32: 161–77.

———. 1996. *Kitchens: The Culture of Restaurant Work.* Berkeley: University of California Press.

———. 1998. *Morel Tales: The Culture of Mushrooming.* Cambridge, MA: Harvard University Press.

———. 1999. "John Brown's Body: Elites, Heroic Embodiment, and the Legitimation of Political Violence." *Social Problems* 46: 225–49.

———. 2000. "Games and Truths: Learning to Construct Social Problems in High School Debate." *Sociological Quarterly* 41: 103–23.

———. 2006. "Notorious Support: The America First Committee and the Personalization of Policy." *Mobilization* 11: 405–26.

———. 2007. *Authors of the Storm: Meteorology and the Culture of Prediction.* Chicago: University of Chicago Press.

———. 2012. *Tiny Publics: A Theory of Group Culture and Group Action.* New York: Russell Sage Foundation.

———. 2015. *Players and Pawns: How Chess Creates Community and Culture.* Chicago: University of Chicago Press.

Fine, Gary Alan, and Michaela DeSoucey. 2005. "Joking Cultures: Humor Themes as Social Regulation in Group Life." *Humor* 18: 1–22.

Fine, Gary Alan, and Patricia Turner. 2001. *Whispers on the Color Line: Rumor and Race in America.* Berkeley: University of California Press.

Fine, Gary Alan, and Lisa-Jo Van den Scott. 2011. "Wispy Communities: Transient Gatherings and Imagined Micro-Communities." *American Behavioral Scientist* 55: 1319–35.

Finkelman, Paul, ed. 1995. *His Soul Goes Marching On: Responses to John Brown and the Harpers Ferry Raid.* Charlottesville: University Press of Virginia.

Fischer, Claude. 1982. *To Dwell Among Friends: Personal Networks in Town and City*. Chicago: University of Chicago Press.

———. 1992. *America Calling: A Social History of the Telephone to 1940*. Berkeley: University of California Press.

Fishkin, James. 2009. *When the People Speak: Deliberative Democracy and Public Consultation*. New York: Oxford University Press.

Fligstein, Neil. 2001. "Social Skill and the Theory of Fields." *Sociological Theory* 19: 105–25.

Fligstein, Neil, and Doug McAdam. 2012. *A Theory of Fields*. New York: Oxford University Press.

Follett, Mary Parker. 1918. *The New State: Group Organization the Solution of Popular Government*. New York: Longmans, Green.

Foucault, Michel. 1981. "Friendship as a Way of Life." Interview for *Gai Pied*, conducted by R. de Ceccaty, J. Danet, and J. Le Bitoux. Translated by John Johnson. http://caringlabor.wordpress.com/2010/11/18/michel-foucault-friendship-as-a-way-of-life. Accessed January 16, 2017.

Fraser, Nancy. 1992. "Rethinking the Public Sphere: A Contribution to the Critique of Actually Existing Democracy." Pp. 109–42 in *Habermas and the Public Sphere*, edited by Craig Calhoun. Cambridge, MA: MIT Press.

Freedman, Jonathan, and Scott Fraser. 1966. "Compliance without Pressure: The Foot-in-the-Door Technique." *Journal of Personality and Social Psychology* 4: 195–202.

Freeman, Jo. 1972–73. "The Tyranny of Structurelessness." *Berkeley Journal of Sociology* 17: 151–64.

Freudenburg, William. 1986. "Sociology in Legis-Land: An Ethnographic Report on Congressional Culture." *Sociological Quarterly* 27: 313–26.

Fuist, Todd Nicholas. 2014. "The Dramatization of Beliefs, Values, and Allegiances: Ideological Performances among Social Movement Groups and Religious Organizations." *Social Movement Studies* 13: 427–42.

———. 2015. "Talking to God among a Cloud of Witnesses: Collective Prayer as a Meaningful Performance." *Journal for the Scientific Study of Religion* 54: 523–39.

Galbraith, John Kenneth. 1964. *The Scotch*. New York: Houghton Mifflin.

Gamson, William. 1992. *Talking Politics*. New York: Cambridge University Press.

Gamson, William, Bruce Fireman, and Steven Rytina. 1982. *Encounters with Unjust Authority*. Homewood, IL: Dorsey Press.

Gannett, Robert, Jr. 2003. "Bowling Ninepins in Tocqueville's Township." *American Political Science Review* 97: 1–16.

Garrido, Marco. 2018. "Populism as Witchcraft." Unpublished manuscript.

Garfinkel, Harold. 1956. "Conditions of Successful Degradation Ceremonies." *American Journal of Sociology* 61: 420–24.

Gebhardt, Jürgen. 2008. "Friendship, Trust, and Political Order: A Critical Overview." Pp. 315–47 in *Friendship and Politics: Essays in Political Thought*, edited by John von Heyking and Richard Avramenko. Notre Dame, IN: University of Notre Dame Press.

Gerlach, Luther, and Virginia Hine. 1970. *People, Power, Change: Movements of Social Transformation.* Indianapolis: Bobbs-Merrill.

Ghaziani, Amin. 2011. "Post-Gay Collective Identity Construction." *Social Problems* 58: 99–125.

Gibson, David. 2012. *Talk at the Brink: Deliberation and Decision During the Cuban Missile Crisis.* Princeton, NJ: Princeton University Press.

Giddens, Anthony. 1984. *The Constitution of Society: Outline of the Theory of Structuration.* Berkeley: University of California Press.

Gilbert, Margaret. 1997. "What Is It for Us to Intend?" *Synthese Library*: 65–86.

———. 2009. "Shared Intentions and Personal Intentions." *Philosophical Studies* 144: 167–87.

Gina. 2006. "Wrapping My Mind Around Yearly Kos." Daily Kos (June 13, 2006).

Glassberg, David. 1990. *American Historical Pageantry: The Uses of Tradition in the Early Twentieth Century.* Chapel Hill: University of North Carolina Press.

Goffman, Erving. 1959. *Presentation of Self in Everyday Life.* Garden City, NY: Anchor.

———. 1967. *Interaction Ritual: Essays on Face-to-Face Behavior.* Garden City, NY: Anchor.

———. 1974. *Frame Analysis.* Cambridge, MA: Harvard University Press.

———. 1983. "The Interaction Order." *American Sociological Review* 48: 1–17.

Goldfarb, Jeffrey. 2006. *The Politics of Small Things: The Power of the Powerless in Dark Times.* Chicago: University of Chicago Press.

Goodman, Dena. 1994. *The Republic of Letters: A Cultural History of the French Enlightenment.* Ithaca, NY: Cornell University Press.

Goodwin, Doris Kearns. 2013. *The Bully Pulpit: Theodore Roosevelt, William Howard Taft, and the Golden Age of Journalism.* New York: Simon and Schuster.

Goodwin, Jeff. 1997. "The Libidinal Constitution of a High-Risk Social Movement: Affectual Ties and Solidarity in the Huk Rebellion, 1946 to 1954." *American Sociological Review* 62: 53–69.

Gordon, Daniel. 1994. *Citizens Without Sovereignty: Equality and Sociability in French Thought, 1670–1789.* Princeton, NJ: Princeton University Press.

Gordon, H. Scott. 1954. "The Economic Theory of a Common-Property Resource: The Fishery." *Journal of Political Economy* 62: 124–42.

Gordon, Linda. 2017. *The Second Coming of the KKK: The Ku Klux Klan of the 1920s and the American Political Tradition.* New York: Liveright.

Gould, Roger V. 1993. "Trade Cohesion, Class Unity, and Urban Insurrection: Artisanal Activism in the Paris Commune." *American Journal of Sociology* 98: 721–54.

———. 1995. *Insurgent Identities: Class, Community, and Protest in Paris from 1848 to the Commune.* Chicago: University of Chicago Press.

———. 2003. *Collision of Wills: How Ambiguity about Social Rank Breeds Conflict.* Chicago: University of Chicago Press.

Grannis, Rick. 2009. *From the Ground Up: Translating Geography into Community through Neighbor Networks.* Princeton, NJ: Princeton University Press.

Granovetter, Mark. 1973. "The Strength of Weak Ties." *American Journal of Sociology* 78: 1360–80.

Graveline, Christopher, and Michael Clemens. 2010. *The Secrets of Abu Ghraib Revealed: American Soldiers on Trial.* Washington, DC: Potomac Books.

Greene, Joshua. 2013. *Moral Tribes: Emotion, Reason, and the Gap between Us and Them.* New York: Penguin.

Guhin, Jeffrey. 2016. "Why Worry About Evolution? Boundaries, Practices, and Moral Salience in Sunni and Evangelical High Schools." *Sociological Theory* 34: 151–74.

Gurbuz, Mustafa. 2015. "Ideology in Action: Symbolic Localization of Kurdistan Workers' Party in Turkey." *Sociological Inquiry* 85: 1–27.

Habermas, Jürgen. 1989. *The Structural Transformation of the Public Sphere: An Inquiry into a Category of Bourgeois Society*, translated by Thomas Burger. Cambridge, MA: MIT Press.

Hackman, J. Richard, and Neil Vidmar. 1970. "Effects of Size and Task Type on Group Performance and Member Reactions." *Sociometry* 33: 37–54.

Haedicke, Michael. 2012. "'Keeping Our Mission, Changing Our System': Translation and Organizational Change in Natural Foods Co-ops." *Sociological Quarterly* 53: 44–67.

Haine, William Scott. 1996. *The World of the Paris Café: Sociability among the French Working Class, 1789–1914.* Baltimore: Johns Hopkins University Press.

Hallett, Tim. 2010. "The Myth Incarnate: Recoupling Processes, Turmoil, and Inhabited Institutions in an Urban Elementary School." *American Sociological Review* 75: 52–74.

Hallett, Tim, Brent Harger, and Donna Eder. 2009. "Gossip at Work: Unsanctioned Evaluative Talk in Formal School Meetings." *Journal of Contemporary Ethnography* 38: 584–618.

Hallett, Tim, and Marc Ventresca. 2006. "Inhabited Institutions: Social Interaction and Organizational Forms in Gouldner's *Patterns of Industrial Bureaucracy.*" *Theory and Society* 35: 213–36.

Harding, David. 2010. *Living the Drama: Community, Conflict, and Culture among Inner-City Boys.* Chicago: University of Chicago Press.

Hardy, Cynthia, and Steve Maguire. 2008. "Institutional Entrepreneurship." In *The SAGE Handbook of Organizational Institutionalism*, edited by Royston Greenwood, Christine Oliver, Roy Suddaby, and Kirsten Sahlin-Andersson. Thousand Oaks, CA: Sage.

Harper, Douglas. 2001. *Changing Works: Visions of a Lost Agriculture.* Chicago: University of Chicago Press.

Hart, Stephen. 2001. *Cultural Dilemmas of Progressive Politics.* Chicago: University of Chicago Press.

Harwood, W. S. 1897. "Secret Societies in America." *North American Review* 164, no. 486 (May): 617–24.

Hassan, Hatem. 2015. "Extraordinary Politics of Ordinary People: Explaining the

Microdynamics of Popular Committees in Revolutionary Cairo." *International Sociology* 30: 1–18.

Hattox, Ralph. 1985. *Coffee and Coffeehouses: The Origins of a Social Beverage in the Medieval Near East.* Seattle: University of Washington Press.

Haug, Christoph. 2013. "Organizing Spaces: Meeting Arenas as a Social Movement Infrastructure between Organization, Network, and Institution." *Organization Studies* 34 (5–6): 705–32.

Herken, Gregg. 2014. *The Georgetown Set: Friends and Rivals in Cold War Washington.* New York: Knopf.

Hobbes, Thomas. 1651. *Leviathan.* Oxford: Clarendon Press.

Hoggett, Paul, and Jeff Bishop. 1986. *Organizing Around Enthusiasms.* London: Comedia.

Honohan, Isault. 2001. "Friends, Strangers or Countrymen? The Ties Between Citizens as Colleagues." *Political Studies* 49: 51–69.

Homans, George. 1941. *English Villagers of the Thirteenth Century.* Cambridge, MA: Harvard University Press.

———. 1946. "The Small Warship." *American Sociological Review* 11: 294–300.

Horgan, John. 2014. *The Psychology of Terrorism.* 2nd ed. New York: Routledge.

Hunt, Jennifer. 2010. *Seven Shots: An NYPD Raid on a Terrorist Cell and Its Aftermath.* Chicago: University of Chicago Press.

Ikegami, Eiko. 2000. "A Sociological Theory of Publics: Identity and Culture as Emergent Properties in Networks." *Social Research* 67: 989–1029.

Jacobson, David. 2001. *Place and Belonging in America.* Baltimore: Johns Hopkins University Press.

Janis, Irving. 1972. *Victims of Groupthink: A Psychological Study of Foreign-Policy Decisions and Fiascoes.* Boston: Houghton Mifflin.

Jasper, James. 2004. "A Strategic Approach to Collective Action: Looking for Agency in Social-Movement Choices." *Mobilization* 9: 1–16.

———. 2010. "Social Movement Theory Today: Toward a Theory of Action?" *Sociology Compass* 10: 965–76.

Jasper, James, and Frédéric Volpi. 2018. "Introduction: Rethinking Mobilization after the Arab Uprisings." Pp. 11–40 in *Microfoundations of the Arab Uprisings: Mapping Interactions between Regimes and Protesters,* edited by Frédéric Volpi and James Jasper. Amsterdam: Amsterdam University Press.

Johnston, Hank. 1991. *Tales of Nationalism: Catalonia, 1939–1979.* New Brunswick, NJ: Rutgers University Press.

———. 2006. "'Let's Get Small: The Dynamics of (Small) Contention in Repressive States." *Mobilization* 11: 195–212.

Johnston, Hank, and Aili Aarelaid-Tart. 2000. "Generations, Microcohorts, and Long-term Mobilization: The Estonian National Movement." *Sociological Perspectives* 43: 671–98.

Junger, Sebastian. 2016. *Tribe: On Homecoming and Belonging.* New York: Twelve.

Kaplan, Danny. 2006. *The Men We Loved: Male Friendship and Nationalism in Israeli Culture.* New York: Berghahn Books.

————. 2018. *The Nation as Social Club: Building Solidarity through Sociability.* New York: Palgrave-Macmillan.

Kaufman, Jason. 2002. *For the Common Good? American Civic Life and the Golden Age of Fraternity.* New York: Oxford University Press.

Kelley, Robin D. G. 2002. *Freedom Dreams: The Black Radical Imagination.* Boston: Beacon Press.

Keohane, Nannerl. 2014. "Civil Society and Good Democratic Leadership." Unpublished manuscript, Princeton University.

Kerbel, Matthew. 2009. *Netroots: Online Progressives and the Transformation of American Politics.* Boulder, CO: Paradigm.

Kim, Jeong-Chul. 2013. *"Indigenous Collaboration under Foreign Occupation: Japanese-Occupied Koreans from 1904 to 1945."* Ph.D. dissertation, Northwestern University.

Kim, Jeong-Chul, and Gary Alan Fine. 2013. "Collaborators and National Memory: The Creation of the Encyclopedia of Pro-Japanese Collaborators in Korea." *Memory Studies* 6: 130–45.

Kjølsrød, Lise. 2013. "Mediated Activism: Contingent Democracy in Leisure Worlds." *Sociology* 46: 1207–23.

Klein, Lawrence. 1996. "Coffeehouse Civility, 1660–1714: An Aspect of Post-Courtly Culture in England." *Huntington Library Quarterly* 59 (1): 30–51.

Klinenberg, Eric. 2018. *Palaces for the People: How Social Infrastructure Can Help Fight Inequality, Polarization, and the Decline of Civic Life.* New York: Crown.

Koshar, Rudy. 1986. *Social Life, Local Politics, and Nazism: Marburg, 1880–1935.* Chapel Hill: University of North Carolina Press.

Kos. "My Yearly Kos Keynote Address." Daily Kos, August 4, 2007; online.

Koselleck, Reinhart. 1988. *Critique and Crisis: Enlightenment and the Pathogenesis of Modern Society.* Cambridge, MA: MIT Press.

Kuzmics, Helmut. 1991. "Embarrassment and Civilization: On Some Similarities and Differences in the Work of Goffman and Elias." *Theory, Culture, and Society* 8: 1–30.

Kretsedemas, Philip. 2000. "Examining Frame Formation in Peer Group Conversations." *Sociological Quarterly* 41: 439–56.

Kuhn, Manford H., and Thomas S. McPartland. 1954. "An Empirical Investigation of Self-Attitudes." *American Sociological Review* 19: 68–76.

Lamont, Michele. 2009. *How Professors Think: Inside the Curious World of Academic Judgment.* Cambridge, MA: Harvard University Press.

Lane, Christel. 1981. *The Rites of Rulers: Ritual in Industrial Society—The Soviet Case.* Cambridge: Cambridge University Press.

Lainer-Vos, Dan. 2013. *Sinews of the Nation: Constructing Irish and Zionist Bonds in the United States.* Cambridge, UK: Polity.

Latour, Bruno. 2005. *Reassembling the Social: An Introduction to Actor-Network Theory.* New York: Oxford University Press.

Laumann, Edward. 1973. *Bonds of Pluralism: The Form and Substance of Urban Social Networks.* New York: Wiley.

Lawrence, Tom, and Roy Suddaby. 2006. "Institutions and Institutional Work." In *Handbook of Organization Studies*, 2nd ed., edited by Stewart Clegg, Cynthia Hardy, Tom Lawrence, and Walter Nord. London: Sage.

Lawrence, Thomas, Roy Suddaby, and Bernard Leca. 2009. "Introduction: Theorizing and Studying Institutional Work." In *Institutional Work: Actors and Agency in Institutional Studies of Organizations*, edited by Thomas Lawrence, Roy Suddaby, and Bernard Leca. Cambridge: Cambridge University Press.

Lee, Caroline. 2007. "Is There a Place for Private Conversation in Public Dialogue? Comparing Stakeholder Assessments of Informal Communication in Collaborative Regional Planning." *American Journal of Sociology* 113: 41–96.

Leenders, Reinoud. 2012. "Collective Action and Mobilization in Dar'a: An Anatomy of the Onset of Syria's Popular Uprising." *Mobilization* 17: 419–34.

Lefebvre, Henri. 1991. *The Production of Space*. Oxford: Blackwell.

Leighly, Jan. 1991. "Participation as a Stimulus of Political Conceptualization." *Journal of Politics* 53: 198–211.

LeMasters, E. E. 1975. *Working Class Aristocrats: Life-Styles at a Working-Class Tavern*. Madison: University of Wisconsin Press.

Levtzion, Nehemia. 2002. "The Dynamics of Sufi Brotherhoods." Pp. 104–18 in *The Public Sphere in Muslim Societies*, edited by Miriam Hoexter, Shmuel N. Eisenstadt, and Nehemia Levtzion. Albany: State University of New York Press.

Lewis, C. S. 1960. *The Four Loves*. New York: Harcourt, Brace.

Lichterman, Paul. 2005. *Elusive Togetherness: Church Groups Trying to Bridge America's Divisions*. Princeton, NJ: Princeton University Press.

———. 2006. "Social Capital or Group Style?" Rescuing Tocqueville's Insights on Civil Engagement." *Theory and Society* 35: 529–63.

Lichterman, Paul, and Nina Eliasoph. 2014. "Civic Action." *American Journal of Sociology* 120: 798–863.

Liebow, Eliott. 1967. *Tally's Corner: A Study of Negro Streetcorner Men*. Boston: Little Brown.

Lipsky, Michael. 2010. *Street-Level Bureaucracies: Dilemmas of the Individual in Public Services*. New York: Russell Sage Foundation.

Lloyd, William Forster. 1980 [1833]. "W. F. Lloyd on the Checks to Population." *Population and Development Review* 6 (3): 473–96.

Lofland, John, and Michael Jamison. 1984. "Social Movement Locals: Modal Member Structures." *Sociological Analysis* 45: 115–29.

Lukes, Steven. 2005. *Power: A Radical View*. 2nd ed. New York: Palgrave Macmillan.

Maffesoli, Michel. 1996. *The Time of the Tribes: The Decline of Individualism in Mass Society*. London: Sage.

Maier, Pauline. 1997. *American Scripture: Making the Declaration of Independence*. New York: Knopf.

Maines, David. 1977. "Social Organization and Social Structure in Symbolic Interactionist Thought." *Annual Review of Sociology* 3: 235–59.

Mallory, Peter. 2012. "Political Friendship in the Era of 'the Social': Theorizing Personal Relations with Alexis de Tocqueville." *Journal of Classical Sociology* 12: 23–42.

Mannheim, Karl. 1952. "The Problem of Generations." In *Essays on the Sociology of Knowledge*. London: Routledge and Kegan Paul.

Manzo, John. 1993. "Jurors' Narrations of Personal Experience in Deliberation Talk." *Text* 13: 267–90.

Mansbridge, Jane. 1980. *Beyond Adversary Democracy*. New York: Basic Books.

Martin, Joanne. 1992. *Culture in Organizations: Three Perspectives*. New York: Oxford University Press.

Martin, John Levi. 2011. *The Explanation of Social Action*. New York: Oxford University Press.

Massey, Doreen. 1991. "The Political Place of Locality Studies." *Environment and Planning* 23: 267–81.

May, Reuben A. Buford. 2001. *Talking at Trena's: Everyday Conversations at an African American Tavern*. New York: New York University Press.

McAdam, Doug. 1988. *Freedom Summer*. New York: Oxford University Press.

McAdam, Doug, and Ronnelle Paulsen. 1993. "Specifying the Relationship between Social Ties and Activism." *American Journal of Sociology* 99: 640–67.

McCarter, Jeremy. 2017. *Young Radicals in the War for American Ideals*. New York: Random House.

McFarland, Daniel. 2004. "Resistance as Social Order: A Study of Change-Oriented Encounters." *American Journal of Sociology* 109: 1249–1318.

McFeat, Tom. 1974. *Small-Group Cultures*. New York: Pergamon.

McGinty, Patrick. 2014. "Divided and Drifting: Interactionism and the Neglect of Social Organizational Analysis in Organization Studies." *Symbolic Interaction* 37: 155–86.

McLean, Paul. 2007. *The Art of the Network*. Cambridge: Cambridge University Press.

McPhail, Clark. 1991. *The Myth of the Madding Crowd*. New York: Aldine.

McPherson, Miller, Lynn Smith-Lovin, and Matthew Brashears. 2006. "Social Isolation in America: Changes in Core Discussion Networks over Two Decades." *American Sociological Review* 71: 353–75.

Mead, George Herbert. 1934. *Mind, Self, and Society: From the Standpoint of a Social Behaviorist*. Chicago: University of Chicago Press.

Meeks, Wayne. 2003. *The First Urban Christians: The Social World of the Apostle Paul*. 2nd ed. New Haven, CT: Yale University Press.

Menzies, Heather. 2014. *Reclaiming the Commons for the Common Good*. Gabriola Island, BC: New Society Publishers.

Merton, Robert, and Elinor Barber. 2004. *The Travels and Adventures of Serendipity: A Study in Sociological Semantics and the Sociology of Science*. Princeton, NJ: Princeton University Press.

Meyer, John, and Brian Rowan. 1977. "Institutionalized Organizations: Formal Structure as Myth and Ceremony." *American Journal of Sociology* 83: 340–63.

Meyer, Robinson. 2013. "It's a Lonely World." *Atlantic* (December 19). http://www
.theatlantic.com/technology/archive/2013/12/its-a-lonely-world-the-median
-twitter-user-has-1-measly-follower/282513/. Accessed February 1, 2015.

Miller, Montana. 2012. *Playing Dead: Mock Trauma and Folk Drama in Staged High School Drunk Driving Tragedies.* Logan: Utah State University Press.

Miller, Stephen. 2006. *Conversation: A History of a Declining Art.* New Haven, CT: Yale University Press.

Mills, C. Wright. 1956. *The Power Elite.* New York: Oxford University Press.

Mische, Ann. 2008. *Partisan Publics: Communication and Contention across Brazilian Youth Activist Networks.* Princeton, NJ: Princeton University Press.

———. 2009. "Projects and Possibilities: Researching Futures in Action." *Sociological Forum* 24: 694–704.

Mische, Ann, and Harrison White. 1998. "Between Conversation and Situation: Public Switching Dynamics Across Network-Domains." *Social Research* 65: 295–324.

Mishler, Paul. 1999. *Raising Reds: The Young Pioneers, Radical Summer Camps, and Communist Political Culture in the United States.* New York: Columbia University Press.

Misztal, Barbara. 2001. "Normality and Trust in Goffman's Theory of Interaction Order." *Sociological Theory* 19: 312–24.

Mitchell, Richard, Jr. 2002. *Dancing at Armageddon: Survivalism and Chaos in Modern Times.* Chicago: University of Chicago Press.

Mitchell, William. 1978. *Mishpokhe: A Study of New York City Jewish Family Clubs.* Chicago: Aldine.

Morrill, Calvin. 1995. *The Executive Way: Conflict Management in Corporations.* Chicago: University of Chicago Press.

Morris, David, and Karl Hess. 1975. *Neighborhood Power: Returning Political and Economic Power to Community Life.* Boston: Beacon Press.

Moskos, Peter. 2008. *Cop in the Hood: My Year Policing Baltimore's Eastern District.* Princeton, NJ: Princeton University Press.

Munson, Ziad. 2008. *The Making of Pro-Life Activists.* Chicago: University of Chicago Press.

Nee, Victor, and Brett de Bary Nee. 1973. *Long Time Californ': Documentary Study of an American Chinatown.* New York: Pantheon.

Nietzsche, Friedrich. 1907. *Beyond Good and Evil.* New York: Macmillan.

Norberg, Jakob. 2014. *Sociability and Its Enemies: German Political Theory after 1945.* Evanston, IL: Northwestern University Press.

Oates, Stephen. 1984. *To Purge This Land with Blood: A Biography of John Brown.* 2nd ed. Amherst: University of Massachusetts Press.

Ober, Josiah. 1989. *Mass and Elite in Democratic Athens.* Princeton, NJ: Princeton University Press.

Oldenburg, Ray. 1989. *The Great Good Place.* St. Paul: Paragon House.

Olick, Jeffrey. 1999. "Collective Memory: The Two Cultures." *Sociological Theory* 17: 333–48.

Oliver, Pamela, and Hank Johnston. 2000. "What a Good Idea! Ideologies and Frames in Social Movement Research." *Mobilization* 5: 37–54.

Olson, Mancur. 1965. *The Logic of Collective Action: Public Goods and the Theory of Groups*. Cambridge, MA: Harvard University Press.

Opie, Iona, and Peter Opie. 1959. *The Lore and Language of School-Children*. Oxford: Clarendon.

Ostrom, Elinor. 1990. *Governing the Commons: The Evolution of Institutions of Collective Action*. New York: Cambridge University Press.

Paik, Anthony, and Kenneth Sanchagrin. 2013. "Social Isolation in America: An Artifact." *American Sociological Review* 78: 339–60.

Parker, John, and Edward Hackett. 2012. "Hot Spots and Hot Moments in Scientific Collaborations and Social Movements." *American Sociological Review* 77: 21–44.

Parker, John, and Ugo Corte. 2018. "Placing Collaborative Circles in Strategic Action Fields: Explaining Differences Between Highly Creative Groups." *Sociological Theory* 34: 261–87.

Pattillo-McCoy, Mary. 1998. "Sweet Mothers and Gangbangers: Managing Crime in a Black Middle-Class Neighborhood." *Social Forces* 76: 747–74.

Payne, Charles. 1995. *I've Got the Light of Freedom: The Organizing Tradition and the Mississippi Freedom Struggle*. Berkeley: University of California Press.

Perrin, Andrew. 2005. "Political Microcultures: Linking Civic Life and Democratic Discourse." *Social Forces* 84: 1049–82.

Perry, Evelyn. 2017. *Live and Let Live: Diversity, Conflict, and Community in an Integrated Neighborhood*. Chapel Hill: University of North Carolina Press.

Petev, Ivaylo D. 2013. "The Association of Social Class and Lifestyles: Persistence in American Sociability, 1974 and 2010." *American Sociological Review* 78: 633–61.

Pettigrew, Thomas, and Linda Tropp. 2011. *When Groups Meet: The Dynamics of Intergroup Contact*. New York: Psychology Press.

Pfaff, Steven. 1996. "Collective Identity and Informal Groups in Revolutionary Mobilization: East Germany in 1989." *Social Forces* 75: 91–118.

Piven, Frances Fox, and Richard Cloward. 1992. "Normalizing Collective Protest." Pp. 301–25 in *Frontiers in Social Movement Theory*, edited by Aldon Morris and Carol Mueller. New Haven, CT: Yale University Press.

Polletta, Francesca. 2002. *Freedom Is an Endless Meeting: Democracy in American Social Movements*. Chicago: University of Chicago Press.

———. 2006. *It Was Like a Fever: Storytelling in Protest and Politics*. Chicago: University of Chicago Press.

Polletta, Francesca, and John Lee. 2006. "Is Telling Stories Good for Democracy? Rhetoric in Public Deliberation after 9/11." *American Sociological Review* 71: 699–723.

Pollner, Melvin. 1987. *Mundane Reason: Reality in Everyday and Sociological Discourse*. New York: Cambridge University Press.

Portes, Alejandro. 1998. "Social Capital: Its Origins and Applications in Modern Sociology." *Annual Review of Sociology* 24: 1–24.

Putnam, Robert. 1993. *Making Democracy Work: Civic Traditions in Modern Italy.* Princeton, NJ: Princeton University Press.

———. 1995. "Tuning In, Tuning Out: The Strange Disappearance of Social Capital in America." *PS: Political Science and Politics* 28: 664–83.

———. 2000. *Bowling Alone: The Collapse and Revival of American Community.* New York: Simon and Schuster.

Putnam, Robert, and David Campbell. 2010. *American Grace: How Religion Divides and Unites Us.* New York: Simon and Schuster.

Quillian, Lincoln, and Devah Pager. 2001. "Black Neighbors, Higher Crime? The Role of Racial Stereotypes in Evaluations of Neighborhood Crime." *American Journal of Sociology* 107: 717–67.

Rawls, Anne. 1987. "Interaction Sui Generis." *Sociological Theory* 5: 136–49.

Rawls, John. 1971. *A Theory of Justice.* Cambridge, MA: Harvard University Press.

Reed, Isaac. 2006. "Social Dramas, Shipwrecks, and Cockfights: Conflict and Complicity in Social Performance." Pp. 146–68 in *Social Performance: Symbolic Action, Cultural Pragmatics and Ritual,* edited by Jeffrey Alexander, Bernhard Giesen, and Jason Mast. Cambridge: Cambridge University Press.

Reed, Isaac Ariall. 2017. "Chains of Power and Their Representation." *Sociological Theory* 35: 87–117.

Reedy, Justin, John Gastil, and Michael Gabbay. 2013. "Terrorism and Small Groups: An Analytic Framework for Group Disruption." *Small Group Research* 44: 599–626.

Reger, Jo. 2002. "Organizational Dynamics and Construction of Multiple Feminist Identities in the National Organization for Women." *Gender & Society* 16: 710–27.

Rhodes, R. A. W. 2011. *Everyday Life in British Government.* Oxford: Oxford University Press.

Rieder, Jonathan. 1985. *Canarsie: The Jews and Italians of Brooklyn against Liberalism.* Cambridge, MA: Harvard University Press.

Riesman, David, Robert Potter, and Jeanne Watson. 1960. "The Vanishing Host." *Human Organization* 19: 17–27.

Riley, Dylan. 2010. *The Civic Foundations of Fascism in Europe: Italy, Spain, and Romania, 1870–1945.* Baltimore: Johns Hopkins University Press.

Ringmar, Erik. 1998. "Nationalism: The Idiocy of Intimacy." *British Journal of Sociology* 49: 534–49.

Rivera, Lauren. 2012. "Hiring as Cultural Matching: The Case of Elite Professional Service Firms." *American Sociological Review* 77: 999–1022.

Robnett, Belinda. 1996. "African-American Women in the Civil Rights Movement, 1954–1965: Gender, Leadership, and Micromobilization." *American Journal of Sociology* 101: 1661–93.

Rochon, Thomas. 1998. *Culture Moves: Ideas, Activism, and Changing Values.* Princeton, NJ: Princeton University Press.

Romani, Gabriella. 2007. "A Room with a View: Interpreting the Ottocento through the Literary Salon." *Italica* 84: 233–46.

Rose, Norman. 2000. *The Cliveden Set: Portrait of an Exclusive Fraternity.* London: Jonathan Cape.

Roy, Donald. 1959–60. "Banana Time: Job Satisfaction and Informal Interaction." *Human Organization* 18: 158–68.

Rubinstein, Jonathan. 1973. *City Police.* New York: Farrar, Straus, and Giroux.

Rymond-Richmond, Wenona. 2006. "Transforming Communities: Formal and Informal Mechanisms of Social Control." Pp. 295–312 in *The Many Colors of Crime,* edited by Ruth Peterson, Laurie Krivo, and John Hagan. New York: NYU Press.

Sacks, Harvey. 1995. *Lectures on Conversation.* Malden, MA: Wiley-Blackwell.

Sageman, Marc. 2008. *Leaderless Jihad: Terror Networks in the Twenty-First Century.* Philadelphia: University of Pennsylvania Press.

Sampson, Robert. 2012. *Great American City: Chicago and the Enduring Neighborhood Effect.* Chicago: University of Chicago Press.

Sampson, Robert, Jeffrey Morenoff, and Felton Earls. 1999. "Spatial Dynamics of Collective Efficacy for Children." *American Sociological Review* 64: 633–60.

Sampson, Robert, Jeffrey Morenoff, and Thomas Gannon-Rowley. 2002. "Assessing Neighborhood Effects: Social Processes and New Directions in Research." *Annual Review of Sociology* 28: 443–78.

Sampson, Robert, and Stephen Raudenbush. 1999. "Systematic Social Observation of Public Spaces: A New Look at Disorder in Urban Neighborhoods." *American Journal of Sociology* 105: 603–51.

Sandra, Jaida, and Jon Spayde. 2001. *Salons: The Joy of Conversation.* Gabriola Island, BC: New Society Publishers.

Santino, Jack. 1994. *All Around the Year: Holidays and Celebrations in American Life.* Urbana: University of Illinois Press.

Sanyal, Paromita. 2009. "From Credit to Collective Action: The Role of Microfinance in Promoting Women's Social Capital and Normative Influence." *American Sociological Review* 74: 529–50.

Sawyer, R. Keith. 2007. *Group Genius: The Creative Power of Collaboration.* New York: Basic Books.

Schegloff, Emanuel. 1992. "Repair After Next Turn: The Last Structurally Provided Defense of Intersubjectivity in Conversation." *American Journal of Sociology* 97: 1295–1345.

———. 2007. *Sequence Organization in Interaction: A Primer in Conversation Analysis.* New York: Cambridge University Press.

Scheler, Max. 1954, *The Nature of Sympathy.* Translated by P. Heath. New Haven, CT: Yale University Press.

Schlesinger, Arthur. 1944. "Biography of a Nation of Joiners." *American Historical Review* 50: 1–25.

Schneider, Beth. 1988. "Political Generations in the Contemporary Women's Movement." *Sociological Inquiry* 58: 4–21.

Schudson, Michael. 1989. "How Culture Works: Perspectives from Media Studies on the Efficacy of Symbols." *Theory and Society* 18: 153–80.

Schutz, Alfred. 1967. *The Phenomenology of the Social World*. Evanston, IL: Northwestern University Press.

———. 1970. *On Phenomenology and Social Relations*. Chicago: University of Chicago Press.

Schwartzenbach, Sibyl. 2009. *On Civic Friendship: Including Women in the State*. New York: Columbia University Press.

Schwartzman, Helen. 1989. *The Meeting: Gatherings in Organizations and Communities*. New York: Plenum.

Scott, James. 1976. *The Moral Economy of the Peasant: Rebellion and Subsistence in Southeast Asia*. Princeton, NJ: Princeton University Press.

———. 1985. *Weapons of the Weak: Everyday Forms of Peasant Resistance*. New Haven, CT: Yale University Press.

———. 1990. *Domination and the Arts of Resistance: Hidden Transcripts*. New Haven, CT: Yale University Press.

———. 2012. *Two Cheers for Anarchism*. Princeton, NJ: Princeton University Press.

Scott, Joan. 1980. *The Glassworkers of Carmaux: French Craftsmen and Political Action in a Nineteenth-Century City*. Cambridge, MA: Harvard University Press.

Selden, John. 1689. *Table Talk: Being the Discourses of John Selden*. London: J. M. Dent and Company.

Sennett, Richard. 1977. *The Fall of Public Man*. New York: Knopf.

———. 2012. *Together: The Rituals, Pleasures, and Politics of Cooperation*. New Haven, CT: Yale University Press.

Shalin, Dmitri. 1988. "G. H. Mead, Socialism and the Progressive Agenda." *American Journal of Sociology* 93: 913–51.

Shenk, Joshua. 2014. *Powers of Two: Finding the Essence of Innovation in Creative Pairs*. Boston: Houghton Mifflin Harcourt.

Shepard, Benjamin. 2015. *Rebel Friendships: "Outsider" Networks and Social Movements*. New York: Palgrave Macmillan.

Sherif, Muzafer, O. J. Harvey, B. J. Hood, and Carolyn W. Sherif. 1961. *Intergroup Conflict and Cooperation: The Robbers Cave Experiment*. Norman: University of Oklahoma Book Exchange.

Shibutani, Tamotsu. 1966. *Improvised News: A Sociological Study of Rumor*. Indianapolis: Bobbs-Merrill.

Silver, Daniel. 2011. "The Moodiness of Action." *Sociological Theory* 29: 199–222.

Silver, Daniel, Terry Nichols Clark, and Clemente Jesus Navarro Yanez. 2010. "Scenes: Social Context in an Age of Contingency." *Social Forces* 88: 2293–2324.

Simmel, Georg. 1950. *The Sociology of Georg Simmel*. Translated and edited by Kurt Wolff. New York: Free Press.

Sinclair, Betsy. 2012. *The Social Citizen: Peer Networks and Political Behavior*. Chicago: University of Chicago Press.

Skocpol, Theda. 1999. "How Americans Became Civic." Pp. 27–80 in *Civic Engagement in American Democracy*, edited by Theda Skocpol and Morris Fiorina. Washington: Brookings Institution Press.

———. 2003. *Diminished Democracy: From Membership to Management in American Civic Life.* Norman: University of Oklahoma Press.

Small, Mario. 2004. *Villa Victoria: The Transformation of Social Capital in a Boston Barrio.* Chicago: University of Chicago Press.

———. 2009. *Unanticipated Gains: Origins of Network Inequality in Everyday Life.* New York: Oxford University Press.

———. 2017. *Someone to Talk To.* New York: Oxford University Press.

Smelser, Neil. 1962. *Theory of Collective Behavior.* New York: Free Press.

Smith, Gregory. 2006. *Erving Goffman.* Abington, UK: Routledge.

Snow, David A., and Leon Anderson. 1987. "Identity Work among the Homeless: The Verbal Construction and Avowal of Personal Identities." *American Journal of Sociology* 92: 1336–71.

Snow, David, and Robert Benford. 1988. "Ideology, Frame Resonance, and Participant Mobilization." Pp. 197–218 in *International Social Movement Research*, vol. 1, edited by B. Klandermans, H. Kriesi, and S. Tarrow. Greenwich, CT: JAI Press.

Snow, David, Daniel Cress, Liam Downey, and Andrew Jones. 1998. "Disrupting the 'Quotidian': Reconceptualizing the Relationship between Breakdown and the Emergence of Collective Action." *Mobilization* 3: 1–22.

Snow, David, and Dana Moss. 2014. "Protest on the Fly: Toward a Theory of Spontaneity in the Dynamics of Protest and Social Movements." *American Sociological Review* 79: 1122–43.

Snow, David, E. Burke Rochford Jr., Steven Worden, and Robert Benford. 1986. "Frame Alignment Processes, Micromobilization, and Movement Participation." *American Sociological Review* 51: 464–81.

Snow, David, Louis Zurcher, and Sheldon Ekland-Olsen. 1980. "Social Networks and Social Movements: A Microstructural Approach to Differential Recruitment." *American Sociological Review* 45: 787–801.

Somers, Margaret. 1993. "Citizenship and the Place of the Public Sphere: Law, Community, and Political Culture in the Transition to Democracy." *American Sociological Review* 58: 587–620.

Stack, Carol B. 1974. *All Our Kin: Strategies for Survival in a Black Community.* New York: Harper & Row.

Stinchcombe, Arthur. 2001. *When Formality Works: Authority and Abstraction in Law and Organizations.* Chicago: University of Chicago Press.

Stivers, Tanya, Lorenza Mondada, and Jakob Steensig, eds. 2011. *The Morality of Knowledge in Conversation.* Cambridge: Cambridge University Press.

Stolte, John, Gary Alan Fine, and Karen Cook. 2001. "Sociological Miniaturism: Seeing the Big Through the Small in Social Psychology." *Annual Review of Sociology* 27: 387–413.

Stone, I. F. 1988. *The Trial of Socrates.* Boston: Little, Brown.

Stoner, James. 1968. "Risky and Cautious Shifts in Group Decisions: The Influence of Widely Held Values." *Journal of Experimental Social Psychology* 4: 442–59.

Stout, Jeffrey. 2010. *Blessed Are the Organized: Grassroots Democracy in America.* Princeton, NJ: Princeton University Press.

Strauss, Anselm. 1978. *Negotiations: Varieties, Contexts, Processes and Social Order.* San Francisco: Jossey-Bass.

Stroebaek, Pernille. 2013. "Let's Have a Cup of Coffee: Coffee and Coping Communities at Work." *Symbolic Interaction* 36: 381–97.

Summers-Effler, Erika. 2010. *Laughing Saints and Righteous Heroes: Emotional Rhythms in Social Movement Groups.* Chicago: University of Chicago Press.

Sunstein, Cass, and Reid Hastie. 2015. *Wiser: Getting beyond Groupthink to Make Groups Smarter.* Cambridge, MA: Harvard Business Review Press.

Suttles, Gerald. 1968. *The Social Order of the Slum: Ethnicity and Territory in the Inner City.* Chicago: University of Chicago Press.

Swidler, Ann. 2001. *Talk of Love: How Culture Matters.* Chicago: University of Chicago Press.

Swyers, Holly. 2010. *Wrigley Regulars: Finding Community in the Bleachers.* Urbana: University of Illinois Press.

Tannen, Deborah. 1984. *Conversational Style: Analyzing Talk among Friends.* New York: Praeger.

Tate, W. E. 1967. *The English Village Community and the Enclosure Movements.* London: Gollancz.

Tavory, Iddo. 2016. *Summoned: Identification and Religious Life in a Jewish Neighborhood.* Chicago: University of Chicago Press.

Tavory, Iddo, and Nina Eliasoph. 2013. "Coordinating Futures: Toward a Theory of Anticipation." *American Journal of Sociology* 118: 908–42.

Tavory, Iddo, and Gary Alan Fine. 2020. "Disruption and the Theory of the Interaction Order." *Theory & Society* 49: 365–85.

't Hart, Paul. 1994. *Groupthink in Government: A Study of Small Groups and Policy Failure.* Baltimore: Johns Hopkins University Press.

Thomas, William I., and Dorothy Swayne Thomas. 1928. *The Child in America: Behavior Problems and Programs.* New York: Knopf.

Thompson, E. P. 1971. "The Moral Economy of the English Crowd in the Eighteenth Century." *Past and Present* 50: 76–136.

Thompson, Leigh. 2014. *The Mind and Heart of the Negotiator.* 6th ed. New York: Pearson.

Thomson, Ken. 2001. *From Neighborhood to Nation: The Democratic Foundations of Civil Society.* Hanover, NH: University Press of New England.

Tilly, Charles. 1996. "Invisible Elbow." *Sociological Forum* 11: 589–601.

———. 2006. *Identities, Boundaries, and Social Ties.* Boulder, CO: Paradigm.

Tönnies, Ferdinand. 2001 [1887]. *Community and Civil Society.* Translated by Jose Harris and Margaret Hollis. Cambridge: Cambridge University Press.

Tuan, Yi-Fu. 1977. *Space and Place: The Perspective of Experience.* Minneapolis: University of Minnesota Press.

Tuomela, Raimo. 2007. *The Philosophy of Sociality: The Shared Point of View.* Oxford: Oxford University Press.

Turner, Jonathan. 2012. *Theoretical Principles of Sociology. Volume 3: Mesodynamics.* New York: Springer.

Turner, Victor. 1969. *Ritual Process: Structure and Anti-Structure*. Chicago: Aldine.

Van Maanen, John. 1988. *Tales of the Field: On Writing Ethnography*. Chicago: University of Chicago Press.

Vargas, Robert. 2016a. "How Health Navigators Legitimize the Affordable Care Act to the Uninsured Poor." *Social Science and Medicine* 165: 263–70.

———. 2016b. *Wounded City: Violent Turf Wars in a Chicago Barrio*. New York: Oxford University Press.

Venkatesh, Sudhir. 1997. "The Social Organization of Street Gang Activity in an Urban Ghetto." *American Journal of Sociology* 1–3: 82–111.

———. 2008. *Gang Leader for a Day: A Rogue Sociologist Takes to the Streets*. New York: Penguin.

Verba, Sidney, Kay Lehman Schlozman, and Henry Brady. 1995. *Voice and Equality: Civic Voluntarism in American Politics*. Cambridge, MA: Harvard University Press.

Vickers, Daniel. 1994. *Farmers and Fishermen: Two Centuries of Work in Essex County, Massachusetts, 1630–1850*. Chapel Hill: University of North Carolina Press.

Viterna, Jocelyn. 2013. *Women in War: The Micro-Processes of Mobilization in El Salvador*. New York: Oxford University Press.

Von Heyking, John, and Richard Avramenko. 2008. "Introduction: The Persistence of Friendship in Political Life." Pp. 1–17 in *Friendship and Politics: Essays in Political Thought*, edited by John von Heyking and Richard Avramenko. Notre Dame, IN: University of Notre Dame Press.

Wagner-Pacifici, Robin. 2000. *Theorizing the Standoff: Contingency in Action*. Cambridge: Cambridge University Press.

Walsh, Katherine Cramer. 2003. *Talking about Politics: Informal Groups and Social Identity in American Life*. Chicago: University of Chicago Press.

Walzer, Michael. 1992. "The Civil Society Argument." Pp. 89–107 in *Dimensions of Radical Democracy: Pluralism, Citizenship, Community*, edited by Chantal Mouffe. London: Verso.

Warner, W. Lloyd. 1953. *The Living and the Dead*. New Haven, CT: Yale University Press.

Watson, Bruce. 2010. *Freedom Summer: The Savage Season that Made Mississippi Burn and Made America a Democracy*. New York: Viking.

Weatherford, J. McIver. 1985. *Tribes on the Hill*. South Hadley, MA: Bergin and Garvey.

Weatherford, M. Stephen. 1982. "Interpersonal Networks and Political Behavior." *American Journal of Political Science* 26: 117–43.

Weber, Eugen. 1976. *Peasants into Frenchmen: The Modernization of Rural France, 1870–1914*. Stanford, CA: Stanford University Press.

Weber, Klaus, and Daniel Wäger. 2017. "Organizations as Polities: An Open Systems Perspective." *Academy of Management Annuals* 11: 886–918.

Weber, Max. 1978. *Economy and Society: An Outline of Interpretive Sociology*. Berkeley: University of California Press.

———. 1920 [2011]. *The Protestant Ethic and the Spirit of Capitalism.* Revised 1920 ed. Translated by Stephen Kalberg. New York: Oxford University Press.

———. 1919 [1946]. "Politics as a Vocation." In *From Max Weber*, edited and translated by Hans Gerth and C. Wright Mills. New York: Free Press.

Weeks, John. 2003. *Unpopular Culture: The Ritual of Complaint in a British Bank.* Chicago: University of Chicago Press.

Weiner, Mark. 2013. *The Rule of the Clan.* New York: Farrar, Straus, and Giroux.

Weiss, Philip. 1989. "Masters of the Universe Go to Camp: Inside the Bohemian Grove." *Spy Magazine* (November): 59–76.

Whitehead, Kevin. 2009. "Categorizing the Categorizer: The Management of Racial Common Sense in Interaction." *Social Psychology Quarterly* 72: 325–42.

Whittier, Nancy. 1997. "Political Generations, Micro-Cohorts, and the Transformation of Social Movements." *American Sociological Review* 62: 760–78.

Whyte, Martin King. 1974. *Small Groups and Political Rituals in China.* Berkeley: University of California Press.

Whyte, William F. 1943. *Street Corner Society.* Chicago: University of Chicago Press.

Whyte, William F., and Kathleen King Whyte. 1991. *Making Mondragon: The Growth and Dynamics of the Worker Cooperative Complex.* Ithaca, NY: ILR Press.

Will, George. 1995. "Look at All the Lonely Bowlers." *Washington Post* (January 5): A29.

Wright, Lawrence. 2013. *Going Clear: Scientology, Hollywood, and the Prison of Belief.* New York: Knopf.

Wuthnow, Robert. 1994. *Sharing the Journey: Support Groups and America's New Quest for Community.* New York: Free Press.

Wuthnow, Robert, ed. 2001. *"I Come Away Stronger": How Small Groups Are Shaping American Religion.* Grand Rapids, MI: Wm. B. Eerdmans.

Wynn, Jonathan. 2016. "On the Sociology of Occasions." *Sociological Theory* 34: 276–86.

Xu, Bin. 2017. *The Politics of Compassion: The Sichuan Earthquake and Civic Engagement in China.* Stanford, CA: Stanford University Press.

Yerkovich, Sally. 1977. "Gossiping as a Way of Speaking." *Journal of Communication* 27: 192–96.

Zerubavel, Eviatar. 1997. *Social Mindscapes: An Invitation to Cognitive Sociology.* Cambridge, MA: Harvard University Press.

Zhao, Dingxin. 2001. *The Power of Tiananmen: State-Society Relations and the 1989 Beijing Student Movement.* Chicago: University of Chicago Press.

Zhao, Shanyang. 2003. "Toward a Taxonomy of Copresence." *Presence* 12: 445–55.

Zimmerman, Joseph. 1999. *The New England Town Meeting: Democracy in Action.* Westport, CT: Praeger.

INDEX

www.ingramcontent.com/pod-product-compliance
Lightning Source LLC
Chambersburg PA
CBHW060031030426
42334CB00019B/2279